# Experiments in Economics

Are humans fair by nature? Why do we often willingly trust strangers or cooperate with them even if those actions leave us vulnerable to exploitation? Does this natural inclination towards fairness or trust have implications in the market-place? Traditional economic theory would perhaps think not, perceiving human interaction as self-interested at heart. There is increasing evidence, however, that social norms and norm-driven behaviour such as a preference for fairness, generosity or trust have serious implications for economics. This book provides an easily accessible overview of economic experiments, specifically those that explore the role of fairness, generosity, trust and reciprocity in economic transactions.

Ananish Chaudhuri approaches a variety of economic issues and problems including:

- pricing by firms;
- writing labour contracts between parties;
- making voluntary contributions to charity;
- addressing issues of environmental pollution;
- providing micro-credit to small entrepreneurs;
- resolving problems of coordination failure in organisations.

The book discusses how norm-driven behaviour can often lead to significantly different outcomes than those predicted by economic theories and these findings should in turn cause us to re-think how we approach economic analysis and policy.

Assuming no prior knowledge of economics and containing a variety of examples, this reader-friendly volume will be perfect reading for people from a wide range of backgrounds including students and policy-makers. The book should appeal to economics undergraduates studying experimental economics, microeconomics or game theory as well as students in social psychology, organisational behaviour, management and other business related disciplines.

**Ananish Chaudhuri** is an Associate Professor of Economics at the University of Auckland, New Zealand.

This is an excellent volume on experiments in economics, demonstrating that expectations for fair outcomes and trust are major driving forces behind economic behavior. Chaudhuri explains themes such as price discrimination, gift exchanges and public goods, neatly including their roles in economic behavior. The many clear examples make the book accessible to a wide audience. I expect this book to find a prominent place in many economic libraries.

Ernst Fehr, *University of Zurich*

Despite the great interest in experimental and behavioral economics over the past 20 years there is still a dearth of books that one can use to teach from and which can be used by laymen to learn what is going on in this rapidly changing field. Ananish Chaudhuri has written a wonderful book which is motivated by real world experiences yet closely tied to the state of the art research in experimental and behavioral problems. Dealing with problems of trust, fairness, social coordination, public goods and social dilemmas Chaudhuri takes the reader on a wonderful adventure from which he or she will certainly benefit. I highly recommend this book.

Andrew Schotter, *Professor of Economics, Director,*
*Center for Experimental Social Science, New York University*

Chaudhuri has written an extremely readable introduction to experimental economics. This is perfect for advanced undergrads or graduate students who want to learn about state of the art research without being smothered by technical details.

David J. Cooper, *Professor of Economics, Florida State University*

With lucid prose and a wonderful set of examples, Ananish Chaudhuri brings important results in experimental economics to life, linking concepts such as trust, fairness and reciprocity to our everyday actions. At the same time, *Experiments in Economics* introduces the reader to the science, with engaging accounts of how economists use experiments to get answers to key questions in strategic decision making.

Gary Bolton, *Professor of Business Economics and*
*Executive Programs Faculty Fellow, Smeal College of Business,*
*Pennsylvania State University*

Are people fair-minded and helpful or selfish in the end? Why and whom do people trust? Why do people engage in community work? Why do people obey social norms and conventions? Not long ago these questions, which are at the heart of social life, were deemed outside the realm of economics. The advent of experimental economics and the interchange with the behavioural sciences has changed this picture entirely. Professor Chaudhuri is to be praised for having written a highly readable and informative account of one of the most exciting developments in the social sciences.

Simon Gaechter, *Professor of the Psychology of Economic*
*Decision Making, University of Nottingham*

Ananish Chaudhuri has produced a masterful guide to the experimental literature on behavioural economics. Full of interesting real world examples, this exceptionally well-written book is accessible to non specialists. Yet, it nonetheless provides important insights into the scientific methodology of experimental economics, examining just how its practitioners go about designing experiments to elucidate the roles that abstract concepts such as fairness, trust, and reciprocity play in explaining human interactions. Regardless of whether one is a behaviourist, experimentalist, or "traditionalist", this is a must read.

John C. Panzar, *Professor of Economics, University of Auckland* and Louis W. Menk, *Professor (Emeritus), Northwestern University*

# Experiments in Economics

Playing fair with money

**Ananish Chaudhuri**

LONDON AND NEW YORK

First published 2009
by Routledge
2 Park Square, Milton Park, Abingdon, Oxon OX14 4RN

Simultaneously published in the USA and Canada
by Routledge
270 Madison Ave, New York, NY 10016

*Routledge is an imprint of the Taylor & Francis Group, an informa business*

Typeset in Simoncini Garamond by Wearset Ltd, Boldon, Tyne and Wear
Printed and bound in Great Britain by Antony Rowe, Chippenham, Wiltshire

*British Library Cataloguing in Publication Data*
A catalogue record for this book is available from the British Library

*Library of Congress Cataloging in Publication Data*
A catalog record for this book has been requested

ISBN10: 0-415-47630-5 (hbk)
ISBN10: 0-415-47631-3 (pbk)
ISBN10: 0-203-88479-5 (ebk)

ISBN13: 978-0-415-47630-0 (hbk)
ISBN13: 978-0-415-47631-7 (pbk)
ISBN13: 978-0-203-88479-9 (ebk)

For Ishannita, Indira, Ila and Utpal
and
for Nayan, who never got to see this book in print

# Contents

# Illustrations

## Figures

## Tables

## Boxes

# Preface

In recent years economists have come to realise that social norms and norm-driven behaviour – such as notions of fairness, willingness to be generous towards strangers or cooperate with them, willingness to trust strangers and reciprocate others' trust – play a crucial role in a variety of economic transactions and have implications for economic theories. There have been a lot of innovative and exciting findings in this area that have raised questions about the conclusions reached by traditional economic theories; findings, that I think, would be of interest to people outside the discipline.

So when Libby Passau of the Centre for Continuing Education at the University of Auckland approached me in January 2007 with the idea of delivering a set of five one-hour public lectures, I thought that it might be worthwhile sharing some of these findings – and my work in the area – with a general audience. These lectures are open to the community at large and are designed to expose members of the wider society to current research being carried out at the University. After some initial hesitation, I finally agreed to talk about how social norms play a role in economic transactions and some of the work I have done in this area.

It is a good thing that I did because the lectures were a delightful experience and have eventually formed the basis for this book. While I am used to giving talks in front of academic audiences, this was the first time I had to stand up in front of a group of people drawn from society at large, many of them with little or no exposure to economics prior to this. The audience was mostly mature, who brought with them an enormous wealth of wisdom and experience. The flow of information was clearly bi-lateral. While I am certain that over the course of the week I did manage to challenge pre-existing notions and provoke new thinking among the audience members, at the same time they kept prodding me with questions about assumptions and conclusions and providing me with valuable anecdotes and insights. These lectures helped me immensely in clarifying my thoughts and arguments. I am grateful to Libby and the attendees at the week-long event for their input. To an extent, I wrote this book because at the end of the week a number of people came up to me and asked me what books they could read on the topic. In talking to them I realised that, with the exception of a couple of textbooks and of course articles in scholarly journals, there really were no books out there that provide an overview of these research findings in non-technical language that would be accessible to a purely general audience.

The book can be used by different types of readers. First, the book can be used as an undergraduate textbook for courses in experimental economics that devote a substantial amount of time to issues such as ultimatum, trust, social dilemma and coordination games. In addition, for a variety of upper-level courses in microeconomics or game theory where the instructor might wish to discuss experimental findings, the book could be a very useful supplementary or recommended text. Third, findings in this area have broad overlaps with social psychology, organisational behaviour, management and other business-related disciplines and as such the book should appeal to researchers and students in those areas as well. The chapter on how to resolve problems of coordination failure in organisations should be of particular interest to human resource managers and might provide insights into ways of motivating their work-force. Last, but certainly not least, and as I mention above, the book is written in a way that it will also be accessible to general readers with no prior knowledge of economics. Thus, anyone who is interested in learning how norm-driven behaviour might affect economic outcomes would find this book interesting as well. As I point out in the introduction, even if you do not know what demand and supply means, you will still be able to follow the arguments contained in this book. As long as you have an inquisitive mind and are open to new ideas and thoughts, this book is for you.

I am grateful to the Department of Economics and the University of Auckland for providing me with the research and study leave during which I worked on this manuscript. The break from teaching and administrative responsibilities provided a welcome respite and allowed me to read, think and write uninterruptedly. A lot of my research in this area has been supported by the University of Auckland Research Council, particularly through a Vice Chancellor's Strategic Research Development grant in 2004. I am thankful for this support. I was also fortunate to have two very supportive heads of department in John Small and Bryce Hool.

I am grateful to a large number of people – both teachers and collaborators – who have shaped my ideas and thinking over the years. These include Dipak Banerjee, Paul Brown, Linda Cameron, Debajyoti Chakrabarty, Ira Gang, Lata Gangadharan, Pushkar Maitra, Richard McLean, Anjan Mukherjee, Thomas Prusa, Erwann Sbai, Andrew Schotter, Paul Strand, Chester Spell, and most of all, my dissertation advisor at Rutgers University, Barry Sopher. I would not have become an experimental economist without Barry's advice and encouragement. I teach a post-graduate course in Experimental Economics at the University of Auckland where we get some very intelligent students from both New Zealand and abroad. My students have always been turned on and tuned in and by asking searching questions have always kept me on my toes and served as a sounding board for my ideas. Two of these deserve special mention – Tirnud (Meg) Paichayontvijit and Geoff Brooke. Over the last few years they have assisted me in my research in countless ways and have also read through the manuscript and provided feedback. I should also acknowledge Sara Graziano and Amy Cruickshank who were students first and became collaborators later.

To a large extent, my interest in experimental economics was kindled during a stay at the University of Arizona's Economic Science Laboratory over the summer of 1995. The Economic Science Laboratory, headed by Vernon Smith, the 2002 Nobel Laureate in Economics, provided an intellectually stimulating and vibrant atmosphere. The visit gave me an opportunity to interact with some of the leading researchers in the area which included, besides Smith, James Cox, Mark Isaac, Amnon Rapoport, Steve Rassenti, Stan Reynolds, Mark Walker and John Wooders.

More immediately, a large number of people read over parts or all of this manuscript and provided valuable suggestions and advice. These include Nandita Basu, Gary Bolton, David Cooper, Asoke Das Sharma, Tony Endres, Ernst Fehr, Simon Gächter, Tim Hazledine, Dmitriy Kvasov, John Panzar and especially Andrew Schotter, whose advice about the contents of this book, as well as other issues, has been absolutely invaluable. When I was first designing my graduate course in experimental economics I had written to Ernst Fehr asking him for a copy of the syllabus for his own course on the topic. What I received in response were *all* the lecture slides from his course! I learned an immense amount from perusing these slides and am extremely grateful to Ernst not only for sharing his slides with me but also for the sage advice he has given me periodically. Colin Camerer took the time to e-mail with advice about how to go about finding a publisher for my book and I am thankful for that.

Two anonymous reviewers and especially, Robert Langham, my editor at Routledge have provided extremely valuable feedback which has led to significant improvements in the book's exposition. I thank them sincerely. Sam Elworthy at the University of Auckland Press also provided valuable pointers.

Lisa Meehan did a superb job proof-reading the final version of the book and putting together the bibliography. Pion Das helped with the proof-reading and digging up references in the early stages of the manuscript. Joe Li helped create the figures for the book.

I worked on parts of this book while I was trying to recover from an accident that resulted in a compound fracture of my right leg. I am forever grateful to the people who put me back on my feet and enabled me to resume normal activities within a time-span that seemed interminable at the time but which I now realise, in retrospect, was actually not that long. These include the orthopaedic surgeon Dr Bruce Twaddle, the plastic surgeon Dr Ashwin Chunilal, our family physician Dr Stephen Gates, as well as my physiotherapist Caroline Stark, Auckland district nurses Hilda Fenti and Jane Tyverton, Pete Oxley of ACC and Aimee, Fiona, Hank, Marie, MaryAnn, Megan, Lindsey, Penny and most of all Rani Joseph at Middlemore Hospital. If you are reading this then you should know that I am tremendously grateful for what you did for me.

I am always and forever grateful for the constant support and encouragement provided by my parents Ila and Utpal. My parents have allowed me to make my own decisions from an early age and stood by those decisions even when they did not necessarily agree. Whatever my accomplishments are, they would not have been possible without their assistance. I am also deeply indebted to my parents-in-law Nandita and Samir for their support.

Finally, I am indebted to my wonderful wife Dr Indira Basu in so many ways that I have no idea where to start. She has made tremendous sacrifices on my behalf and marrying her was by far the smartest thing that I have ever done. Over the years she has been forced to listen patiently as I tried out all my ideas and arguments on her. She also read through many of the chapters and provided invaluable pointers. Of course, life is made constantly interesting, enchanting and challenging by my beautiful daughter Ishannita, without whose active interest in every thing that I do, many of my papers and this book would have been finished much earlier.

Of course at the end of it all, as we say in all our academic papers, I alone am responsible for any errors that may appear in the following pages. The views expressed in these pages are my opinion and I could be wrong. Feel free to write and tell me if you do not agree with something I have said and you have counter-examples. Also feel free to let me know if you know of other applications or anecdotes that might be relevant. I hope I have managed to convey some of the passion and excitement that characterises research in these topics and I hope you enjoy reading the book.

Ananish Chaudhuri
University of Auckland
Auckland, New Zealand
May 2008
ananish.chaudhuri@gmail.com

# Part 1
# Introduction

The starting point of much economic thinking is the assumption of individual rationality. While the word rationality often implies different things in different disciplines, in economics this term means that in situations involving strategic decision making, the people making those decisions care mostly about their own monetary payoffs; or they care about their own satisfaction (or "*utility*" as economists refer to it) where that utility is primarily a function of the monetary payoffs accruing to them or their kin. In other words, humans are primarily motivated by "*self-regarding*" preferences. But we now have voluminous evidence that in a wide variety of economic transactions social norms and norm-driven behaviour, such as notions of fairness, willingness to be generous towards or cooperate with strangers, willingness to trust strangers and reciprocate others' trust, play a crucial role.

This can work both ways. Sometimes perfectly feasible deals may not get made because one side believes that the other side is being deliberately unfair. But at the same time deals that should not get made do get made because people are perfectly willing to trust strangers with their money. Enterprises such as eBay or TradeMe essentially rely on such willingness to trust strangers and are making money out of it. Sometimes notions of what is fair or unfair may act as a constraint on firms maximising their profit. Buyers may refuse to buy something they desperately need if they think that firms are taking advantage and charging unnecessarily high prices (a practice often known as "price gouging") – for instance doubling the price of snow-shovels immediately after a snow-storm. Sometimes it might prevent people from getting jobs in the midst of a recession because firms are unwilling to cut the wages of existing workers even though the unemployed ones are willing to work for a much lower wage.

These are some of the things that I will talk about in this book. But before that I need to take you through some preliminary ideas and concepts. I hasten to add that this book is written for people with no background in economics. Don't worry if you don't know what the words "*demand*" and "*supply*" mean – in fact the words "*demand*" and "*supply*" appear rarely in this book – it won't matter. As long as you have an inquisitive mind and are open to new ideas and thoughts, this book is for you.

A large number of decisions in our day to day lives require us to engage in "*strategic decision making*". What does strategic decision making mean? It means that what I decide to do in a particular situation will affect the well-being of another person (or a group of people) – and in turn what someone else does will crucially impact upon my own well-being. Here are some examples of such situations:

- people trying to decide whether to contribute money towards building a local park or another similar charity;
- the local bakery offering a discount on pastries just before closing;
- a Persian-rug seller haggling over the price and deciding how quickly to lower the price;
- a Hadza man in Tanzania deciding whether to join another hunter in order to jointly hunt a stag for the day or to try catching a rabbit on his own;
- an employee deciding how hard to work when the employer is away;
- people bidding for art, oil-leases or knick-knacks on eBay.

Economists (and increasingly others in evolutionary biology, political science, sociology and business-related disciplines such as management, organizational behaviour and marketing) routinely rely on a set of tools called "*game theory*" to understand how people make decisions in such situations. Game theory is essentially a language for describing strategic interactions when what happens to one person is affected by another person. Thus a number of situations that confront us in our day to day lives – such as the ones listed above and many others – can be thought of as "games" with us as "players", and they can be analysed using the tools of game theory.

While it is always hard to pin-point when exactly a particular set of ideas arose, most scholars would agree that the origins of game theory can be traced back to the publication of the book *The Theory of Games and Economic Behavior* written by John von Neumann and Oskar Morgenstern in 1944. Subsequently other scholars have added to our understanding of strategic decision making including John Nash, John Harsanyi, Reinhard Selten, Robert Aumann and Thomas Schelling. Nash, Harsanyi and Selten were honoured with the Nobel Prize in Economics in 1994 while Aumann and Schelling were similarly honoured in 2005.[1]

---

1   John Nash was the subject of an Oscar winning film *A Beautiful Mind* where Russell Crowe portrayed Nash – surely one of very few films based on the life of a mathematician, if not the only one. Directed by Ron Howard, the film was also a huge

Let me highlight why many of these situations involve *strategic* decision making by looking at the first example listed above. Close to where I live in the city of Auckland is a playground for small children called "Little Rangitoto Reserve". I go there often with my young daughter. Surprisingly the equipment in this playground – the slides, the swings, the jungle gym and the monkey-bars – were not provided by the Auckland City Council but were rather bought by local residents on the basis of voluntary contributions. On the face of it, this is probably not surprising to any of you since you may have experience with similar such ventures or others which rely on voluntary charitable contributions for a good cause. It happens all the time and as a result we tend to forget that this is actually quite an accomplishment.

Let me explain why. Suppose you want to build a similar public park in your neighbourhood and you decide to approach local households for a certain contribution. Not everyone in the neighbourhood has to contribute for the park to get built. As long as *some* of the families contribute you will have enough money for the park.

What are the chances that you will be able to raise enough money? The chances are actually good but there is an inherent *social dilemma* here. For the time being suppose (as economists often tend to do) that by and large people are self-interested and care (mostly) about their own welfare. It is obvious that if everyone does chip in with a contribution then the park will get built and everyone in the neighbourhood can take their children there. Collectively then we will all be better off if everyone cooperated.

But let us think for a minute about an individual (who cares primarily about her own well-being and those of her close ones) trying to decide whether to contribute or not. Suppose she does not contribute any money to the pot and the park does not get built. Then she is not better off but she is not worse off either since there was no park there before and there will not be one in the future. But suppose she does *not* contribute but enough money is raised to build the park. Now a park is quite different from (say) a health club because once the park is built it is extremely difficult to keep anyone out regardless of whether she has paid or not. Typically you cannot really have a membership for a public

box-office success. The film, though, bears little resemblance to reality and those who are interested in Nash's life and his contributions to game theory should certainly read Sylvia Nasar's captivating book with the same title.

park. So even if someone has *not* paid, this person cannot be prevented from going to the park once it is built. So she has not contributed anything but still gets to enjoy a walk in the park with her child or her dog. This person is then better off since she has not paid anything out of her own pocket but still gets to enjoy the open air of the park and the verdant surroundings. So then it appears that whether the park gets built or not – for an individual who cares primarily about her own self-interest – the practical course of action is not to contribute any money.

Economists refer to this type of behaviour as *"free-riding"* – taking advantage of other people's contributions. But if everyone reasoned along the same lines then no one will contribute and the park will never get built!

Joseph Heller summed up this phenomenon eloquently in *Catch 22* while discussing Yossarian's reluctance to help build the officers' club:[2]

> *Sharing a tent with a man who was crazy wasn't easy but Nately didn't care. He was crazy, too, and had gone every free day to work on the officers' club that Yossarian had not helped build.*
>
> *Actually, there were many officers' clubs that Yossarian had not helped build, but he was the proudest of the one on Pianosa. It was a sturdy and complex monument to his powers of determination. Yossarian never went there to help until it was finished; then he went there often, so pleased was he with the large, fine, rambling, shingled building. It was truly a splendid structure, and Yossarian throbbed with a mighty sense of accomplishment each time he gazed at it and reflected that none of the work that had gone into it was his.*

In the economist's parlance Yossarian is *free-riding* on the effort put in by the other officers, an occurrence not altogether uncommon in many economic settings, which require a group of people to collaborate. Many of you who are used to working with groups of people and are aware of the problems that arise will recognise Yossarian's behaviour. Economists typically argue that faced with a group enterprise, such as building the officers' club or a local park or contributing to charitable causes in general, self-interested humans will inevitably behave like

---

2   In the event that you have not read *Catch 22*, then it is imperative that you remedy this egregious mistake immediately, but preferably after you have bought and finished reading this book.

Yossarian and, therefore, such enterprises are doomed to failure. Economists go on to suggest that in *equilibrium* – the usual term used is a "*Nash equilibrium*" after John Nash who first proposed the idea – all self-interested actors will free-ride and no one will contribute towards building the park! Here the phrase "*equilibrium*" suggests a lack of any tendency or desire to change. If no one contributes and the park does not get built then collectively everyone is worse off and everyone realises that everyone is worse off. But no individual wishes to change his behaviour. A single individual contributing will not change the outcome (the park will most likely not get built) while this individual will be out of some cash from his own pocket at no additional benefit to himself. Everyone realises that it is better if everyone contributes but once they are caught in the free-riding trap – the *equilibrium* – it is extremely difficult to get out of it. The only way to get out of the trap will be for everyone to change their minds *simultaneously* which again creates a similar collective decision-making problem which led to us falling into the trap in the first place.

Once again our intrepid hero Yossarian of *Catch 22* sums up the nature of this equilibrium succinctly in the following conversation with Major Major Major Major[3]:

> "*Suppose we let you pick your missions and fly milk runs,*" Major Major said. "*That way you can fly the four missions and not run any risks.*"
>
> "*I don't want to fly milk runs. I don't want to be in the war any more.*"
>
> "*Would you like to see our country lose?*" Major Major asked.
>
> "*We won't lose. We've got more men, more money and more material. There are ten million people in uniform who can replace me. Some people are getting killed and a lot more are making money and having fun. Let somebody else get killed.*"
>
> "*But suppose everybody on our side felt that way.*"
>
> "*Then I'd certainly be a damned fool to feel any other way. Wouldn't I?*"

---

3  For those yet to read the book, this gentleman's first name, middle name and last name are all Major and he also has the rank of Major.

Everybody refusing to fly missions is the least desirable outcome in this case – at least from Major Major's and the country's perspective – but if one person does not fly missions while others do then the person not flying is better off and eventually the others will stop flying as well – a *Nash equilibrium*.

At this point you might be thinking that everyone is not like Yossarian or, for that matter, not like an economist! ("*No wonder people call it the 'dismal science'*," you might be muttering under your breath.) If you do not agree with this assumption that is fine because, as I will show you shortly, this assumption is mostly wrong. Yes, people donate large amounts to charity. They donate blood and organs to others. Across a vast majority of transactions, humans routinely cooperate with non-related strangers. Maybe because they believe that this is the behaviour expected of them and not to comply with that expectation imposes psychological costs. But I do need to point out that if you are someone who perceives human beings as being essentially kind and cooperative – altruistic – across the board then, as I will show you (and as many of you probably know from experience), that view would be incorrect as well. People are neither purely self-interested nor purely altruistic but rather they are conditional co-operators whose behaviour is determined to a large extent by what they think their peers will do. I will talk about this at length in Part 4. But we need to start somewhere if we want to build a model of human behaviour that generates accurate predictions and economists feel that the assumption of rational self-interest is a good place to start. So let us start there and see where and how far that gets us.

Suppose we want to find out the real motivations behind people's actions. Why do some people routinely cooperate? Why do some free-ride? How would you go about answering these questions? Traditionally researchers have followed two different paths. The first of these is to rely on surveys where we ask people questions about what motivates them. Why did someone do what he did? Surveys are straight-forward and usually yield valuable insights. But at the same time there are drawbacks to this approach as well. The problem is that sometimes people's response to what they would do in a particular situation does not predict accurately what they would really do when actually placed in that situation. In technical terms we sometimes say that people's attitudes do not always *correlate* well with their behaviour. This essentially means the following: suppose I ask you whether you were willing to contribute $50 for a good cause and you said yes. But when eventually the envelope gets passed around and you have to actually part with the money you may renege on that promise completely or put in less than $50. I am not saying that you *will* do it, but it has been *known to happen.* Moreover, responses in these questionnaires may differ substantially from behaviour not because the respondent is trying to mislead the researcher but because the respondent may possess an incorrect perception of his own and others' views or reactions. That is, the respondent might honestly think that he will behave in a certain way in a particular situation but when that specific situation comes to pass he behaves quite differently.

Here is an example of such dichotomy between attitudes and behaviour taken from the literature in social psychology. In the early 1930s Richard LaPierre wanted to discover if people who had various prejudices or negative attitudes towards members of other ethnic groups would actually demonstrate these behaviours in an overt manner. For approximately two years LaPierre travelled around the US with a young Chinese couple. They stopped at 184 restaurants and 66 hotels. They were refused service only once and on the whole received a better than average standard of service from the establishments visited. After returning from two years of travelling around, LaPierre wrote to all the businesses where he and the Chinese couple had dined or stayed. In a letter, which gave no indication of his previous visit, he enquired whether they would offer service to Chinese customers. While virtually none of the establishments had actually refused service, in the survey the majority expressed the opinion that they would not serve the Chinese visitors. There are many other examples of such dissonance between attitudes and behaviour.

The second avenue of exploration, as opposed to relying on survey questionnaires, has been to look at naturally occurring field-data generated by a real-life economic phenomenon. That is, if you wanted to understand whether and why people contribute to charity then you might dig up data on charitable contributions and analyse that data. This has been the more traditional and usual approach in economics. In order to understand behaviour one needs to look at data that pertained to a particular phenomenon. In fact the famous American economist and the recipient of the Nobel Prize in 1970, Paul Samuelson wrote in his undergraduate textbook (which until recently was the most popular text in universities not only in the US but across the world):

> *(e)conomists cannot perform the controlled experiments of chemists or biologists because (they) cannot easily control other important factors. Like astronomers or meteorologists, (economists) generally must be content largely to observe.*

The problem with field, i.e. naturally occurring, data is that this data may not always be available or not available in the exact form that is needed to answer a particular question. Moreover, since the data is generated by a one-time economic phenomenon it may not necessarily be in the form that allows us to make causal inferences; i.e. whether a particular phenomenon X caused another phenomenon Y. Furthermore, if one is trying to understand people's preferences and beliefs, it is often very difficult to do this using natural data since beliefs or preferences cannot easily be observed.

Economic experiments provide an alternative way of addressing these questions about people's motivations. Contrary to what Samuelson thought, economists found out that it is indeed possible to create laboratory experiments in economics as in other hard sciences and these experiments can be extremely valuable in unravelling the mysteries of motivations, preferences and beliefs. The idea is to take a fundamental economic problem and then design a suitable decision-making experiment. Then you recruit participants to take part in the experimental game and afterwards you analyse the data to see whether people's behaviour corresponds to what economic theory says should happen in this situation. If there are deviations from predicted behaviour then you can try to identify what causes these deviations. Is one or more of our assumptions about human behaviour incorrect? Which part of the puzzle are we missing out? Because the experimenter can control and manipulate the rules of the game and the institutional details in an experiment, we might feel more confident in making causal inferences using experiments.

But how is this different from asking people to fill out survey questionnaires? The difference is that the decisions that participants make in these experimental games are not *hypothetical*. In these experiments participants are paid money based on their performance in the task. The rewards are designed to be large enough and salient enough in order to compensate participants for the opportunity cost of their time (i.e. whatever they might have earned in an alternative job for the duration of the experiment). These payments make the decisions made in the experiment *real* since there is now a substantial amount of money riding on those decisions. Furthermore, this compels the participants to pay attention to the task at hand rather than cavalierly checking off boxes on a questionnaire. Thus, while answers on survey questionnaires can often be no better than self-serving *"cheap talk"*, by paying people money on the basis of their decisions and thereby inducing participants to pay close attention to what they (and others in their group) are doing, decisions made in economic experiments are better able to elicit true preferences and beliefs. Essentially, experimental economists ask participants to put their money where their mouth is.

The above is not meant to suggest by any means that either surveys or work done using naturally occurring data are not valuable. All I am saying is that there are many instances when field data are not available. This is particularly true in the case of situations involving strategic decision making. In many such situations the participants have to anticipate what another person will do and what will be the best way to respond to that anticipated course of action. The actions that participants take in such situations are often affected by their beliefs about the actions of others. But such beliefs are not observable and getting natural data on them is nearly impossible. But if one designs a suitable experiment where people's decisions determine how much they get paid then their actions may allow us to draw conclusions about their beliefs. Experiments then are particularly useful in studying situations that require strategic decision making. This is one reason why the rise of research in experimental economics has coincided with the prominence of game theory in economic analysis. I talk about this more when I provide a brief history of the evolution of experimental economics.

An excellent example of trying to anticipate the actions of others in order to figure out how best to respond comes from Rob Reiner's film *The Princess Bride* starring Cary Elwes. The film buffs among the readers will probably recall the scene where Cary Elwes (the *"man in black"*) is locked in a battle of intellect with Vizzini, the Sicilian played by Wallace Shawn. The battle of wits begins with Cary Elwes putting Iocane powder (a poison) into one of two glasses of wine and Vizzini has to figure out which glass has the poison. Of course, getting it wrong means death. In one memorable passage Vizzini says

*"But it's so simple. All I have to do is divine from what I know of you: are you the sort of man who would put the poison into his own*

*goblet or his enemy's? Now, a clever man would put the poison into his own goblet, because he would know that only a great fool would reach for what he was given. I am not a great fool, so I can clearly not choose the wine in front of you. But you must have known I was not a great fool, you would have counted on it, so I can clearly not choose the wine in front of me." ... "You've beaten my giant, which means you're exceptionally strong, so you could've put the poison in your own goblet, trusting on your strength to save you, so I can clearly not choose the wine in front of you. But, you've also bested my Spaniard, which means you must have studied, and in studying you must have learned that man is mortal, so you would have put the poison as far from yourself as possible, so I can clearly not choose the wine in front of me."*

Vizzini's intellect does not help much as finally he picks a glass, drinks the contents and drops down dead. Of course the dénouement of this scene is that Cary Elwes put poison in both glasses but the poison does not affect him since he has built up immunity to it.

Surveys can provide valuable data in such situations as well, but as I pointed out above, surveys cannot always distinguish opportunistic or self-serving responses from genuinely honest ones. The availability of experiments in economics has revolutionised the study of a number of topics, especially the ones which rely upon individual decision making in the context of strategic decisions and which require an understanding of people's beliefs and expectations. Economic experiments hold out a number of advantages over field studies with naturally occurring data.

First, an experiment can be *replicated*. Suppose you wanted to study the impact of a large scale influx of immigrants into a particular area and you were interested in understanding the impact of such immigration on the wages of local workers and more specifically, whether such immigration puts downward pressure on those wages.

An excellent way to study this would be to find a situation where this happened and then analyse that event. A good example of this would be to look at what happened to local wages in Florida following the Mariel boatlift.[4] Now this event certainly provides an invaluable opportunity to study the impact of immigration on local wages. But the problem is that this is a once-in-a-while event which cannot be replicated by the researcher at a later date in any shape or form. But with economic experiments, if you do not like or believe the results of a particular experiment, you can replicate it to see if the results hold up.

Second, if you think that a researcher left out something important in carrying out an experiment then you can re-run the experiment after rectifying the mistake. For instance if you think that paying more money would make a difference in behaviour, you can run experiments where you do so. If you think that in a particular context – say trading of company shares – investment bankers would behave differently from members of the general public you can recruit people who work on Wall Street and have them participate in an experiment. Or if you think MBAs will be better at making strategic decisions than undergraduate students you can recruit your preferred participants.

Third, in an experiment designed by a researcher you can change the design and the numbers to see how that changes behaviour. For instance, you may want to see if a person behaves in one way when no one is watching as opposed to when others can see him. I may routinely cross the street against a red light or not wear my seat-belt when I am on my own but never do it in front of my children. Along the same lines I might behave differently when dealing with a man as opposed to a woman. If I am a boss hiring a worker I might offer a lower wage to a woman who has the exact same qualifications as another male worker – a common occurrence in many jobs. Used car salesmen routinely quote a higher price to prospective female buyers compared to male buyers.

4  The Mariel boatlift was a mass movement of Cubans who departed from Cuba's Mariel harbour for the United States between April 15 and October 31, 1980. The boatlift was precipitated by a sharp downturn in the Cuban economy, leading to simmering internal tensions on the island and a bid by up to 10,000 Cubans to gain asylum in the Peruvian embassy. The Cuban government subsequently announced that anyone who wanted to leave could do so, and an impromptu exodus organised by Cuban-Americans with the agreement of Cuban President Fidel Castro was underway. The exodus was ended by mutual agreement between the two governments in October 1980. By that time up to 125,000 Cubans had made the journey to Florida, most of whom were placed in refugee camps. The Mariel boatlift features prominently in *Scarface*, a 1983 film directed by Brian De Palma, and starring Al Pacino as Antonio "Tony" Montana, a fictional Cuban refugee who comes to Florida in 1980 as a result of the Mariel Boatlift. It turns out that in spite of this massive influx of immigrants, wages did not go down. The reason as to why those wages did not decline are complex and far beyond the scope of this book.

*Box 1.1* Criticisms of experimental economics

The experimental approach has its detractors. Here is a partial list:

1   In many experiments the participants are college/university students who are typically young and less experienced than an average member of the population. This raises the question: How *representative* are these students of the population as a whole? Do the decisions made by undergraduate students in laboratory experiments provide clues regarding the thinking of CEOs of multi-national corporations or stock-brokers or even the average person on the street? Do the results obtained from these experiments allow us to make inferences about the behaviour of others outside the laboratory? That is to say do these experimental results have *external validity*?

2   While participants do get paid for their participation (often at rates that are significantly higher than the going hourly wage rate or what they might earn in an alternative venture) still the amounts involved are small. Do the decisions made on the basis of these small amounts allow us to generalise about decisions involving millions of dollars?

3   Many experiments are run under artificial laboratory conditions where the instructions given to the participants are written using abstract, context-free and non-emotive language. There is mounting evidence that providing a context for the decisions enables people to understand the underlying problem better and make more informed decisions.

4   Sometimes, in designing an experiment, one worries about the possibility of *"experimenter demand effects"*. This refers to the fact that the very design of a particular experiment, or the instructions provided, might unwittingly provide signals to the participants about a preferred course of action. That is, participants may come to believe that the experimenter wishes them to behave in a particular manner. As a result participants may end up acting in the way they think they are *expected* to, rather than in the way they would actually like to behave.

5   Finally, do experiments allow us to make causal inferences? That is, if outcome Y is associated with institution X, then can we say that Y is caused by X?

These are all valid criticisms. But it is important to note that not all of these are criticisms of the experimental method *per se*. Some of these are essentially arguments for carrying out more elaborate experiments with participants drawn from other parts of the population. As a result, in recent years experimental economists have started undertaking experiments that are far more elaborate in their design, that involve much larger (and often very large) sums of money. As I point out in the next section on ultimatum games, very often larger sums of money do not make any or much of a difference, contrary to what critics think.

If a critic believes that data generated with student participants is not reliable in predicting behaviour among other parts of the population or for special sub-groups, then one can easily run experiments with participants recruited from those groups. And experimental economists routinely and increasingly do so. For instance in trying to understand how markets for financial assets often lead to speculative bubbles, experimental economists have had experienced asset traders participate in their experiments. The short answer is that in some experiments student participants behave differently from those with greater experience but in a lot of experiments involving strategic decision making the differences are not as stark as people might think. Experience can also be a two-edged sword. People with experience in a particular area might wrongly apply those lessons and their wisdom to a problem that appears similar but is actually quite different.

As I note above, one oft-repeated criticism of the experimental approach is that experiments with university students in the sterile conditions of the laboratory using non-emotive and context-free language may not tell us much about real-life phenomena. In response, experimental economists have also started gathering data using participants other than university students and outside the laboratory. In the next section I talk about a very broad study funded by the MacArthur Foundation that collected data for experiments using the members of 15 primitive societies from literally all over the world. Other researchers have looked at the levels of trust among CEOs or among villagers in Peru. Increasingly experimental economists are venturing out into the real-world to run more elaborate experiments many of which also use emotive language and provide an explicit context to the decision-making task at hand.

Experimenter demand effects should not be a concern as long as an experiment is carefully designed. The important point is to design appropriate control treatments and to make sure that in creating experimental treatments, one does not vary too many things at the same time. Varying too many things at once might introduce confounds and make experimenter demand effects a reality. Rather, by making small, incremental and careful changes to the experimental design, and doing so one at a time, one can tease out how changes in the underlying factors lead to changes in behaviour, without sending unwanted signals to the participants about a preferred course of action.

Do experiments allow causal inferences? (Incidentally this criticism can be applied with equal force to empirical studies as well.) Suppose every time you eat Mexican food you get heartburn. Does this allow you to make the inference that you will get heartburn the next time you consume a burrito? Not really. Nevertheless, almost all people will arrive at this conclusion. This is the essence of *inductive* reasoning, the act of going from the specific to the general. No experiment can *prove* that under the same circumstances the same regularities will prevail. Yet, if we design a suitable experiment with proper controls and many such experiments show that – given a certain set of conditions – robust and replicable regularities emerge, we can have faith that the same regularities will occur in reality when those same conditions are satisfied. That is probably why the next time you eat at a Mexican restaurant you will have a roll of antacid tablets handy.

What this essentially means is that carefully designed experiments can often be a very useful complement to conclusions drawn on the basis of surveys or natural data. They can also serve as a means of testing the robustness of conclusions drawn by other means. Increasingly, many experimental economists are resorting to collecting data using multiple methods. They use both survey data as well as experimental data in order to understand decision making. In Part 3, I will talk about one such study undertaken by Dean Karlan of Yale University which examines loan re-payments among members of a rotating savings-and-credit association in rural Peru and uses both surveys and experiments to understand who repays and who defaults. There are now many such examples of elaborate field experiments using non-students.[5]

---

5  John List at the Department of Economics of the University of Chicago is one of the pioneers in the area of such elaborate field experiments. If you are interested then you can find out more about his work from his website: http://home.uchicago. edu/~jlist/.

Here is a real-life example. Many associations such as Red Cross or UNICEF try to attract donations from people and they often hire professional fund-raisers for this purpose. Now, when it comes to fund-raising what kinds of strategies work better than others? James Andreoni and Ragan Petrie of the University of Wisconsin carried out an experiment with paid participants. They look at two strategies that are often used by fundraisers. First, what happens when participants can choose to contribute to one of two charities – one where their contributions are anonymous and another where their contributions are made public? Second, what happens when there is "category reporting", i.e. rather than providing information about actual contributions, contributions are reported in categories such as less than $100, $101 to $500, $501 to $1,000, etc. For the first question, Andreoni and Petrie find that participants contribute very little when their contributions are anonymous while they contribute a lot more when their contributions are made public. Also, when contributions are reported in categories, many more participants increase their contributions to enter the lower end of a higher category. This suggests that along with the warm glow of donating to charity, there is a bit of vanity involved as well. Experiments allow researchers to look at many of these phenomena and also allow us to make changes to the design to tease out differences – something which would be, and typically is, very difficult to do with naturally occurring data. Experiments also allow economists to focus much more carefully on individual motivations and decision making and the nuances in those decisions.

But in doing so, economists began to make some surprising discoveries. Economists began to realise that notions of fairness, willingness to be generous towards strangers or cooperate with them, willingness to trust strangers and reciprocate others' trust play a crucial role in economic transactions and at times may lead to very different outcomes from those predicted by economic theory. This is what I will talk about in the next few chapters.

In the next part I will talk about the "*ultimatum game*" which is designed to illustrate that notions of fairness make a serious difference in economics. People may routinely scupper a deal that will yield substantial monetary gains if they feel that the other side to the deal is being unfair or that in relative terms the other side will make a lot more.

In Part 3, I will look at our willingness to trust strangers – even if that leaves us vulnerable to exploitation – and also our willingness to behave in a trustworthy manner, i.e. reciprocate the trust that another person – often a stranger – has placed in us.

In Part 4, I will introduce the *"public goods game"* which simulates the decision to make voluntary contributions to charity and will explore fundamental questions of cooperation and selfishness. In each part, after discussing the findings of economic experiments I will talk about the implications of those results for economics.

In Part 5, I focus on a slightly different phenomenon, albeit one where norms and conventions play a major role. A range of phenomena in life – both economic and non-economic – require coordinated action by multiple agents. Such coordination problems arise when workers must decide whether to work hard or shirk when the employer is away; or when members of the public decide whether to join a demonstration against an unpopular regime. Under-development in some countries may result from an inability to take coordinated action. Countries may fail to develop when such development requires the simultaneous industrialisation of many sectors of the economy but no sector can break even industrialising alone. In a macroeconomic context, an economy can experience unemployment when no firm wishes to expand production unless it can be assured that others will do so; yet not doing so leads to an outcome that is worse for everyone concerned. In all these cases, people or organisations need to figure out successful interventions that might alleviate pervasive coordination failures. In this part of the book, I discuss how experimental economics can provide insights into resolving such coordination failures.

Finally in Part 6, the epilogue, I provide some further examples of how notions of fairness, trust, reciprocity and altruism can have an enormous impact on a variety of economic phenomena. I discuss the emergence of the Grameen Bank in Bangladesh, which has come to serve as a model of micro-credit organisations in other nations. I will also discuss how the traditional economic approach of providing explicit rewards and punishments for following a desired course of action can *reduce* intrinsic motivations to undertake the same and how we need to think carefully in designing such incentive schemes. For instance, people's willingness to accept the location of a noxious facility, such as a nuclear power plant, in their own neighbourhood (often referred to as *Not-In-My-Backyard (NIMBY)* projects) goes down when they are offered compensation in return for their acceptance as opposed to when they accept this out of a sense of civic duty. Finally, I discuss how mutual trust and reciprocity among a country's citizens can have implications for the country's overall economic performance. Along the way I point out how experimental findings in this area have the potential to change the way we think of, approach and solve diverse economic problems. Of course, there are many applications and I have time and space to talk about only a few of those – the ones I am aware of and understand well.

---

*Box 1.2* How does the approach of experimental economists differ from those of experimental psychologists?[6]

Experimental economists are generally interested in how human beings make decisions in a variety of economic interactions, especially those requiring strategic thinking. Given that experimental economists wish to study the processes of human interactions, the research agenda of experimental economists has broad overlaps with those of both cognitive and social psychologists. But there are often, though not always, substantial differences in their approaches. This does not make one approach superior to the other and in many instances researchers use an eclectic mix of the two in an attempt to synthesise the two approaches, which is both possible and desirable.

- First, economic experiments tend to be much more theory-based and many if not most experiments emanate from a theoretical basis – often as an attempt to test said theories. In psychology, however, the data often takes precedence and a new theory or concept finds acceptance if it is better able to explain a body of empirical findings.
- Economists often focus on behaviour in specific institutions such as markets while psychologists often prefer to study behaviour in the absence of such institutional constraints.
- Experimental economists take great pains to establish a clear incentive structure in the laboratory where the payments to participants are directly related to the decisions that they

---

6   This discussion borrows heavily from Friedman, D. and Sunder, S. (1994). "Chapter 9, Section 9.8", in *Experimental Methods: A Primer for Economists* (pp. 132–134). Cambridge, UK: Cambridge University Press.

make. Psychologists are less concerned about providing incentives to their participants and often do not feel the need for such rewards. Instead they often rely on *intrinsic* motivation on the part of their participants. Some psychologists even argue against providing salient rewards which are designed to provide *extrinsic* motivation suggesting that such extrinsically provided motivations to participants might in fact crowd-out their intrinsic motivations. As we will see in Part 3 and again in the Epilogue (Part 6), this issue of extrinsic versus intrinsic motivation is an interesting one and there are times when intrinsic motivation does work well and extrinsic financial rewards might indeed be counter-productive.

- Finally, economists are extremely reluctant to use deception in their experiments, psychologists less so. Economists believe that participants, who have been deceived in one experiment, might be much less inclined to take the instructions at face-value in the next one and might assume that the experimenter *really* wants to study something other than what the instructions suggest. Psychologists take a more casual view of deception and believe that deception does not make a difference in behaviour and extensive de-briefings at the end of the session will take care of mistaken impressions and assumptions on the part of the participants.

I need to tell you a few other things before we start. First, there is a vast literature in every single topic discussed in this book. My aim here is not to provide a comprehensive overview of all the papers written on these issues. Thus, I had to choose which articles to discuss and which to ignore because I do not wish to snow you under with an overload of information. In doing so, I have had to leave out many deserving and important papers. I offer my apologies to the authors of those papers. In building my arguments in this book, I have chosen only those papers that I felt were the *most relevant* to my thesis.

While discussing papers I have often indicated the institutional affiliation of the paper's author. In some cases this information is dated where the author has moved on to another institution since then. In indicating affiliations, I have usually pointed out where the author was at the time the research for the paper was carried out. In some cases, though, this poses a bit of a problem where authors have changed institutions a number of times. I have tried to indicate the correct affiliations as far as possible.

Second, in presenting the results of studies I have decided not to present them in chronological order but rather discuss them in a way that will enable me to tell a coherent story. Thus, papers that appeared in print earlier are often discussed after papers that were published later to maintain a logical progression.

Third, in making my arguments I have, once in a while, resorted to using figures and tables. I realise that these can be a turn-off for some. But I do not want you to put the book down because you are not comfortable with figures and tables. In most cases I have relied on these because I felt that they are the best way of making my case succinctly. And as they say, sometimes a picture *is* worth a thousand words. But regardless of how essential the figures and tables are, I will talk you through them and often reiterate the information presented in them so that you can still follow my arguments clearly even if you do not quite understand what a particular figure or table is saying. Thus, if you prefer you may ignore the figures and tables and you will still be able to understand the point I am trying to make.

That is all I have to say in the way of an introduction. It is time to get started.

---

*Box 1.3* A brief history of experimental economics[7]

It was not until the last two decades of the 20th century that experimental economics really became a part of the mainstream. Prior to that the attitude towards experiments was exemplified by the quote from Paul Samuelson above and economics was viewed as an essentially non-experimental discipline. This was in sharp contrast to a long and firmly established tradition of experiments in psychology.

It is difficult to provide a short review of the historical development in all areas of experimental economics. I am therefore going

---

7 This section borrows heavily from Roth, A. (1995). "Introduction to Experimental Economics", in J. Kagel and A. Roth (eds), 1995, *Handbook of Experimental Economics* (pp. 3–109), Princeton, NJ: Princeton University Press and Friedman, D. and Sunder, S. (1994). "The emergence of experimental economics", in *Experimental Methods: a Primer for Economists* (Chap. 9: pp. 121–142), Cambridge, UK: Cambridge University Press.

to confine this review primarily to experiments that deal with strategic decision making.

John von Neumann and Oskar Morgenstern published their book *Theory of Games and Economic Behavior* in 1944. This book brought to wide attention a more powerful theory of individual choice and a new theory of interactive strategic behaviour and had a profound influence on subsequent experimental work. In January 1950 Melvin Drescher and Merrill Flood conducted an experiment which introduced the game which subsequently became known as the *Prisoner's Dilemma*. (However, some believe that Al Tucker, a Princeton mathematician, was the first to suggest this game.) I discuss this game in greater detail in the Appendix to this part. Drescher and Flood found behaviour in this game to be much more cooperative than theory predicted which led to an attempt to better understand and explain how people approached these situations in real life.

Around the same time a circle of talented mathematicians at Princeton including John Nash, Lloyd Shapley and John Milnor began an empirical tradition they called "gaming"; and an overlapping group of mathematicians and psychologists at RAND Corporation in Santa Monica and other groups around the country began to conduct experiments informed by the emerging literature in game theory.

In 1952 an inter-disciplinary conference was organised at the RAND Corporation which was supported by a number of organisations including the Ford Foundation and the Office of Naval Research. A large part of the discussion at the conference and a number of papers presented dealt with reporting and interpreting the results of experiments. At least three of the participants had a major subsequent impact on the development of experimental economics – Jacob Marschak, Roy Radner and Herbert Simon (winner of the Nobel Prize in Economics in 1978).

In 1957, Thomas Schelling (who would go on to win the Nobel Prize in Economics in 2005) reported on a series of experiments and pointed out that in many situations the problem facing economic agents is predominantly one of coordinating their actions. (I discuss this topic in detail in Part 5.) In such situations it is often the case that people might be able to coordinate their actions better by focusing on actions that are "prominent". For instance Schelling asked a group of students the following question: "*Tomorrow you have to meet a stranger in NYC (New York City). Where and when do you meet them?*" Schelling found the most common answer was "noon (at the information booth) at Grand Central Station". There is nothing that makes Grand Central Station a location with a higher payoff but its tradition as a meeting place makes it prominent and therefore a focal point.[8]

The beginning of experimentation into the process of price formation in markets can be traced back to the work of Edward Chamberlin at Harvard in the 1940s. Chamberlin wanted to study how markets worked and prices were formed. In order to do so he had his students participate as buyers and sellers in simulated markets. Buyers were assigned values for a fictitious good being sold by the sellers who were in turn assigned costs of production. The underlying assumption is that both parties are interested in making the maximum profit. Chamberlin allowed buyers and sellers to walk around the room and engage in bilateral trades and did not use any monetary rewards. His aim was to understand how a process of bargaining between these hypothetical buyers and sellers led to the determination of prices in these markets.

The end of the 1950s and the early years of the 1960s saw a number of experimental studies looking at the behaviour of prices and quantities in different market structures. Of these the most extended experimental study was that carried out by Sidney Siegel and Lawrence Fouraker who reported on a series of experiments in which participants bargained in pairs until they reached agreement over a price and quantity which in turn determined their profits. Two methodological aspects of this work are noteworthy in the context of our discussion. First, Siegel and Fouraker took pains to ensure that the participants interacted anonymously. Second, they followed the practice of paying the participants on the basis of their decisions. They also looked carefully at how decisions change when the underlying payoffs were changed.

---

8 Of course, fans of *An Affair to Remember* (1957) with Cary Grant and Deborah Kerr or *Sleepless in Seattle* (1993) with Tom Hanks and Meg Ryan might respond that the best place would be the top of the Empire State Building, possibly at sunset. I guess it depends on what you know about the person you have to meet. Did she read Schelling or is she a fan of romantic comedies? If the answer to the question is both then you are back to square one.

Separately from developments in the US, there was a pronounced experimental movement in Germany led by the noted theorist Reinhard Selten (awarded the Nobel Prize in Economics in 1994 for his contributions to game theory) at the University of Bonn starting in the 1950s. This line of work, often not published in English until the later years of the 20th century, tended to focus on issues of bargaining and bounded rationality.

Vernon Smith, who would go on to win the Nobel Prize in Economics in 2002, specifically for his work in experimental economics, was one of the students who took part in Chamberlin's experiments. As an assistant professor at Purdue University a few years later, Smith realised that one could analyse propositions derived from economic theory by using experimental tests. Smith embarked on an extensive project that tried to understand the formation of market prices and the convergence to equilibrium in perfectly competitive markets. The first set of Smith's results was published in 1962. However, it would still be many years before experimental methods became common-place in economic analysis.

In the late 1960s Charles Plott was a young theorist at Purdue and a friend of Smith's. In 1971 Plott moved to the California Institute of Technology (Caltech) and began to realise that experimental techniques were relevant not only to studying the formation of prices but also to social choice theory, public economics and political science.

In 1975 Smith joined the University of Arizona and started on a number of experimental projects pertaining to studying markets with Arlington Williams and auction design with James Cox.

By this time, game theoretic models had become solidly entrenched in economic analysis. These models, which placed demands on human cognition and brought issues of beliefs, learning and bounded rationality to the fore, lent themselves readily to experimental validation. Experimental economics gradually began to find greater acceptance and a number of leading game theorists, including Reinhard Selten, increasingly turned to experiments to put their theories to the test.

By the 1990s experimental economics had become part of the mainstream. Besides the extensive experimental work being carried out at Arizona, Bonn and California Institute of Technology (Caltech), there were a number of other researchers and laboratories. These included Alvin Roth, John Kagel and Jack Ochs at Pittsburgh, Shyam Sunder at Carnegie Mellon, Daniel Friedman at UC-Santa Cruz, Raymond Battalio at Texas A&M, Robert Forsythe at Iowa, Arlington Williams and James Walker at Indiana and Andrew Schotter at New York University.

## Appendix: a very brief and very simple introduction to game theory

As I mentioned above, many day-to-day decisions require strategic decision making. That is, they require us to anticipate the actions of others because actions taken by them crucially affect us in terms of our earnings, profit or utility. Economists (and game theorists) represent such situations as "*games*" with us – the participants – as the "*players*" in those games. In any particular game, each particular player has a number of strategies that she can choose from. Once everyone has chosen what she thinks is her best strategy given what she thinks others will choose, we get an outcome of the game where each participant receives a pay-off.

In what follows, for the sake of simplicity, I will restrict myself to games with only two players where these players can pick one of two strategies. I will also assume that players care only about making the most money. I have argued above that this assumption is not necessarily true but for the time being I am going to make this assumption to establish a bench-mark and worry about violations of this assumption later. Let us see what we can say *if* we assume that players are purely self-interested and wish to maximise their monetary earnings.

The trick in any game is to pick the strategy that you think will earn you the most money given what you think everyone else will choose. Of course the pay-offs you get can take non-monetary forms but, for the sake of simplicity, I will assume that we can assign a monetary value to all pay-offs received.

Let us think about the game between Nately and Yossarian. Each of them can choose one of two strategies: (1) work on building the officers' club; I will call this strategy "*work*"; (2) not work on building the officers' club, that is shirk and free-ride on the effort put in by others. I will call this strategy "*shirk*". The second strategy is analogous to not contributing towards the public park and free-riding on the contributions made by others hoping that the park will get built any way.

I will also assume that the officers' club will get built as long as one person works on the project except if both of them work then the club gets built faster. (If you think it is unrealistic for a club to be built by one man then think of Nately as the leader of a group of co-operators who always choose to "work" and Yossarian as the leader of a group of free-riders who always "shirk".)[9]

For each strategy – "work" or "shirk" – adopted by Nately and Yossarian they get a pay-off. Suppose we could assign a monetary amount to these. If both Nately and Yossarian (or their respective groups) work then the club gets built quickly. Suppose the pay-off to each (or each group) from having the club built is $12. (Maybe this is the monetary equivalent of the satisfaction they will get from using the club on any given day; or maybe this is the amount they were willing to pay in order to go there and have a drink at the end of the day.) But now suppose only Nately works but Yossarian does not. Remember the club will still get built in that case but now Yossarian is better off because he can now go there for a drink but has expended no effort in building the club and thus has not incurred any physical or psychological costs. Say this increases his pay-off to $16 at the expense of Nately who has expended effort. Because effort is costly (in terms of time and physical exhaustion) and Nately has had no help from Yossarian, Nately now gets only $2. The situation is similar if, by some strange quirk of fate, only Yossarian worked and Nately shirked. Then Nately gets $16 while Yossarian gets $2. Finally if they both shirk then the club does not get built and they are neither better off nor are they worse off. Suppose the pay-off to each in this case of both shirking is $6 each.

9  One can very easily visualise Nately and Yossarian in the following scenario from Jerome K. Jerome's *Three Men in a Boat*:

> *There is nothing does irritate me more than seeing other people sitting about doing nothing when I'm working.*
>
> *I lived with a man once who used to make me mad that way. He would loll on the sofa and watch me doing things by the hour together, following me round the room with his eyes, wherever I went. He said it did him real good to look on at me, messing about. He said it made him feel that life was not an idle dream to be gaped and yawned through, but a noble task, full of duty and stern work. He said he often wondered now how he could have gone on before he met me, never having anybody to look at while they worked.*

It is not difficult to visualise which role would be played by Nately and which by Yossarian.

We can represent this game in the following box, which is referred to as a *pay-off matrix* (see Figure 1.1).

In this pay-off matrix Yossarian chooses one of the two row strategies – work or shirk – while Nately chooses one of the columns – work or shirk. Each of them makes a choice at the same time and before knowing what the other person has decided. Once they have each chosen a strategy they get a particular monetary payoff created by the intersection of those two strategies.

It is clear that collectively Yossarian and Nately (or their respective groups) are better off if they both choose to work. They each get $12. But is that what individual rationality (as embodied in the decision to maximise monetary pay-off) suggests? It turns out that the answer is no. Here is why. Let us look at this game from Yossarian's perspective. (Since the situation is symmetric, all the arguments that apply to Yossarian, apply with equal force to Nately.)

Suppose Yossarian is convinced that Nately will work. What we need to figure out is this: What is Yossarian's best response to the strategy that Nately has chosen? In this case Nately has chosen "work". Should Yossarian work too? The answer is no. Yossarian is actually better off – gets a better pay-off – by shirking. To understand this look at the pay-off matrix again, but this time with Nately's pay-offs covered up (see Figure 1.2).

Suppose Nately chooses to *work*; then Yossarian gets $12 from working also but he gets more – $16 – from shirking. This implies that if Yossarian is only interested in maximising his pay-off then he should

| | Nately's strategy | |
|---|---|---|
| Yossarian's strategy | Work | Shirk |
| Work | Y's profit = $12<br>N's profit = $12 | Y's profit = $2<br>N's profit = $16 |
| Shirk | Y's profit = $16<br>N's profit = $2 | Y's profit = $6<br>N's profit = $6 |

*Figure 1.1* The game played by Yossarian and Nately.

| Yossarian's strategy | Nately's strategy | |
|---|---|---|
| | Work | Shirk |
| Work | Y's profit = $12 | Y's profit = $2 |
| Shirk | Y's profit = $16 | Y's profit = $6 |

*Figure 1.2* Yossarian's payoff for each of Nately's strategies.

shirk. So Yossarian's *best response* to Nately's decision to work is to *shirk*.

Suppose Nately chooses to *shirk*; then Yossarian gets $2 from working but he gets more – $6 – from shirking as well. This implies that if Yossarian is only interested in maximising his pay-off then he should shirk as well. So Yossarian's *best response* to Nately's decision to shirk is to also *shirk*.

This then implies that regardless of what Nately does, Yossarian is better off shirking. Game theorists call this a "*dominant strategy*", a strategy that does better, i.e. yields a higher payoff, against each of the opponent's strategies. Shirk, then, is a dominant strategy for Yossarian. If Yossarian is only concerned with making the most money then he should choose to shirk no matter what Nately chooses. The presence of this dominant strategy actually makes Yossarian's decision-making problem easier because now he really doesn't need to worry about what Nately is doing. Yossarian should always choose to shirk. If Nately *works*: then Yossarian gets $16 from shirking and only $12 from working. So if Nately works then Yossarian should shirk. But if Nately *shirks*: Yossarian gets $2 from working (a very bad outcome for Yossarian) and he gets $6 from shirking too. Yossarian therefore has a clear, indeed a dominant, strategy: shirk.

But since the situation is symmetric and the same argument applies equally well to Nately, he should always shirk too. To see this, look at

| | Nately's strategy | |
|---|---|---|
| Yossarian's strategy | Work | Shirk |
| Work | N's profit = $12 | N's profit = $16 |
| Shirk | N's profit = $2 | N's profit = $6 |

*Figure 1.3* Nately's payoff for each of Yossarian's strategies.

the payoff matrix again and focus on Nately's payoffs from different strategies only (see Figure 1.3).

It is clear that if Nately always chooses to shirk then he makes either $16 (if Yossarian chooses to work) or $6 (if Yossarian chooses shirk); whereas, if Nately chooses to work then he can make either $12 (if Yossarian chooses to work) or $2 (if Yossarian chooses to shirk). Therefore, the payoff to Nately from shirking is *always greater* compared to that from working, regardless of what Yossarian does. Nately is always better off choosing to shirk just like Yossarian!

This in turn implies that neither will work on building the club and the club will never get built; just as I argued above, if everyone is only interested in his own payoff then no one would contribute to the public park and the park will never get built.

Moreover, once both of them have decided to shirk, they both end up with $6 which is worse than the $12 that they could have obtained by working together. But, unilaterally neither wishes to change his mind. This is because if one player continues to shirk then the other player gets even less – $2 – by changing his mind and choosing to work. And so even though they both realise that collectively they are worse off by choosing to shirk, no one wishes to change his strategy. We have reached the equilibrium – a *Nash equilibrium* (see Figure 1.4).

In this game then the Nash equilibrium comes about when each player chooses to shirk as their best response to what they think the

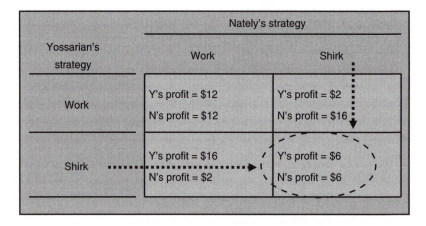

| | Nately's strategy | |
|---|---|---|
| Yossarian's strategy | Work | Shirk |
| Work | Y's profit = $12<br>N's profit = $12 | Y's profit = $2<br>N's profit = $16 |
| Shirk | Y's profit = $16<br>N's profit = $2 | Y's profit = $6<br>N's profit = $6 |

*Figure 1.4* The unique outcome in the game played by Yossarian and Nately.

other player will do. More generally then, we get a *Nash equilibrium* when players choose that strategy which they think is their best response – will do the best or yield the highest payoff – against what their opponent will choose.

In this game, often called a *"Prisoner's Dilemma"*, the crux of the problem is that both players can be better off if they cooperate; but individual rationality and the desire to maximise pay-offs dictates the use of the dominant strategy "shirk" and when they both rely on their dominant strategies they are collectively worse off. There is, thus, a tension between cooperating and maximising the joint benefit or free-riding and trying to maximise one's own pay-off at the expense of others.

Here is the reason why a game like the one played between Yossarian and Nately is called a *"prisoner's dilemma"*. It seems that when the game was first introduced, it was placed in the context of the following story where a crime has been committed. The police arrest a couple of likely suspects. Let us call them Bonnie and Clyde. The police bring Bonnie and Clyde over to the station and put them in different cells where they can neither see nor talk to one another. One police officer says to Bonnie:

> *look, we know you guys did it. But we are pretty sure that Clyde was the primary instigator; you just went along for the ride and then things got out of control. It is not too late to save yourself. All you*

*need to do is to rat on your mate and finger him for the crime; then we can convict him and he will get ten years in prison, and we will let you go free. But you need to make up your mind quickly, because all we need is one confession. So if Clyde rats on you first, then he gets the deal and you go away for ten years.*

At the same time another officer makes the exact same offer to Clyde. *"But what if I keep mum and so does my mate?"* asks Bonnie (or Clyde). *"Then you can't convict, can you?"* *"That's true,"* admits the police officer. *"But even then we will still have enough to convict you of a lesser crime and put each of you in jail for a year."* *"And if we both rat on each other?"* asks Bonnie (or Clyde). *"Then we can put both of you away for five years,"* says the officer.

We will assume that Bonnie is *"rational"*, meaning that she wants to do that, which serves her own self-interest (and the arguments that apply to Bonnie apply with equal force to Clyde). Bonnie considers each possible action by Clyde and figures out her best reaction in each case. So if Clyde rats on Bonnie, then Bonnie's best move clearly is to rat on Clyde. If Clyde confesses, then by staying mum Bonnie gets ten years in jail, but by also confessing she gets five years instead of ten. But suppose Clyde *doesn't* rat; even then Bonnie's best move is to rat on Clyde. Because this guarantees that Bonnie will go free instead of one year in prison, while Clyde gets ten years. So if Bonnie is self-interested, then it is always in Bonnie's interest to rat on Clyde. Essentially, this means that for Bonnie, ratting on Clyde is the *dominant strategy*; she should do this regardless of what Clyde does. But since a similar argument applies to Clyde, his best move (*dominant strategy*) is to rat on Bonnie. But if they both rat on each other *then they will both go to prison for five years! Except if only both could have kept their mouths shut, they would both be better off and spend only one year in jail!* This particular scenario is, in fact, a regular feature of cop shows on TV such as *NYPD Blue*. So in the Nash equilibrium of this game, we would expect both Bonnie and Clyde to rat on each other. This is exactly like Yossarian and Nately both choosing to shirk in the Nash equilibrium of their game.

There are many situations in life when we confront a prisoner's dilemma like this. As I mentioned above, the decision whether to contribute to a public park or not is one such situation. Everyone is better off if everyone contributes, but individually I can do better if I free-ride. But if everyone thinks like that, then no one contributes.

All countries are better off if every country chooses to reduce their greenhouse gas emissions. But reducing emissions is costly and requires sacrifices. If one country does not reduce its emissions while others do, then this country is better off at the expense of others. But when every country figures along the same lines no one reduces its emissions and we get massive global warming.

If all fishermen abide by their assigned quotas and one fisherman cheats and exceeds his quota then he is better off – he catches more fish – at the expense of those who are abiding by the quota. But if everyone chooses to do so – since it is a dominant strategy to over-fish if everyone else is abiding by the quota – then we get massive over-fishing and depleting stocks of fish (or other resources).

If all of us throw our garbage in designated garbage bins – which might involve some work – then we are all better off. But if one person throws his garbage out on the street then he is better off since he has saved himself the extra effort. But if everyone does the same thing then we get utter chaos and really dirty streets.

In all these cases, collectively we are better off if we cooperate, but the cooperative outcome is often hard to sustain since if every one is cooperating then one person can be better off by reneging and free-riding. But if it makes sense for one person to free-ride then it does so for others as well; so we all free-ride in equilibrium and we end up with global warming, fast depleting oceans and forests and dirty streets.

And once we arrive at that bad outcome, we might regret it but we are often unable or unwilling to change the situation because we would need everyone to change at the same time. One person choosing to cooperate while everyone else shirks does not change things and makes the one co-operator worse off. But getting everyone to change their minds at the same time poses similar problems of collective action which led to the Nash equilibrium in the first place.

Before moving on I need to point out that prisoner's dilemma like situations often arise when the interactions are one-off and players have no or limited ability to make binding commitments, meaning that they can say that they will do one thing but when the time comes to take action they are free to renege and cannot be held to their promises. This – especially the absence of binding commitments – is often the case in real life. If players know that they will interact over and over again or they can make binding commitments that can be enforced by a third party, then the outcome might be different. But that is beyond our scope at the moment.

Before I end this section I need to emphasise that not all games are like the prisoner's dilemma. Not all games have dominant strategies and neither do they lead to a unique outcome as in the prisoner's dilemma game. In Part 5, I will discuss another type of game where players do not have a dominant strategy. Furthermore in these games, when each player chooses his best response to the other player's strategy choice, we will end up with more than one feasible outcome; that is these games will allow for multiple equilibrium outcomes.

# Part 2
# The ultimatum game

## 2.1 The ultimatum game

In 1994, the players of Major League Baseball in the US went on strike. This led to the cancellation of 938 games overall, including the entire post-season and the World Series. Team owners were demanding a salary cap and came up with a new revenue-sharing plan, which required the players' approval. The players' union rejected the offer, which they thought was unfair to the players and merely a way to address problems of disparity among the owners. After prolonged negotiations failed to break the impasse, the acting commissioner Bud Selig called off the rest of the season on September 14. The move to cancel the rest of the season meant the loss of $580 million in owner-ship revenue and $230 million in player salaries. Thus, the players essentially walked away from $230 million collectively – the average salary of players at this time was about $1.2 million per year – because of what they considered was an unfair offer. This in turn resulted in a loss of more than twice that amount for the owners.

In February 2007, shareholders of the Tokyo Kohtetsu Company blocked a takeover by a rival steel producer, the Osaka Steel Company, the first time in Japan that shareholders have vetoed a merger approved by the companies' boards. An investment fund, Ichigo Asset Management, started a rare proxy fight against what it saw as an unfair offer from Osaka. Ichigo, which owns 12.6% of Tokyo Kohtetsu, had not been against the takeover *per se*, only against the fairness of the offer. Yoshihisa Okamoto, senior vice-president at Fuji Investment Management, said the vote *"sends the message that such unfair offers are unacceptable."*[1]

Colin Camerer, a leading experimental economist at Caltech, tells the following story:

> *I once took a cruise with some friends and a photographer took our picture, unsolicited, as we boarded the boat. When we disembarked hours later, the photographer tried to sell us the picture for $5 and refused to negotiate. (His refusal was credible because several other groups stood around deciding whether to buy their pictures, also for $5. If he caved in and cut the price, it would be evident to all others*

---

1   Reuters (2007, February 22). "A first in Japan: shareholders block a takeover", *New York Times* (World Business).

*and he would lose a lot more than the discount to us since he would
have to offer the discount to everyone.) Being good game theorists,
we balked at the price and pointed out that the picture was worthless
to him. (As I recall, one cheapskate (either Dick Thaler or myself)
offered $1.) He rejected our insulting offer and refused to back down.*

The picture is essentially valueless to the photographer (worth less than
$1) and of significant value to Camerer (certainly more than $5). Therefore there are many ways to divide the gains from exchange which
would leave both parties with a profit. Yet the photographer was
unwilling to accept any price less than $5 and walked away from a prof-
itable deal.

In all of these examples, people are willing to forego money because
they consider a particular offer to be unfair. This raises the questions:
Are humans fair by nature? Does this sense of fairness have economic
implications? These are things that I will talk about in this part.

Bargaining (haggling, negotiating) is a frequent part of many economic transactions including bargaining for a higher salary in job contracts or haggling over the price of a carpet or a used-car or
negotiations between owners and striking workers of a company. Often
as a part of the bargaining process, especially in cases where agreement
is proving to be elusive, one party makes an ultimatum offer, a situation
where that party says *"this is my best offer, take it or leave it…"*. This
happens, for instance, in the case of binding arbitration where two
sides are dead-locked and have failed to arrive at a compromise despite
repeated attempts. If that ultimatum offer is accepted then it leads to a
resolution, but if not, then it sometimes means substantial financial
losses for both parties involved.

In many such situations where the two sides in a dispute – players
and owners, management and union – have reached an impasse, one
side, that may have greater bargaining power or less to lose, might
make a *"take-it-or-leave-it"* offer to the other side – an *ultimatum*. For
instance team owners may join together to lay down an ultimatum to
the players' union and threaten the entire season if the players do not
agree to the owners' ultimatum. If however, the recipient of the ultimatum does decide to "leave it" – possibly because they are unhappy with
the offer and the way the available amount on the table is being split,
then it usually implies that both sides end up losing money. Rejecting
an offer in these circumstances means that the aggrieved person is

willing to forego a substantial amount of money in order to make sure that the other side loses as well. This is akin to cutting off one's nose to spite one's face.

In the early 1980s, Werner Güth, Rolf Schmittberger and Bernd Schwarze, three economists at the University of Cologne, were studying bargaining behaviour. More specifically, Güth and his colleagues looked at what happens when one party makes such a "take-it-or-leave-it" ultimatum offer to the other. What Güth and his colleagues were interested in understanding was: How do people – especially the recipients of such an ultimatum – respond to it? And do the people who make an ultimatum offer anticipate that response?

In order to study this problem, Güth and his colleagues recruited a group of graduate students at their university and had them take part in a simple game which has subsequently become well-known as the *Ultimatum Game*. Forty-two participants were paired into groups of twos to form 21 pairs. One player in each pair is called the "*proposer*" while the other is called the "*responder*".[2]

Each proposer was given a sum of money which ranged from 4 marks to 10 marks. Three proposers received 4 marks, three received 5 marks, three received 6 marks, three received 7 marks, three received 8 marks, three received 9 marks and finally three proposers received 10 marks. Each member of the pair knew *exactly* how much money the proposer of the pair was given. Their task was simple. Each proposer was asked to suggest a split of this initial endowment between him and the responder he was paired with. But there was a catch: the responder had to agree for either to receive any money!

That is, suppose a proposer who received 10 marks said "*I want to keep 8 marks and give 2 marks to the responder*" then that offer would be communicated to the paired responder and the responder would have to decide whether to accept this offer. If the responder accepted then the proposer got to keep the 8 marks while the responder received 2 marks. But if the responder did not accept the proposer's offer then they both got nothing! In the latter case, if the responder turned down the proposer's offer, then they both ended up with zero marks. Figure 2.1 illustrates the situation:

---

2  Actually Güth and his colleagues called them Player 1 and Player 2, respectively. Different authors use different terms in their papers. Rather than use different terms all the time I will stick to the convention of calling the first player, the proposer and the second player, the responder in the rest of this part.

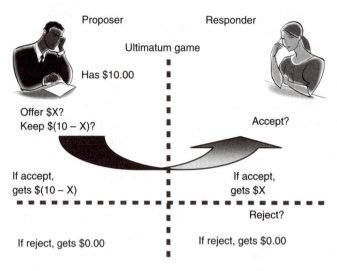

*Figure 2.1* The structure of the ultimatum game.

The proposers and the responders were seated at opposite ends of a large room and while they were placed in identifiable groups, no proposer ever learned which responder he was paired with. So what happened? Before you proceed, you might want to put the book down for a couple of minutes and think of the following: Suppose you were a proposer and had 10 marks (or 10 dollars), what would you do? How much would you keep? How much would you offer to the responder – someone who is most likely a complete stranger to you and someone you will possibly not meet or interact with in the future? Next, put on your responder hat. You know how much money the proposer you are paired with was given. What is the minimum amount you are willing to accept? 1 cent? 5 cents? 1 dollar? Remember that if you reject the proposer's offer then you both get zero.

Now what should we expect to happen? Before that, let me briefly tell you how economists think through situations like these. Economists, in these cases, rely on the principle of "*backward induction*" which says: start with the decision to be made by the last person and work your way backwards. (If you have ever tried to solve one of those maze-puzzles that appear in newspapers and magazines, then you will know what I am talking about. If you have tried, then it is highly likely that once in a while you have "cheated" and started from the end, i.e. you looked at where you had to go and then figured out how to get there starting from the beginning by working your way *backwards* through the maze.) That's backward induction! In this case then, let us start with the second decision maker – the responder. When the responder is offered an amount of money what should she do? Well, if she is someone who believes that some money is better than no money then she should accept any offer that gives her some money (*even if she is offered a relatively small sum*) because the consequence of turning down the offer means that she will get nothing. So the responder should be willing to accept most offers – even meagre ones! (Of course if the offer is really small – say 10 cents – the responder might be indifferent between making 10 cents and making nothing, in which case the responder might turn the offer down. But we would expect the responder to accept most non-trivial amounts.) Therefore, if the proposer *anticipates* the responder's reaction – that the responder will be willing to accept most non-trivial amounts, even small ones – then the proposer should offer exactly that, a small amount because the less the proposer offers to the responder, the better off the proposer is (since he gets to keep more of the money) as long as the responder agrees to that division. Suppose we constrain the proposers to making offers in 50 cent increments. Then we really expect those proposers to offer relatively small amounts to the responder – maybe 50 cents, maybe a dollar. Thus in a *Nash equilibrium* of this game we expect that proposers will offer a very small amount to the responder and the responder will accept whatever amount is offered.

In Figure 2.2, I show the various percentages such as 10%, 20%, 30% etc. (out of the initial amount) that the 21 proposers offered to their paired responders. Since different proposers received different starting amounts I need to put all these numbers in percentage terms rather than absolute numbers. The lighter-shaded bars show the number of proposers (out of 21) who offered a particular percentage amount such as the number of proposers who offered 10%, number of proposers who offered 20%, etc. The darker shaded bars show the number of rejections, i.e. the number of times a particular offer was turned down. The graph is quite striking. One-third of the proposers (seven out of 21) offered exactly half (50%) of the initial amount to the responder. Seventeen out of 21 proposers (slightly more than 80%) offered the responder *at least 20% or more* of the total amount available. This was surprising to say the least, since the proposers seemed to be offering way more than they had to. The one other puzzling bit here

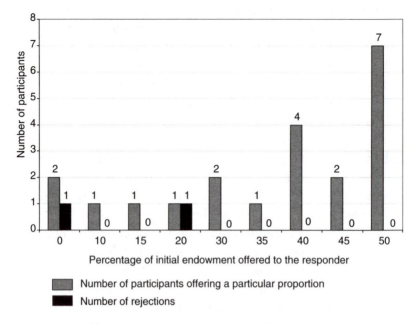

*Figure 2.2* Güth *et al.* (1982): proportional offers made by proposers and rejection rates (*inexperienced* subjects). Figure created by author on the basis of data provided in the original study.

was the rejections. Two of the 21 offers were rejected. As you can see from Figure 2.2, at the extreme left, there are two proposers who wanted to keep the entire amount (100%) and offered the responder nothing (0%). One of these zero offers is turned down by the responder. This is hardly surprising since the responder would have obtained nothing in either case whether he accepted or rejected the offer. But the surprise is that in one case, a proposer wanted to keep 80% of the available amount and offered the responder 20% but the responder turned this offer down! The proposer in this case had been given 6 marks to start with and he wanted to keep 4.80 marks and offered 1.20 to the responder. But the responder turned down the 1.20 marks in order to make sure that the proposer did not get the 4.80 marks!

Surprised and intrigued, Güth and his colleagues decided to carry out the exercise again. They brought back the same 42 participants – 21 proposers and 21 responders – a week later and asked them to play the exact same game as before with the same instructions. The only difference was that this time the proposers most likely received a different amount at the start compared to what they received a week earlier (say 8 marks rather than 5) and they were very likely paired with a different responder this time around. The results – presented in Figure 2.3 – were possibly even more striking. Figure 2.3 is very similar to Figure 2.2. As before, the lighter-shaded bars show the number of proposers (out of 21) who offered a particular percentage amount, such as the number of proposers who offered 10%, number of proposers who offered 20%, etc. Again, as before, the darker-shaded bars show the number of rejections, i.e. the number of times a particular offer was turned down.

A number of things stand out in this figure. First, there were fewer 50–50 splits offered by the proposers (three out of 21, or 14%, as opposed to seven out of 21, or 33%, a week before). But the offers were still very generous. Eighteen out of 21 proposers (close to 86% and almost the same number as a week before) offered at least 20% of the available amount to the responder. Even more striking were the rejections. Six of the 21 offers are rejected. In a number of cases, where the proposer wished to keep 80% or more of the available amount and offered the responder 20% or less, the responders turned down the offer.

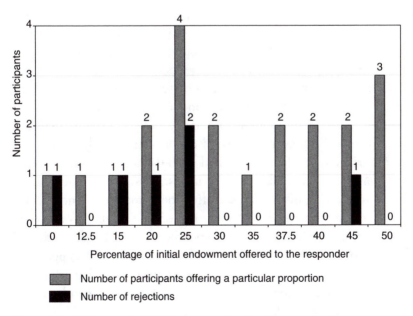

*Figure 2.3* Güth *et al.* (1982): proportional offers made by proposers and rejection rates (*experienced* subjects). Figure created by author on the basis of data provided in the original study.

But two responders said "*no*" when the proposer offered them 25% of the pie. In absolute amounts, in both cases the proposer had 4 marks to start with and had offered the responder 1 of those 4 marks and the responder turned them down. And in one case a proposer, who had received 7 marks to start with, wanted to keep 4 marks (55%) and offered the responder 3 marks (45%) but was turned down giving both zero!

In order to make sure that these results were not being caused by the inability of the participants to understand the instructions, Güth and his colleagues had them participate in a more difficult decision-making problem to test their analytical skills. Their performance in this more difficult task convinced the researchers that lack of understanding was not driving these results.

In reporting these results Güth and his colleagues commented

> . . . *subjects did not deviate from the optimal outcome because of their difficulties in solving the game. The main reason seems to be that the rational solution is not considered as socially acceptable or fair.*

They went on to add that the typical consideration of the responder in this game seems to be as follows: If the proposer left me a fair amount then I will accept; if not and the amount to be sacrificed is not large then I will reject the proposer's offer. Correspondingly, a proposer possibly reasoned like this: Even if I offer the responder a small amount, I need to give him a sufficient amount so that he is better off accepting this amount rather than turn me down and force us both to get nothing.

In order to get a better handle on the psychology of the participants, Güth and his colleagues then carried out a further study. Here, they had 37 participants who were asked to allocate 7 marks, but each person was asked to make two decisions. First, how much would someone in the role of a proposer offer the responder? And second, what was the minimum amount each person was willing to accept as the responder? The idea is this: If someone says that I want to keep 5 marks out of 7 and give the responder 2 marks (and expects the responder to accept that offer) then we would expect that when this same person was a responder and was offered 2 marks then he would gladly accept that amount.

It turns out that the majority of people were remarkably consistent. Fifteen participants out of 32 – as the proposer – offered the exact same amount to the paired responder that they were willing to accept as the responders themselves. That is, if they offered 2 marks out of 7 to the responder then in their role as responder they were willing to accept 2 marks as well. In many of these cases the actual split proposed was 50:50. Seventeen participants showed an explicit recognition of the fact that in this game, the proposer essentially has the upper hand and thus can be excused for wishing to retain a larger proportion of the available amount. These participants were willing to accept a smaller amount in their role as the responder than they offered to the responder in their role as proposer. That is, suppose as proposers, they offered 3 marks out of 7 to the responder, then as responders they were willing to accept 3 marks *or less* in a clear recognition of the power asymmetry between the two. But while these participants were perfectly willing to make allowances for this asymmetry as the responder, they were often more reluctant to exploit this power as the proposer. (I will have more to say later about this reluctance to fully exploit one's market power to garner more money for one's own self.) There were only five participants out of 37 who offered the responders less money than the minimum amount they were willing to accept as the responder.

These results clearly demonstrated that people's decisions were not being caused by an inability to understand the game or mistakes, but rather that participants obviously had clearly defined notions of what constituted a fair or unfair offer. Proposers were reluctant to make offers that would be construed as being unfair and responders had no hesitation about turning down unfair offers, when made, even if that meant sacrificing substantial amounts, as long as that sacrifice also caused the person making that unfair offer to suffer.

These results caused a stir. To a large extent, this was because neither unfairness nor a concern for relative payoffs was part of the economist's lexicon at that point. Economists typically tend to rely on the assumption of a rational *homo economicus* who is primarily interested in maximising his monetary returns in a particular situation or more generally his utility (with monetary payoffs featuring as the prominent component of utility). These results suggested that people seemed to care a lot about normative outcomes such as whether an allocation was fair or not, and more importantly, they seemed to be quite obsessed about relative payoffs – i.e. how much do I get as the responder vis-à-vis the proposer – and were willing to give up non-trivial amounts of money to avoid inequitable outcomes. So, for instance, responders seemed to be happy to give up 2 dollars to spite the proposer out of 8 dollars. This leads to the conclusion that people care considerably about the fairness of outcomes. Responders are willing to turn down money if they believe that a particular allocation is unfair. In making allocations proposers make allowances for the fact that an offer may get turned down if it appears unfair to the responder, even if it gives the responder a relatively large payoff in absolute terms.

## 2.2 Intentions, as well as outcomes, matter

One potential confound here is this: When responders turn down inequitable offers – that is, offers which give the proposer a much larger share of the pie compared to the share of the responder – what is it that they are protesting about? Is it the unfairness of the offer – that the proposer is trying to take more of the money to make himself better off at the expense of the responder? That is, are they acting in accordance to some implicit social norm that prescribes what behaviour is acceptable in a given situation and what is not? Or are the responders dissatisfied with the outcome of the bargaining process and the fact that they are relatively worse off compared to the proposers and it is this relative standing that bothers them? It is conceivable that preferences and reactions to allocations are affected not only by the final outcome of the process but also by how the current decision context transpired. People may be far more willing to put up with unfair outcomes if they are the result of environmental or chance factors than the result of a deliberate act by another person. For instance, people are more willing to exact retribution when a plane crashes because a faulty part was not replaced rather than when the crash is caused by a storm.

Sally Blount at the University of Chicago's Graduate School of Business decided to examine this phenomenon of aversion to unfair acts as opposed to protesting unfair outcomes. She had MBA students take part in an ultimatum game under different conditions.

The first condition was the usual ultimatum game, where participants were randomly assigned to the role of proposers and responders. Proposers had US$10 and got to offer a split of the initial pie and the responders had the right to accept or reject. In the event of a rejection, neither the proposer nor the responder got any money. In a second treatment – called the "*third party*" treatment – participants were divided into proposers and responders but the actual allocation of the initial amount (US$10) was decided not by the proposer, but by another disinterested participant who stood to gain nothing from the allocation. The responders had the option of rejecting the allocation decided by the disinterested third party and in the event of rejection, neither the proposer nor the responder got any money. Finally there was a third – "*chance*" – treatment where once again participants were divided into proposers and responders. There was US$10 to be divided as before, but rather than the proposer or a third party getting to decide, the allocation of the money in this treatment was decided by the spin of a roulette wheel which put an equal chance on each outcome (for instance $10 for the proposer and $0 for the responder, $9 for the proposer and $1 for the responder and so on).

Before playing the actual game, Blount also asked each participant to state the minimum amount he was willing to accept if assigned to the role of the responder in the game to be played immediately thereafter. If all that the respondents cared about was their *relative standing* vis-à-vis the proposers, that is, they did not want to be too worse off in monetary terms compared to the proposer, then the minimum acceptable amounts stated by participants in these three treatments should not be different. However, if it is the *intentionality* of the act that matters and people care more about intentional acts of unfairness rather than how much money they get relative to another, then we would expect people to be willing to accept inequitable allocations when the allocation is made by chance (by spinning a roulette wheel) than when the allocation is made by a proposer who stands to gain from the inequity of the offer.

The results clearly demonstrated that it is the *unfairness* of offers, rather than relative payoffs that people care about. In the first treatment, where the offers were decided by the proposer who got to keep more money by offering the responder less, the minimum amount responders were willing to accept was $2.91 (out of $10). In the case where the allocations were determined by a disinterested third party, the minimum acceptable amount was $2.08. But in the case when the offer is decided by chance, the minimum acceptable amount was $1.20. Thus, people were far less concerned by the unfairness of the outcome and the inequity of final payoffs when the division was decided by chance than when it was decided by another human, especially a human who stood to gain by making an inequitable offer. Furthermore, in the first treatment where the proposer got to allocate the money, nine out of 17 proposers offered a 50–50 split to the responder, four offered between $4 and $4.50, two offered between $2.50 and $3 and two offered the responder only $0.50. It became quite clear that participants were much less willing to accept large disparities in the payoffs in the condition where the proposer, who had a vested interest in the outcome, decided on the allocation, compared to the participants in the condition where the allocation was decided by chance.

Further evidence that intentions matter came from Armin Falk, Ernst Fehr and Urs Fischbacher of the University of Zürich. They had 90 participants take part in four separate, slightly modified ultimatum games. In each game the proposer is asked to suggest a split of 10 points. (Total points accumulated by the proposers and the responders were later redeemable for cash payments.) But rather than choosing any possible split of the 10 points, Falk and his colleagues restricted their proposers to making *only one of two choices*. I will call these choices A and B. Furthermore, choice A was *always the same in all four games*. Choice A gave 8 points out of 10 to the proposer and 2 points to the responder. Choice B, however, varied from one game to the next. In one game, choice B gave 5 points to the proposer and 5 points to the responder, i.e. in this game the proposer had a choice between keeping 8 for himself and giving 2 to the responder (choice A) or making an equal split giving 5 to each (choice B). Let us call this the "5/5 game". In a second game, choice B gave 2 points to the proposer and 8 points to the responder, i.e. in this game the proposer could choose to retain the lion's share of the pie (8 for him and 2 for the responder) or give away 8 to the responder keeping only 2. Let us call this the "2/8 game". Finally, in another game, choice B gave 10 points to the proposer and nothing to the responder. This game then offered two inequitable choices to the proposer – one inequitable offer where he kept 8 and offered the responder 2 and one even more inequitable choice where he kept all 10 and gave the responder nothing. I will call this the "10/0 game".

They also ran a game which provided the proposer with a trivial choice where both choice A and choice B gave 8 points to the proposer and 2 points to the responder. Here the proposer had no choice but to keep 8 and offer 2. I am not going to discuss this game since a discussion of the other three games will suffice to make my point.

In each and every game the responder could reject the proposer's offer, in which case, they both ended up with nothing. Before I tell you the results, and it is quite likely that you have an intuitive feeling for what to expect, let us think of what we expect to happen in this game in terms of acceptance or rejection by the responders. Once again, if responders are only concerned with their monetary payoffs then we expect that the 8/2 offer (8 points for the proposer and 2 for the responder) will never be rejected. Intuitively, we would expect that in the "5/5 game" a proposal of 8/2 is clearly perceived as unfair because the proposer could have proposed the egalitarian offer of 5 points for the proposer and 5 for the responder. In the "2/8 game" offering 8/2 may still be perceived as unfair but probably less so than in the "5/5 game" because the only alternative available to 8/2 gives the proposer only 2 points as opposed to 8 points to the responder. Thus, we would expect that the rejection rate of the 8/2 offer in the "5/5 game" is higher than in the "2/8 game". Finally, offering 8/2 in the "10/0 game" may even be perceived as a fair (or less unfair) action so that the rejection rate of 8/2 is likely to be lowest in this game.

The results were exactly as expected. The rejection rate of the inequitable 8/2 offer was the highest in the first "5/5 game" (44.4%). The 8/2 offers were rejected 27% of the time in the "2/8 game" and only 9% of the time in the "10/0 game". The variations in these rejection rates suggest that *intentions* driven reciprocal behaviour is a major factor behind them. The rejection rates of the alternative offers (5/5), (2/8) and (10/0) are as follows: nobody rejected the 5/5 offer and only one subject rejected the 2/8 offer. Almost 90% rejected the 10/0 offer when made.

Chimpanzees (*Pan troglodytes*) do not seem to share this human penchant for fairness. In 2007, Keith Jensen, Josep Call and Michael Tomasello at the Max Planck Institute for Evolutionary Anthropology had 11 chimpanzees participate in an ultimatum game with the exact same format as the Falk, Fehr and Fischbacher study described here except the chimpanzees were dividing 10 raisins rather than money. But, just as in the human study, the proposer chimpanzees had to choose between two offers A and B. Offer A always gave 8 raisins to the proposer and 2 to the responder while choice B varied from one game to the next. In one game, offer B gave 5 raisins to each ("5/5 game"), in a second, offer B gave 2 raisins to the proposer and 8 to the responder ("2/8 game") and in a third, it gave 10 raisins to the proposer and none to the responder ("10/0 game"). Unlike their human counterparts who routinely turn down 8/2 offers when the alternative is

5/5, chimpanzee responders *"did not reject unfair offers when the pro-poser had the option of making a fair offer; they accepted all non-zero offers; and they reliably rejected only offers of zero"*.

## 2.3  Criticisms of the findings of Güth and his colleagues

There were a number of criticisms aimed at the validity and interpreta-tion of these results. Broadly speaking, these questions could be classified into the following categories. First, the critics suggested that we are con-ditioned from childhood onwards to be sociable and cooperative. Thus, when confronted with a relatively novel situation of the ultimatum game proposers do not quite catch on that they have the upper hand in the transaction and can therefore earmark a larger portion of the available amount, giving the responders a smaller share. That is, proposers make generous offers because they are being altruistic and this does not really have anything to do with the fairness or unfairness of offers. This, of course, does not quite explain why the responders turn money down.

The second criticism was somewhat related to the first and grew out of it. Suppose you brought a group of people into a room and made half of them proposers and half responders. You gave the proposers $10 to divide between the two. This was like manna from heaven. Clearly the proposer is in a position of strength vis-à-vis the responder. But what entitles the proposer to be a proposer and therefore gain this position? The assignment to roles is purely a matter of chance. In this rather ambiguous situation the proposers might feel less entitled to the money and more inclined to share it fairly with the responders – after all the proposer could easily have been a responder. Elizabeth Hoffman, Kevin McCabe and Vernon Smith, who have done extensive work in the area, put it in the following way. *"It is as if you and I are walking along the street, and we see an envelope on the sidewalk. I pick it up. It contains ten $1 bills. I hand five to you and keep five."*

The third criticism was aimed at the relatively small stakes involved. These critics argued that ten marks was not a large amount and there-fore the participants may not even have taken the game seriously. Behaviour would be different and more "rational" if the amounts involved were larger, that is, proposers will keep a larger fraction and responders will not be so quick to turn offers down if larger amounts were involved. Turning down a dollar or two is one thing but who would turn down $10 or $20?

The fourth criticism involved a more subtle issue and had to do with what is often called "*experimenter demand effects*". This suggests that even if a proposer is interested in pocketing most of the amount given to him, he may not do so because he knows that the experimenter can see his decisions and he does not want the experimenter to think of him as greedy. Thus, it is embarrassment that is preventing the proposers from pocketing most of the money. And similarly being observed by the experimenter may compel the responder to reject small amounts because he does not want to appear desperate or look like a push-over.

## 2.4 Behaviour in the ultimatum game: fairness or altruism?

Let us take these criticisms in turn and see if they hold water. First, are proposers motivated by a desire to share? Robert Forsythe, Joel Horowitz, N. E. Savin and Martin Sefton of the University of Iowa answered this question by looking at the differences in behaviour in the ultimatum game and an even simpler game called the *Dictator Game*. The dictator game is similar to the ultimatum game in that participants are paired into proposers and responders. The proposers are then given an amount of money such as $10. They are then told to decide on an allocation of this money between the two. But now the responder does not have a say at all! Thus, any amount the proposer gives to the responder, the latter would have to accept without any option of reject-ing that offer.

Here the prediction based on self-interest is clear. The proposer should simply take all the money and give nothing to the responder. But, comparing the behaviour of the proposers in the ultimatum and dictator games can tell us about the motivations of the proposers. Suppose proposers in the ultimatum game were merely motivated by altruism – a desire to share – rather than fear of rejection. If that is that case, then the offers by the proposers in the two games – the ultimatum game and the dictator game (the latter being purely a decision to share the money) – should be similar. But if proposers in the ultimatum game are motivated by the fear of being punished in the event of unfair offers then we would expect much more generous offers in this game than in the dictator game.

In Figure 2.4, I show the behaviour of the participants from one of the experiments carried out by Forsythe and his colleagues. The

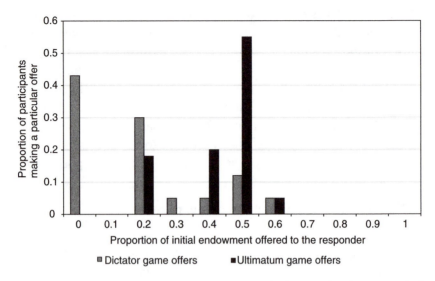

*Figure 2.4* Forsythe *et al.* (1994): comparison of offers in the dictator and ultimatum games. Figure created by author on the basis of data provided in the original study.

darker-shaded bars show the offers made in the ultimatum game while the lighter-shaded bars show the offers made in the dictator game – both in terms of the percentage of the initial amount that the proposer offered to the responder. In both games the proposers were given US $5 and were asked to suggest an allocation out of this.

It is quite clear from looking at the darker-shaded bars in this figure that the proposers in the ultimatum game offer the responders a lot more money than the proposers in the dictator game. It is clear that the modal offer – i.e. the offer made by the majority of participants – in the ultimatum game is 50% of the initial amount available. Fifty-five per cent of the proposers offered the responder $2.50 out of the $5.00 given to the proposers at the start of the game. Another 20% offered 40%, i.e. $2.00 out of $5.00. Thus three-quarters of proposers in the ultimatum game offered between $2.00 and $2.50 out of $5.00 (i.e. between 40% and 50%) to the responders. In contrast, if you look at the lighter-shaded bars then you can see that the modal offer in the dictator game is nothing. Forty-two per cent of the proposers in the dictator game offered nothing to the responder. Another 30% offered 20% of the available amount, i.e. $1.00. So while 75% of proposers in the ultimatum game offered $2.00 or more (40% or more) out of $5.00, just about 70% of the proposers in the dictator game offered a dollar or less (20% or less).

This was powerful evidence against an explanation based on proposer altruism and lent further credence to the argument that both proposers and responders were reacting in accordance with implicit social norms that dictate fairness in allocations. The conclusion was unequivocal. In the dictator game where there is no threat of being punished, proposers are rather parsimonious. But in the ultimatum game, the proposers clearly anticipate the fact that if they make unfair offers to responders then many responders will react adversely to that unfairness by turning down the offer even if the responder has to forego a substantial amount by doing so. Both proposers and responders exhibit that they have a very clear notion of what constitutes fair or unfair in a particular situation and respond accordingly.

## 2.5  Raising the monetary stakes in the ultimatum game

Would behaviour in the ultimatum game be different with higher stakes? Here, one unresolved issue of course is how large is large enough? In 1996, Elizabeth Hoffman, Kevin McCabe and Vernon Smith decided to try the same game with US$10 and US$100. US$100 was certainly a nontrivial amount then, as it is now, especially if you are a student whose opportunity cost of time (whatever is the most they can earn if they do something else during that time rather than participate in the experiment) is certainly less than $100 – especially given that the experiment took around 20 minutes to run. Hoffman, McCabe and Smith decided to examine the question of entitlement as well. So besides carrying out one treatment where participants are assigned to a role as proposer or responder randomly exactly as in prior studies, they looked at another treatment where these roles were decided on the basis of performance in a trivia quiz. Those who scored high in the quiz got to be proposers while the rest got to be responders. The proposers in this ultimatum game were told that they have "won" the right to divide this money with the idea that having won this right would imply a greater sense of entitlement among the proposers and might lead to more parsimonious offers.[3]

---

3  It is, of course, debatable whether a trivia quiz creates a genuine sense of entitlement. Those who end up as the "losers" might feel aggrieved and question whether performance in a trivia quiz is an appropriate or adequate way of creating a legitimate entitlement for those who "won".

What Hoffman, McCabe and Smith found was startling. In those experiments where participants were randomly assigned to the role of proposers and responders, as in the original study by Güth and his colleagues, the offers made by proposers to responders in the game played with $100 are *remarkably similar* to the offers made in the $10 game. There are 24 proposers in the $10 game and 27 in the $100 game. In both cases the modal offer (i.e. the offer made by a majority of proposers) is 50% – either $5 out of $10 or $50 out of $100. And in both games, pretty much all the offers ranged between 30% and 50%, i.e. between $3 and $5 in the $10 game and between $30 and $50 in the $100 game. Except, in the $100 game, there was one person who wished to keep the entire $100 (which was acceptable to the responder) while no proposer wanted to keep it all in the $10 game. And in the $100 game there were two subjects who offered $60 (60%) to the paired responder – that is these two were willing to give up $60 and keep $40! Little wonder that these offers were accepted.

When it came to the games where people have "earned" the right to be proposers by doing well on the trivia quiz, offers were more parsimonious. There were 24 proposers who played the $10 game and 23 who play the $100 game. There were fewer offers that gave the responder 40% or more and more offers that gave the responder 10%. In this case, a number of proposers appeared to believe that the responders would be willing to accept a smaller portion of the pie, such as 10% (probably because the proposers have "won" the quiz and feel entitled to claim a larger share of the booty). But quite surprisingly, the responders were clearly not willing to accede to this sense of entitlement on the part of the proposers. This was because the rejection rates (i.e. the rate at which proposed offers were turned down by the responders) were much higher in the $100 game as well. In the $10 game only three out of 24 offers were rejected while in the $100 game five out of 23 offers were rejected. Three out of four offers where the responder received $10 were rejected and out of five cases where the responder was offered $30 with the proposer keeping $70, two were rejected! Thus, a number of participants in the $100 game rejected amounts of money that were greater than or equal to the entire stake in the $10 game. This suggests that the expectations of what constitutes fair is different between the $10 and $100 games.

The Hoffman, McCabe and Smith study suggested that if the roles of proposer and receiver are assigned randomly then offers tended to cluster around 50% and this was true whether the stakes are $10 or $100. Thus, multiplying the stakes ten-fold did not lead to any appreciable changes in proposer behaviour. When the roles were assigned on the basis of performance in a trivia quiz, proposers seem to feel entitled to keep more of the money and make more parsimonious offers, but this legitimacy was not necessarily accepted by the responders and, especially in the $100 game, the parsimony of the proposers led to discord and higher rejection rates.

These results went a long way to answering the proposition that behaviour would be different and more in keeping with the self-interest assumption if only the stakes were higher. It turns out that this is not true, and in fact, if roles are assigned randomly then there is a slight movement towards more equitable offers with increased stakes. But is $100 high enough? Would behaviour be different if the sum of money was even larger?

One problem with using really large sums of money is that these studies are funded by research grants and most researchers do not have unlimited amounts of money at their disposal. But there is a way out of this and that is to run these experiments in a poorer country. Given that there are large differences in purchasing power, even small sums in developed countries amount to much larger sums in less developed ones. Thus, the same amount of dollars go a much longer way in poorer countries and allows the researcher to run experiments with stakes that amount to many times the monthly income of participants.

Lisa Cameron decided that to really answer the question about stakes, we need to look at behaviour with even greater amounts of money. In 1994, she travelled to Gadjah Mada University in Yogyakarta, Indonesia. At that time, the per capita gross domestic product of Indonesia was US$670, which was about 3% of the gross domestic product in the US. Cameron had participants play the ultimatum game with 5,000, 40,000 and 200,000 Indonesian rupiahs (approximately 2.50, 20 and 100 American dollars, respectively with the then exchange rate of US$1 = 2,160 Indonesian rupiahs). The largest of these three stakes were approximately three times the average monthly expenditure of the participants. These were unarguably high stakes.

It is possible, behaviour may be different if we were dealing with millions of dollars but most of us are not dealing with millions on an everyday basis. Furthermore, it is not clear if that would make a difference either. If Bill Gates was playing an ultimatum game with

Warren Buffet – those are the people who can afford to play the ultimatum game with millions of dollars – and Buffet offered Gates US$200,000 out of US$1 million then it is quite conceivable that Gates might turn the offer down. $200,000, after all, does not mean as much to Gates as it does to most of us.

Table 2.1 shows the offers made by the proposers using the three different amounts. The average amount offered is around 40% in all three cases and the modal amount is 50% in each case.

Surprisingly, or in the light of what I have said above, not surprisingly, in the game with 200,000 rupiahs, offers of 10% and 20% of the available amount (20,000 and 40,000 rupiah, respectively) were rejected by the responders. In the 40,000-rupiah game, offers of 25%, 30% and 35% (10,000, 12,000 and 14,000 rupiahs, respectively) were turned down as well. Cameron's conclusion: the examination of proposer behaviour in these games does not show any movement towards the Nash equilibrium outcome as the stake increases. Remember, Nash equilibrium reasoning suggests very small offers by proposers and acceptance by responders. Cameron goes on to conclude that "...*proposer behaviour is invariant to stake changes*", i.e. offers do not become more parsimonious even where large sums of money are concerned. Possibly because, as I pointed out above, in the case of inequitable offers of 25% of the available amount or less, responders routinely turn down substantial amounts of money if they feel that the offer is unfair.

Cameron also found that there was an increase in the rates of acceptance of offers as the stakes increase but she suggests that this may not necessarily reflect a greater willingness on the part of the responders to

*Table 2.1* Cameron (1995): offers made in high stakes ultimatum games

|  | Game 1 (5,000 rupiah) (%) | Game 2 (40,000 rupiah) (%) | Game 3 (200,000 rupiah) (%) |
| --- | --- | --- | --- |
| Average proportion offered | 40 | 45 | 42 |
| Modal offer (offer made by a majority of participants) | 50 | 50 | 50 |
| Acceptance Rates | 69 | 91 | 90 |

Source: Table created by author on the basis of data provided in the original study.

accept a given amount but is rather due to the fact that as the stake size grows, proposers in general tend to make more generous offers which makes those offers more likely to be accepted. So, if Warren Buffet did get together with Bill Gates to play the ultimatum game chances are Buffet will offer Gates 40–50% of the pie and Gates will accept!

## 2.6 Fear of punishment or fear of embarrassment?

What about the criticism that generous offers by proposers are caused by an unwillingness to appear "greedy" in the eyes of the experimenters who can observe the decisions made? Elizabeth Hoffman, Kevin McCabe, Keith Shachat and Vernon Smith ran some dictator game experiments using a complicated *"double-blind"* protocol. Normally, in experiments, a participant is not aware of who he is paired with but the experimenter can see all the decisions. Thus, there is anonymity between the participants but not between the participants and the experimenter. This protocol is called *"single-blind"*. A double-blind protocol refers to a situation where the decisions made by all particip-ants are completely anonymous in that neither the other participants nor the experimenter learns what a particular participant decided.[4] Usually experimental economists carry out double-blind protocols by assigning letters or numbers to participants and participants then picking a letter or number at random. Participants then make decisions on pieces of paper which are deposited into a locked box so that the experimenter cannot see those decisions. The experimenter then pays the participants on the basis of the numbers or letters assigned and deposits these payments into another locked box. Participants pick up the payment that matches their letter or number from the locked box using keys given to them at the beginning of the session. The experi-menter does not know which participant was assigned a particular letter or number and therefore has no way of matching the decisions with a particular participant.

---

4  Double-blind protocol in medical studies refers to an even more stringent condition where even the principal researcher does not know which patient is assigned to which group – for instance, which patient is in the treatment group and which is in the placebo group. This would dictate that all experimental sessions are run with research assistants who have no idea about the researcher's hypotheses or purpose. While this is feasible, it is often not practicable and in any case the evidence, at least in the case of studies in experimental economics, suggests that this does *not* make a big difference.

Using this complex protocol guarantees that the participants will be convinced that no one – neither the other participants nor the experimenter – will ever learn what each individual participant decided. Hoffman and her colleagues actually ran another even more stringent double-blind protocol where they used one of the experimental participants as the monitor for the entire session. This participant, who was taught what to do at the beginning of the session, was in charge of running the entire session and did not have any prior knowledge about the experimenters' purpose. Furthermore, Hoffman and her colleagues also looked at a treatment where not only did they use a double-blind protocol but also reinforced the proposer's sense of entitlement to the money by having them participate in a trivia quiz where those in the top half of the group got to be proposers while the rest were responders.

In previous dictator experiments, around 20% of proposers offered nothing to the responder, while another 20% offered half the available amount. When Hoffman and her colleagues looked at dictator games where the right to be a proposer was "earned" on the basis of performance in the trivia quiz, 40% of the proposers offered nothing and another 40% offered only 10 or 20% of the pie to the responder. When they added the double-blind protocol on top of that – i.e. proposers earned the right by winning in the trivia quiz and there was anonymity between both participants and between the participant and the experimenter – over two-thirds of proposers offered nothing and 84% offered 10% or less. Hoffman and her colleagues suggested that being observed by the experimenter – and possibly thought "greedy" – seemed to matter and that it is conceivable that it is this fear of being thought greedy that leads to generous offers in the ultimatum game rather than allowances for implicit social norms of fairness or the fear of being punished for unfair offers.

Of course, this elaborate double-blind protocol coupled with a sense of entitlement generated by winning the quiz might have created a different type of experimenter demand effect. It is possible that participants may have construed the elaborate procedures as a "signal" that they really should keep the money given that most transactions in real-life are often not nearly as anonymous as this.

Gary Bolton at Penn State and Rami Zwick at the University of Auckland provided an eloquent answer to this question and demonstrated beyond doubt that it was the fear of punishment that was driving behaviour in the ultimatum game. Bolton and Zwick compared the behaviour of participants in the ultimatum game with another game that they called the *"impunity game"*. Let me explain the impunity game first. In the impunity game players are paired up into proposers and responders exactly as in the ultimatum game. Also, exactly as in the ultimatum game, the proposer is given a certain sum of money and asked to suggest a split of this money between the proposer and the responder. The responder is informed about the split offered by the proposer and asked whether he accepted or rejected that allocation. If the responder accepts the offer then the allocation is implemented with the proposer keeping the amount he wanted to and the responder getting the rest. However if the responder rejects the offer, *then the proposer still gets the amount he wanted to keep but the responder gets nothing.* So the difference with the ultimatum game is that in the impunity game a rejection by the responder does not have the power to hurt the proposer by taking money away from him. The threat of punishment to the proposer for making an unfair offer is removed in the impunity game.

Here is what Bolton and Zwick proposed to do. They decided to look at behaviour in the ultimatum game, first, with a double-blind protocol which preserves anonymity between the participants and the experimenter and then, with a single-blind protocol where the experimenter gets to observe participant decisions. They also decided to compare the behaviour of the proposers in the ultimatum game with that in the impunity game. The reasoning is as follows: suppose proposers make generous offers in the ultimatum game because they do not want to be perceived as being greedy or unfair by the experimenter. Then we should expect to see less generous offers in the double-blind ultimatum game where the experimenter could not observe individual decisions as compared to the single-blind protocol where the experimenter could see all decisions. On the other hand, if generous offers in the ultimatum game are driven by the fear of being punished in the event of making an unfair offer, then we should observe far more parsimonious offers in the impunity game where there is no threat of punishment (since even if the responder rejects the offer in this game the proposer still gets to keep the amount he wanted for himself) compared to the ultimatum game where the responder's rejection will cost the proposer his share of the pie.

Bolton and Zwick also made a change to the way the games were carried out. In most prior studies proposers were given an amount (say US$10) and asked to suggest a split of this amount between the proposer and the responder. The changes made by Bolton and Zwick included the following. First, each proposer played the game ten times but each time the proposer was paired with a different responder. In each round the proposer had US$4 and in each round the proposer could make one of two choices – an *equitable* choice which gave US$2 to both the proposer and the responder and an *inequitable* choice which gave the proposer more money than the responder.

But this inequitable choice was different in different rounds. Sometimes the inequity in payoffs was small, while in other cases the difference was larger. More specifically the proposer could choose one out of five inequitable offers – {$2.20, $1.80}, {$2.60, $1.40}, {$3.00, $1.00}, {$3.40, $0.60}, {$3.80, $0.20}. Since each proposer played ten games, he faced each of these above five choices twice. Notice that, in each of the five choices, the sum adds up to $4 and that the first of these five offers is more equitable than the last which gives the responder only $0.20 (i.e. 5% of the pie) and the level of inequity increases between the first and the last choice. Once again, if participants are motivated by purely monetary considerations then the obvious self-interested preferences dictate that the proposer should choose the {$3.80, $0.20} split and the responder should accept. More generally we would expect the proposer to choose the inequitable payoffs predominantly and regardless of which inequitable offer is chosen, we expect the responder to accept.

Again, to remind you about the central comparison here, if it is experimenter observation that matters then we would expect proposers to choose the inequitable offer more frequently in the double-blind ultimatum game as compared to the single-blind ultimatum game. On the other hand, if it is the fear of punishment that is the primary motivation behind proposer choices then we expect more inequitable choices in the impunity game, where the responder cannot retaliate to the inequity by rejecting the offer, compared to the ultimatum game where rejection is meaningful and deprives the proposer of his payoff. The results clearly supported the punishment hypothesis. In the single-blind ultimatum game, 56% of all proposer choices were one of the inequitable choices and around 20% of these offers were rejected. The equitable offer of $2 each for the proposer and the responder was never rejected by the responder. Rejection rates were also higher as the offers became more inequitable. The choices in the double-blind ultimatum game were not all that different from those of the single-blind ultimatum game. There was a small increase in the proportion of

*Table 2.2* Bolton and Zwick (1995): percentage of inequitable offers rejected by the responder

| Inequitable offers to the responder | $1.80 | $1.40 | $1.00 | $0.60 | $0.20 |
|---|---|---|---|---|---|
| Single-blind ultimatum game | 7.7 | 11.8 | 57.1 | 77.8 | 100.0 |
| Double-blind ultimatum game | 13.3 | 7.1 | 67.0 | 70.0 | 100.0 |

Source: Table created by author on the basis of data provided in the original study.

inequitable offers by the proposers – 63% of the offers were inequitable ones in the double-blind protocol as opposed to 56% in the single-blind protocol. Once again there were also substantial rejections by the responders. Bear in mind what we said before. It is possible that responders may reject small offers in the ultimatum game in order not to be seen as desperate or a push-over by the experimenter. Using this logic we would expect many more responders to accept small offers in the double-blind ultimatum game as opposed to the single-blind ultimatum game. Remember that the responder could be offered $1.80, or $1.40, or $1.00, or $0.60, or $0.20 out of $4. Table 2.2 provides a break-down of rejection rates

A few things stand out from this table. First, offers that were grossly inequitable – offering the responder only 20 cents out of the $4 available – were turned down in every single case regardless of whether the experimenter could observe actions (single-blind protocol) or not (double-blind protocol). Furthermore, more than 50% of offers that gave the responder $1 or less are turned down. Overall the differences between the two treatments – single-blind versus double-blind – were not very pronounced. To observe really different behaviour one must look at the impunity game where the threat of punishment was removed. Here 98% of the offers made by the proposers were inequitable offers and *none of these – not even when the proposers offered the responder $0.20 out of $4 – were turned down!* The evidence was incontrovertible. When the responders could not retaliate by rejecting unfair offers the proposers felt no compunction in making inequitable offers; and when the responders knew that their rejection was not going to hurt the proposer, the responders did not bother engaging in such punishment either.

## 2.7  Do norms of fairness differ across cultures?

Most of the above studies used university students as participants and were concentrated on participants in the US and, in the case of the original study by Güth and his colleagues, Germany. It should be clear from the discussion above that the prevailing norm as to what constitutes a fair offer influences behaviour in the ultimatum game. But different cultures may have very different ideas of what constitutes "fair". Thus while the above studies may provide us with clues regarding what university students in western market-based economies conceive as fair, is it possible to generalise those results to other countries and other cultures?

The first attempt to answer this question was undertaken by Alvin Roth and his colleagues, Vesna Prasnikar, Masahiro Okuno-Fujiwara and Shmuel Zamir during 1989–1990. Roth and his colleagues decided on an ambitious project which involved recruiting university students across four different locations – Pittsburgh, Ljubljana (in Slovenia which used to be part of Yugoslavia), Tokyo (in Japan) and Jerusalem (in Israel). This was one of the first attempts to look at behaviour in the ultimatum game across a number of (very) different cultures. A typical session had 20 participants and they were divided into ten pairs of proposers and responders. Each of the ten proposers interacted with each of the ten responders so that by the end of the session each participant had participated in ten rounds of play. Needless to mention, proposers and responders were anonymous to one another and were identified by numbers only. In the US, in every round, each proposer had US$10 to divide. In keeping with purchasing powers prevailing at the time, the amount to be divided was made equal to 400,000 dinars in Slovenia, 20,000 yen in Japan and 20 shekels in Israel. However, because these amounts were different, proposers in each country were asked to suggest a division of 1,000 tokens where total tokens earned by a participant was converted into real money at the end of the session.

An ambitious cross-country project like this poses a number of ancillary problems. Two of these are language effects and experimenter effects. The first one refers to the fact that, since the instructions to participants are written in four different languages (English, Hebrew, Japanese and Slovenian), this might lead to differences in behaviour. For instance, as these authors point out, the words "bargaining", "negotiating" and "haggling" are roughly synonymous but quite possibly convey very different messages depending on which word is being used. Pepsi for instance, much to its chagrin, found out about the pitfalls in translation when Pepsi's tag-line *"Come alive with the Pepsi generation"* translated into *"Pepsi brings your ancestors back from the grave"* in Chinese. Along the same lines Frank Perdue's chicken slogan, *"It takes a strong man to make a tender chicken"* was translated into Spanish as *"It takes an aroused man to make a chicken affectionate."* Coors beer's slogan, *"Turn it loose"* was translated into Spanish to read as *"Suffer from diarrhoea".*[5]

This problem is handled by first writing out the instructions in English and then translating them to the language of the country concerned and then back-translating them into English to make sure that the act of translating the instructions does not distort the meaning of the instructions. The initial translation and back-translations are done by different people. The second problem arises from the fact that different people are running the experiments in different countries and there is a chance (possibly low) that the participants may respond differently to the different demeanours or personalities of the different experimenters. This problem was solved by having each of the experimenters run sessions in Pittsburgh. By keeping the location fixed, any differences in behaviour due to a particular experimenter's personality can be pin-pointed. The Slovenian data was gathered by Prasnikar, who also ran the first Pittsburgh sessions, with Roth observing. The remaining Pittsburgh data were gathered by Zamir (who also ran the experiments in Jerusalem) and Okuno-Fujiwara (who ran the sessions in Tokyo as well) with Roth and Prasnikar observing. There were no systematic differences in behaviour based on who was running the session.

Figure 2.5 shows the types of offers made in the four locations. In this figure I show what happened only in the tenth (and last) round of interactions. It is conceivable that participants, particularly proposers, engage in some amount of experimentation – i.e. trying out different things – in the first few rounds. Furthermore, they probably learn valuable information from both acceptances and rejections of offers during those early rounds. Thus it stands to reason that the offers made in the very last round reflect in-built preferences and norms better than the data from the first few rounds.

5  I need to thank Nandita Basu for providing me with these examples.

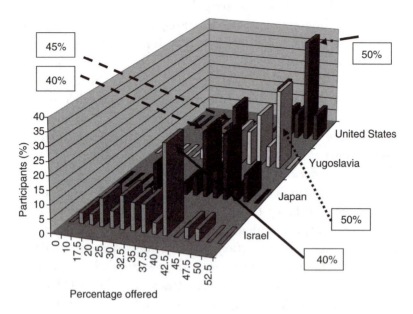

*Figure 2.5* Roth *et al.* (1991): offers made in the ultimatum game in Israel, Japan, Yugoslavia and the United States. Figure created by author on the basis of data provided in the original study.

The graph looks complicated but really is not. The horizontal axis shows the percentage of the amount available that the proposer offered to the responder. The vertical axis shows the proportion of offers that offered a particular percentage to the responder. There are four sets of bars. The first set shows the offers that were made in Israel. The second set shows the offers made in Japan. The third shows the offers in Slovenia and the final set of bars (at the very end) shows the offers made in the US. So looking at the bars for Israel – the very first set – we find that no one offered 0% to the responder. About 5% of offers gave the responder 10% of the pie while another 5% offered 17.5%. Ten per cent of offers gave the responder 20% and 32% offered the responder 40%.

A few things stand out from these figures. Not surprisingly the proposers seldom offered more than 50% of the pie to the responder. (There is one exception. In the US – look at the very last set of bars – around 10% of all offers in the last round were "hyper-fair" in that these proposers offered 52.5% of the pie to the responder keeping only 47.5%, a lower share. Of course these offers were all accepted.)

Second, overall the offers look similar in that in no country do we see extremely parsimonious offers as the theory predicts.

But if we look more closely then there are differences. One thing that you should notice is that in Israel (the very first set of bars) the modal offer (i.e. the offer made by the most subjects) is 40%. Around one-third of all offers gave the responder 40% of the pie. In Japan (the second set of bars) there are two modes – 40% and 45%. Roughly 25% of offers each were of either 40% or 45%. However in Slovenia and the US, the modal offer is 50%. Thirty per cent of all offers in the last round gave the responder 50% in Slovenia and 40% of offers gave 50% to the responder in the US. Statistical tests confirmed the following: offers in the US and Slovenia were equally generous, while the offers in these two countries were more generous than the offers in Japan which in turn was more generous than the offers in Israel.

If we now look at the rejection rates then we find that across all rounds, roughly 28% of all offers were rejected in the US, 29% in Slovenia, 22% in Japan and 28% in Israel. Thus while the rejection rates were broadly similar across countries, what was surprising is that if we look at the tenth and final round only, then we find that the rejection rates in the two low-offer countries – Japan and Israel – were actually lower than the other two. Rejection rates in the tenth and final round were 14% and 13%, respectively, in the two low-offer countries, Japan and Israel, and these rates were lower than the 19% and 23% rejection rates in the US and Slovenia, respectively. Looking at these patterns of behaviour one could hypothesise that the difference among subject pools is in something like their "aggressiveness" or "toughness". But if it is indeed the case that there are differences in aggressiveness across the four countries then we would expect the responders to share that characteristic. This should then lead to high rates of disagreement and rejected offers in the two countries (Japan and Israel) where the offers are low in general. But that is not the case. Instead, the two countries where offers are low (Japan and Israel) do not exhibit any higher rates of disagreement than the high-offer countries (the US and Slovenia).

The authors conclude:

> *This suggests that what varies between subject pools is not a property like aggressiveness or toughness, but rather the perception of what constitutes a reasonable offer under the circumstances. That is,*

*suppose that in all subject pools it seems reasonable for the first mover to ask for more than half the profit from the transaction and that what varies between subject pools is how much more seems reasonable. To the extent that offers tend towards what is commonly regarded as reasonable, and assuming that offers regarded as reasonable are accepted, there would be no reason to expect disagreement rates to vary between subject pools, even when offers do. Our data thus lend some support to the hypothesis that the subject-pool differences observed in this experiment are related to different expectations about what constitutes an acceptable offer.... Consequently, we offer the conjecture that the observed subject-pool differences are cultural in character.*

The work done by Roth and his colleagues went a long way towards addressing the issue of cultural differences. Their results showed that there were both similarities and differences across cultures. The similarity was that in no country were the proposers as parsimonious as the theory would suggest and the vast majority of offers gave the responders 20% or more of the pie. But there were differences. The modal offers were lower in Japan and Israel compared to Slovenia and the US and offers in general were less generous in the former two countries compared to the latter two.

## 2.8 An even more ambitious cross-cultural study

But, while it is true that the four above countries do represent very different cultures, are students across these countries all that different? Maybe the students are much more alike than the citizens of these nations at large. If so, then maybe we should look further and deeper to search for cultural differences in behaviour. In the mid-1990s a far more comprehensive cross-cultural study of behaviour in the ultimatum game than anything attempted before was initiated under the auspices of the MacArthur Foundation Norms and Preferences Network.

Joseph Henrich, an anthropologist at the University of California–Los Angeles (UCLA) was undertaking field work among the Machiguenga, a group of horticulturalists in the tropical forests of south-eastern Peru. Henrich had heard about the ultimatum game results discussed above from his advisor Robert Boyd. Henrich decided to have the Machiguenga play the ultimatum game. Henrich's findings were surprising and deviated substantially from the findings of studies prior to this. The Machiguenga behaved very differently from the participants in the studies mentioned above. The most common offer made by Machiguenga proposers was 15% and despite many low offers, not a single offer was rejected. This was doubly surprising given that Machiguenga live in small villages where people interact with other village members quite regularly and have very limited contact with strangers – an environment that we would expect would make the people more pre-disposed towards sharing, reciprocal motivations and fairness.

Henrich shared his findings with Robert Boyd, a noted anthropologist at UCLA and Colin Camerer, a leading experimental economist at Caltech. Both Boyd and Camerer were also members of the Norms and Preferences Network. The obvious question was this: Were the Machiguenga results anomalous or were these results indicative of far more substantial cultural variations in behaviour that is not captured by the predominantly student participants in the previous studies? Boyd and Herbert Gintis, who were at this time the directors of the Preferences Network, decided to organise and fund a tremendously ambitious programme of cross-cultural experimental work.

They put together a group of 12 experienced field researchers working in 12 countries over five continents and gathered data for 15 small-scale societies exhibiting a wide variety of economic and cultural conditions. The 15 societies studied included the Orma in Kenya, the Hadza and the Sangu in Tanzania, the Torguud Mongols and the Kazakhs in Mongolia, the Lamalera in Indonesia, the Au and the Gnau in Papua New Guinea, the Achuar in Ecuador, the Machiguenga in Peru, the Tsimane in Bolivia, the Mapuche in Chile and the Ache in Paraguay. Three of these are foraging societies, six practise slash-and-burn horticulture, four are nomadic herding groups and three are sedentary, small-scale agricultural societies.

Needless to mention, given the complexity of the task involved it was impossible to control for differences in language or experimenters (as Roth and his colleagues did). Thus the researchers, who were already involved in anthropological field work in these countries, carried out the experiments on their own in these respective societies using the local language or local dialect. The experimenters tried to maintain anonymity by having proposers make offers and responders make acceptance/rejection decisions in seclusion, still given the small-knit nature of many of these communities the level of anonymity is certainly less than in usual laboratory studies of behaviour.

The findings, published in 2004 in the book *Foundations of Human Sociality* edited by Joseph Henrich, Robert Boyd, Samuel Bowles, Colin Camerer, Ernst Fehr and Herbert Gintis, suggested that (1) there is no society where behaviour is commensurate with the extreme self-interest hypothesis that posits that proposers would keep a lion's share of the pie; (2) there is much more variation between groups than has been previously reported. The norm of what constitutes fair behaviour varies substantially across these societies and, more importantly, this variation coincides with differences in the patterns of interaction in everyday life.

Table 2.3 provides a broad overview of behaviour in the ultimatum game across these diverse societies. I have arranged the societies in increasing order of the average offers made. As you can see the variations are substantial. At the low end we have the Machiguenga, Quichua and Hadza (small camp) where the average offers are around 25% of the pie and the modal offer also hovers around the 25% mark. (Remember in the Roth *et al.* study the lowest mode was in Israel and that mode was 40% of the pie.) At the other end of the spectrum we have the Achuar, Orma, Ache and Lamalera. Among the Achuar and the Orma, proposers on average offer a little more than 40% of the pie which is very similar to what we find in the industrialised country studies. The Ache and the Lamalera are even more generous and on average make "hyper-fair" offers where the proposers on average offer a larger share of the pie (51% and 58%, respectively) to the responders.

Looking at the column for rejection rates we find that these rates tend to be low. In industrialised nations on average five out of 10 (50%) offers that give the responder less than 20% are rejected. But regardless of whether the offers are in general parsimonious, as among the Machiguenga and the Quichua, or very generous, as among the Achuar, Orma, Ache and Lamalera, very few offers are rejected. This suggests broad agreement among the proposers and responders as to what constitutes a fair offer in these societies. Strangely enough among the Machiguenga and the Quichua where the average offer is around 25% and the modal offer is also around 25%, these low offers are readily accepted by the responders as are the much more generous offers made among the Achuar, Orma, Ache and Lamelera where the average and modal offers hover around half the pie.

*Table 2.3* Henrich *et al.* (2004): offers across the diverse small-scale societies

| Group | Country | Mean offer | Modes | Rejection rates | Low offer (less than 20%) rejection rates |
|---|---|---|---|---|---|
| Machiguenga | Peru | 0.26 | 0.15/0.25 | 0.05 (1 of 21) | 0.10 (1 of 10) |
| Hadza (small camp) | Tanzania | 0.27 | 0.20 | 0.28 (8 of 29) | 0.31 (5 of 16) |
| Quichua | Ecuador | 0.27 | 0.25 | 0.15 (2 of 13) | 0.50 (1 of 2) |
| Mapuche | Chile | 0.34 | 0.33/0.50 | 0.07 (2 of 30) | 0.20 (2 of 10) |
| Torguud Mongols | Mongolia | 0.35 | 0.25 | 0.05 (1 of 20) | 0.00 (0 of 1) |
| Gnau | Papua New Guinea | 0.38 | 0.40 | 0.40 (10 of 25) | 0.50 (3 of 6) |
| Hadza (big camp) | Tanzania | 0.40 | 0.50 | 0.19 (5 of 26) | 0.80 (4 of 5) |
| Achuar | Ecuador | 0.42 | 0.50 | 0.00 (0 of 16) | 0.00 (0 of 1) |
| Au | Papua New Guinea | 0.43 | 0.30 | 0.27 (8 of 30) | 1.00 (1 of 1) |
| Orma | Kenya | 0.44 | 0.50 | 0.04 (2 of 56) | – (0 of 0) |
| Ache | Paraguay | 0.51 | 0.40/0.50 | 0.00 (0 of 51) | 0.00 (0 of 8) |
| Lamalera | Indonesia | 0.58 | 0.50 | 0.20 (4 of 20) | 0.38 (3 of 8) |

Source: Table created by author on the basis of data provided in the original study.

The large variations across the different cultural groups suggest that preferences or expectations are affected by group-specific conditions, such as social institutions or cultural fairness norms. While it is difficult to pin-point the causes of behavioural differences across these extremely diverse societies, to the researchers involved in this work, two reasons stood out. The first of these, that seems to predict whether offers are generous or stingy, is the payoff to cooperation – i.e. how important and how large is a group's payoff from cooperating in day-to-day economic production. For instance, among the Machiguenga, who are entirely economically independent and rarely engage in productive activities that involve others besides family members, the proposers made very low offers. On the other hand, Lamalera whale hunters, who go to sea in large canoes manned by a dozen or more individuals requiring close cooperation between them, make more generous offers.

The second factor that seemed to have predictive power in explaining offers was the extent of market integration. How much do people rely on market interaction in their daily lives? The researchers found that by and large those who engage in greater interaction make more generous offers in the ultimatum game. It seems then, that the more market oriented a society is, the more equitable are the offers made by the proposers. The researchers tentatively suggest one plausible explanation of this behaviour. When faced with a novel situation (the experiment), the participants looked for analogues in their daily experience asking *"What familiar situation is this game like?"* and then act in a manner appropriate for that situation.

Once again the primary lesson arising from this very broad and ambitious cross-country study is that a social norm regarding what is a fair allocation – rather than pure self-interest – is the primary driving force behind offers in the ultimatum game even though that actual norm is substantially different from one society to another. Thus, offers in some societies such as the Machiguenga and the Quichua are very low while those among the Ache and Lamalera are more generous but in all cases there is little conflict between proposers and responders showing that while the idea of what is fair may be different *across* these societies, *within* those societies there is broad agreement regarding this and both proposers and responders behave in accordance with this mutually shared understanding of what constitutes a fair offer.

## 2.9  What does a preference for fairness have to do with economics?

As I pointed out in the introduction, the starting point of much economic thinking is the assumption of individual rationality implying that in most situations involving strategic decision making, the people making those decisions care primarily about their own monetary payoffs or their utility where that utility is mostly a function of the monetary payoffs accruing to them or their kin. In most economic transactions, individuals (or households) are attempting to maximise their utility while businesses are attempting to maximise their profit. Typically such attempts at maximising utility or profit do not involve overt moral or ethical considerations or notions of what is fair. This idea is not new. Two hundred and thirty years ago, in 1776, Adam Smith, generally considered the progenitor of modern economics, writing in his book *An Inquiry into the Nature and Causes of the Wealth of Nations* put it thus:

*It is not from the benevolence of the butcher, the brewer, or the baker, that we expect our dinner, but from their regard to their own self-interest. We address ourselves, not to their humanity but to their self-love, and never talk to them of our own necessities but of their advantages.*

While moral philosophers may object to this rather Hobbesian view of human nature, as I pointed out in the introduction, in order to build models which can deliver realistic predictions about behaviour in real life one needs to start somewhere and see how far that gets us. The assumption of rational self-interest is the one that economists start with. As I have shown you this is not *always* wrong and does predict the behaviour of some. And, as I also pointed out in the introduction, if you started with a rosy-hued view of human cooperation you would be disappointed as well and more importantly make incorrect predictions. The truth, as with most things in life, is more nuanced and lies somewhere in the middle. More importantly, as I have tried to convince you, very often tendencies towards rampant self-interest are moderated by notions of fairness.

### 2.9.1 *Fairness as a constraint on profit-making*

One of the early attempts to understand whether norms of fairness may act as an active constraint on profit-seeking or might lead to different outcomes than the ones predicted by the self-interest model was undertaken by Daniel Kahneman, a psychologist at Princeton, and two economists Jack Knetsch of Simon Fraser University and Richard Thaler of Cornell in the mid-1980s. They used an extensive questionnaire to understand people's predispositions towards a multitude of strategies adopted by businesses. Here is an example:

> *A hardware store has been selling snow shovels for $15. The morning after a large snowstorm, the store raises the price to $20.*

Respondents were asked to rate this move as (1) completely fair; (2) acceptable; (3) unfair and (4) very unfair. Out of 107 respondents to this question, 82% considered this unfair or very unfair.

Their findings illustrate the role that norms of fairness play in day to day pricing decisions and how these norms can serve as a constraint on unfettered profit-making. Kahneman and his colleagues provide a number of examples of this phenomenon. Below I discuss some of these.

#### 2.9.1.1 *Exploitation of increased market power*

The market power of a business reflects the ability of the business to charge its customers a higher price. For instance, in the event of a snow-storm the seller obviously has increased power to raise the price because people's need for the shovels has increased. Very often, faced with an emergency people wish to stock up on essentials; this creates an opportunity for the seller to jack up the prices of those commodities. By and large respondents seem to believe that such price-gouging is unfair because such an action would constitute opportunistic behaviour. There are a number of examples of the opposition to exploitation of shortages:

> *A severe shortage of Red Delicious apples has developed in a community and none of the grocery stores or produce markets has any of this type of apple on their shelves. Other varieties of apples are*

*plentiful in all of the stores. One grocer receives a single shipment of Red Delicious apples at the regular wholesale cost and raises the retail price of these Red Delicious apples by 25% over the regular price.*

Only 37% of 102 respondents considered this price increase acceptable. Similarly, firms with market power often use that power to increase profits by charging different customers different prices depending on their willingness to pay a higher price. Movie theatres charge a much higher price for admission on evenings during the week and weekends than during a week day. Airline companies charge a much higher price to those customers buying tickets at the last minute compared to those who bought their tickets way in advance for the same class of service. This is referred to as "*price discrimination*" where the seller is essentially trying to get from each customer the most that he is willing to pay for the good.

But the survey results suggest the addition of a further restraint. Many forms of price discrimination were considered outrageous.

*A landlord rents out a small house. When the lease is due for renewal, the landlord learns that the tenant has taken a job very close to the house and is therefore unlikely to move. The landlord raises the rent $40 per month more than he was planning to do.*

Out of 157 respondents only 9% thought this was acceptable while a whopping 91% considered this unfair. On a different question, a majority of respondents thought it unfair for a popular restaurant to impose a $5 surcharge for Saturday night reservations. The near unanimity of responses to questions like these indicates that pricing strategies that deliberately exploit the dependence of a particular individual is generally considered offensive by most.

### 2.9.1.2 The context for pricing decisions

The next two questions look at what happens when a business increases price in an attempt to protect its profit.

*Suppose that, due to a transportation mix-up, there is a local shortage of lettuce and the wholesale price has increased. A local grocer has bought the usual quantity of lettuce at a price that is 30 cents per head higher than normal. The grocer raises the price of lettuce to customers by 30 cents per head.*

*A landlord owns and rents out a single small house to a tenant who is living on a fixed income. A higher rent would mean the tenant would have to move. Other small rental houses are available. The landlord's costs have increased substantially over the past year and the landlord raises the rent to cover the cost increases when the tenant's lease is due for renewal.*

These increases were considered acceptable by 79% and 75% of the respondents, respectively. This suggests that it is acceptable for firms to protect themselves from losses even if this means raising prices.

But 77% of 195 respondents thought the following was unacceptable.

*A small company employs several workers and has been paying them average wages. There is severe unemployment in the area and the company could easily replace its current employees with good workers at a lower wage. The company has been making money. The owners reduce the current workers' wages by 5%.*

The rule seems to be that the seller can certainly protect himself against losses. But in the last instance the firm is lowering wages not to cover losses but to exploit the fact that workers are now finding it more difficult to find jobs in the region and this places the worker at a disadvantage vis-à-vis the firm.

### 2.9.1.3 *Enforcement*

Sixty-eight per cent of respondents in this survey said they would switch their patronage to a drugstore five minutes further away if the one closer to them raised its prices when a competitor was temporarily forced to close; and, in a separate sample, 69% indicated they would switch if the more convenient store discriminated against its older workers. In traditional economic theory, compliance with contracts depends on enforcement. But buyers and sellers may be willing to abide by norms of fairness even in the absence of any explicit enforcement. The following scenarios illustrate:

*If the service is satisfactory, how much of a tip do you think most people leave after ordering a meal costing $10 in a restaurant that they visit frequently?*

The average tip (as stated by 122 respondents) was $1.28

*... in a restaurant on a trip to another city that they do not expect to visit again?*

Here there are 124 respondents and the average tip is $1.27. The respondents evidently do not treat the possibility of enforcement as a significant factor in the control of tipping. This is entirely consistent with the widely observed adherence to a 15% tipping rule in the US even by one-time customers who have little reason to fear embarrassing retaliation by an irate server.

My first job out of graduate school was at Washington State University in the Pacific North-West of the United States. When I left my position at Washington State to start a new job at Wellesley College, my wife and I decided to drive across the country from Washington to Boston. The first night we stopped at Butte, Montana. I had never been to Butte before this and I sincerely doubt that I will go back there again. I don't even remember the name of the restaurant where we ate dinner. But I do remember leaving a 15% tip after dinner. We did the same thing over the next few days in places like Rapid City, South Dakota and Youngstown, Ohio – places that I doubt we will visit again.

The important question though is: Do firms, which the theory assumes maximise profits, also fail to exploit some economic opportunities because of unenforceable compliance with rules of fairness? The following questions elicited expectations about the behaviour of a garage mechanic dealing with a regular customer or with a tourist:

*[A man leaves his car with the mechanic at his regular]/[A tourist leaves his car at a] service station with instructions to replace an expensive part. After the [customer/tourist] leaves, the mechanic examines the car and discovers that it is not necessary to replace the part; it can be repaired cheaply. The mechanic would make much more money by replacing the part than by repairing it. Assuming the [customer/tourist] cannot be reached, what do you think the mechanic would do in this situation?*

Roughly the same proportion of respondents (60% in the case of the *regular customer* and 63% in the case of the *tourist*) thought that the mechanic will make more money by replacing the part. Here again, there is no evidence that the public considers enforcement a significant factor. The respondents believe that most mechanics (usually excluding their own) would be less than saintly in this situation. However, they also appear to believe that the mechanics that would treat their customers fairly are not motivated in each case by the anticipation of sanctions.

### 2.9.1.4  Fairness in labour markets

Given that norms of fairness seem to apply to a variety of pricing decisions, we would expect that this might extend to labour markets as well. In labour markets it is often observed that the wages paid to workers do not decline even in the face of persistent unemployment when firms could easily hire workers more cheaply and therefore could choose to offer lower wages even to the existing workers. But very often whether a particular transaction is considered fair or not depends on what the relevant reference point is. Market prices and the history of previous transactions between a seller and a buyer can serve as reference transactions. The role of prior history in wage transactions is illustrated by the following question:

> *A small photocopying shop has one employee who has worked in the shop for six months and earns $9 per hour. Business continues to be satisfactory, but a factory in the area has closed and unemployment has increased. Other small shops have now hired reliable workers at $7 an hour to perform jobs similar to those done by the photocopying shop employee. The owner of the photocopying shop reduces the employee's wage to $7.*

Out of 98 respondents 17% thought this was acceptable while 83% considered this unfair. I will have more to say on this particular topic of fairness in labour markets in Part 3.

### 2.9.2 *Economic consequences*

The findings of the study by Kahneman and his colleagues suggest that

> *many actions that are both profitable in the short run and not obviously dishonest are likely to be perceived as unfair exploitations of market power.... Further, even in the absence of government intervention, the actions of firms that wish to avoid a reputation for unfairness will depart in significant ways from the standard model of economic behaviour.*

The above is all fine and good but after all, the results reported above are based on responses to survey questions and, as I pointed out in the introduction, at times actual behaviour does deviate from stated attitudes. For instance, a respondent might say that he will not patronise a firm that is engaging in price-gouging by jacking up the price of an essential commodity in an emergency but when push comes to shove the buyer might easily give in. Now the problem here is that it is very hard to show that people are *not* buying something in protest since it is impossible to prove a negative.

Bradley Ruffle, of Ben Gurion University in Israel, decided to set up an experiment to test if buyers do indeed refrain from buying at prices they consider to be unfair. Ruffle focused on situations where the seller puts a price-tag on his product and the buyer has the option of either buying at that price or not buying at all. In economics these are referred to as "posted-offer" institutions. Most retail stores operate on this principle in the sense that when you walk into the store each item has a price tag and you can either buy at the indicated price or not and there is no scope for haggling over the price. The car company Saturn in the US, for instance, has a no haggling policy as opposed to most other car-sellers who allow for negotiations over the price. Honda has a similar no-haggling policy in New Zealand with a fixed price for their cars. Such a no-haggling policy turns the sale of these cars into a posted-offer institution. Economists have usually tended to focus exclusively on the behaviour of sellers in such a context without realising that if buyers are motivated by norms of fairness and care about relative payoffs then they might actually refrain from buying which in turn has implications for these markets.

In a posted-offer market sellers post prices which buyers can either accept or reject. Acceptance yields the seller a payoff determined by the difference between the price he posts and his cost on each unit sold. The buyer earns the difference between his valuation for the good and the price that he pays. If the buyer rejects the price then neither party earns any surplus. Thus a posted-offer institution is a natural multi-player extension of the ultimatum game.

What does valuation of a good mean? The idea behind valuation is this: economists assume that when a person buys a good, that person has a maximum price he is willing to pay depending on the satisfaction (happiness/utility) that he gets from it. Suppose you are willing to pay $200 to go see Bruce Springsteen play at Giants stadium. Why are you willing to pay $200? Because you have thought about the satisfaction you will derive from attending this event and you think that at the most this is worth $200 to you. Now suppose you manage to get a ticket for $150. Then, in the parlance of the economist, you have enjoyed a surplus of $50, which is your "*consumer surplus*". So anytime you are willing to pay a certain amount for something and you end up paying less than the maximum you were willing to pay, you enjoy a surplus. The "*producer surplus*" on the other hand is the difference between the price at which a seller sells the good and the cost of producing it. "*Producer surplus*" is essentially an alternative term for profit.

Ruffle recruited 92 participants at the University of Arizona and set up a series of posted-offer markets with buyers and sellers. It is assumed that the sellers are selling a homogeneous good. In each market buyers and sellers interact for 20 rounds. In each round the sellers have a number of units of a homogeneous good available for sale. In each round the buyers are assigned a particular valuation for each unit of the good that he buys. Similarly in each round the seller is assigned a particular cost for each unit that he sells. Ruffle looks at the impact of a number of different conditions:

1   *Number of buyers and sellers.* In some cases there are *two* buyers in the market while in other cases there are *four* buyers. The number of sellers is always held constant at *two*.
2   *Relative profits of the buyers and the sellers.* Compared to the buyer, the seller always enjoys a much larger share of the profit on each unit sold. In some cases the seller's share is *three* times that of the buyer. Suppose it costs the seller $12 to produce a t-shirt. The buyer is willing to pay as much as $20 for it. In this case the total surplus to be split is ($20 − $12) = $8. Suppose the seller puts a

price of $18 on the shirt and the buyer agrees to buy it. Then the seller gets a surplus of ($18 – $12) = $6 while the buyer gets a surplus of ($20 – $18) = $2. Thus the seller's share of the surplus ($6) is three times that of the buyers ($2). In other cases the seller's share of the profits is *six* times that of the buyer. Suppose, as in the previous example, the buyer's valuation is $20 while the seller's cost is $13 rather than $12. In this case the total surplus is ($20 – $13) = $7. Suppose the seller quotes a price of $19 and the buyer buys at that price. Then the seller's share of the surplus is ($19 – $13) = $6 while the buyer's share is ($20 – $19) = $1; therefore the seller's share of the surplus is six times that of the buyer's.

3   *Information available to buyers and sellers.* Finally, in some cases the buyers know the sellers' costs and the sellers know the valuations of the buyers while in other cases the buyers and the sellers not only know the costs and valuations respectively but *in addition they are shown the profit that each party will make for various transactions.* The intention here is to make *"the earnings inequality salient to the buyers in an attempt to incite them to forego profitable purchases"*.

What Ruffle finds is that indeed *"demand withholding"* by buyers – where the buyers essentially refuse to buy at prices which gives most of the surplus to the sellers – is a factor in these markets. The effect of such withholding is more pronounced when (1) there are two buyers rather than four; (2) when the surplus accruing to the seller is six times that accruing to the buyer; and (3) when the buyers are made aware of this inequitable distribution of the surplus by providing them with information about the profits accruing to each party. In one session of this particular treatment, one buyer boycotted the market *entirely* for six out of 20 periods thereby foregoing the possibility of earning any money. Bear in mind that if the buyer participates then the buyer will make positive profit but these profits will be small compared to the ones that the seller will make. By not participating at all the buyer is making sure that neither he nor the seller makes any money at all. This is very similar to turning down small offers in the ultimatum game except here such rejection comes in the explicit context of a market transaction.

Such demand withholding does often induce the sellers to lower the price charged in later periods and a lower price in turn implies a more equitable sharing of the surplus between the buyer and the seller. The fact that two buyers are often more successful in acting in a coordinated manner and withholding demand compared to four buyers can be explained by appealing to the fact that the choice to withhold poses a free-rider problem for the buyers. Buyers benefit from withholding prices (since that would result in lower prices and a greater share of the surplus for them later on) but each buyer prefers the other buyers to do the withholding. Such coordinated action to withhold demand proves more successful when there are two buyers as opposed to four buyers. Four buyers are often much less successful in upholding the covenant with sellers resisting buyers' attempts at demand withholding and charging higher prices. Eventually one or more of the buyers gives in. Two buyers, on the other hand, manage to coordinate much better and are successful at driving prices down.

Ruffle concludes:

> For a given price, the punishment to sellers of rejecting a profitable purchase is greater the more extreme the earning inequality. The observation that, for a given number of buyers, withholding is more frequent the larger the surplus inequality is therefore consistent with fairness.

## 2.10  Concluding remarks

In this part I have provided evidence that people are willing to turn down a deal offering substantial monetary amounts if they believe that they are being treated unfairly. This unfairness can take two forms. At one level people care about relative payoffs in the sense that they might reject offers that give the other party a lot more than them. To paraphrase the economist Robert Frank, this concern for relative standing can be summed up succinctly by saying that a person would feel quite happy if he is driving a BMW if everyone around him is driving a Toyota but the same person would be quite unhappy if the people around him were driving Porsches. (Or as Frank humorously comments: A person is happy as long as he makes more than his wife's sister's husband.)

But at the same time I have shown that rejection of offers cannot be attributed to a concern for relative standing only. Intentions matter as well. People are perfectly happy to accept inequitable offers generated by computers (where no attribution of intentions is possible) but unwilling to accept the same offers if made by another human, especially if that human stands to benefit from the offer being accepted.

However, I should point out that a recent study by Gary Bolton, Jordi Brandts and Axel Ockenfels suggests that at times a fair procedure can be a substitute of a fair outcome. That is, people might be willing to accept an unfair offer if they believe that the offer was the result of implementing a fair policy. In their study proposers in an ultimatum game have three choices initially – (A) a hyper-fair offer of (200, 1800) i.e. 200 experimental dollars for the proposer and 1,800 for the responder; (B) an equitable offer of (1,000, 1,000); and finally (C) an inequitable offer of (1,800, 200). They found that 41% of the inequitable offers (C) were rejected. In a second study the offers were generated by throwing dice rather than being generated by an actual human proposer. They looked at an *asymmetric* lottery which puts a very high (98%) probability on the inequitable offer (C) and a *symmetric* lottery which puts an equal 33% probability on all three choices. They found that the rejection rates of the inequitable offer (C) were very similar with the *asymmetric* lottery and with human proposers but the rejection rates were much lower for the *symmetric* lottery. The authors conclude that the fairness of the outcomes and the fairness of the procedures both matter and that a fair procedure may be a substitute for a fair outcome.

This study appears to be quite similar to the one conducted by Sally Blount, yet there is a subtle difference. In Blount's study people were willing to accept unfair offers when these offers were chosen by a lottery but not when they were made by other participants. In the study by Bolton and his colleagues, people were willing to commit *beforehand* to accepting the outcome of a lottery knowing full well that the outcome may be bad for them *as long as they were certain that the lottery itself was fair, that is the lottery placed a roughly equal probability on the fair and unfair outcomes.*

Finally, I have also shown that notions of fairness may vary across cultures in that offers that are considered unfair and routinely turned down in one society are readily accepted in others. Social norms operational in different societies may dictate what is fair and what is not.

# Part 3

# Trust and trustworthiness in everyday life

## 3.1 Trust and trustworthiness in everyday life

In Victor Hugo's *Les Misérables*, Jean Valjean, an ex-convict recently released from prison and overwhelmed by the vicissitudes of life, shows up at the doorstep of Monseigneur Myriel. To his surprise, the bishop welcomes him warmly, inviting him to share his supper and offering him a bed for the night. Even more remarkable, he treats Valjean with unfailing courtesy and ignores the stigma of his past. But rising stealthily in the middle of the night, Valjean steals the bishop's silver. Later he gets caught by the police, who bring him back to the bishop. This time his crime will bring him life imprisonment. However, Monseigneur Myriel pretends that the silverware is a legitimate gift and in a gesture of supreme kindness he takes his most prized possessions, a set of candlesticks, and gives them to Valjean as well. As Valjean is leaving, the bishop says: *"Don't forget that you promised me to use this silver to become an honest man."* This level of trust reposed – and kindness shown – to a complete stranger would be beyond most of us.

Yet many day-to-day transactions in life require us to trust strangers. For instance every time we buy things on eBay (http://www.ebay.com) or TradeMe (http://www.trademe.co.nz) and hand over our credit card details we are essentially assuming that the seller will honour that trust and not rip us off. Similarly when we pay our lawyer or accountant or auto-mechanic on the basis of hours of work, we trust these individuals to correctly represent their total hours. The concept of trust cuts across disciplines. Besides economists, people in many other disciplines such as politics or sociology or management sciences talk about the role of trust – trust among nations, among groups, among workers in organisations, between unions and management. In economic transactions, trust is often important in reducing the costs of transacting deals. So much so that economists have now come to believe that such trust among strangers has implications for the economy's performance as a whole. Countries whose citizens are more trusting experience faster economic growth compared to those whose citizens are less trusting. I will discuss the implications of trust among citizens for a country's development later in the book.

Such trust is ubiquitous in many situations. In 2002, I was attending the Annual Meeting of the American Economic Association in Atlanta, Georgia. I was interviewing for jobs at the meeting. I took a cab to a hotel where I was supposed to meet the representatives of a particular university only to realise upon arrival at the hotel that I neither had their room number nor their phone number. In order to get this information I had to go back to the main conference hotel. I had very little time left before the appointment. I asked the cab driver to take me to the main conference hotel. Once there I told him to wait while I ran inside to get this information from the bulletin board. Now this was a bustling hotel with hundreds of conference attendees milling around. Once I went in I could have easily walked out via another door and stiffed the cab driver out of his fare. He could have never found me once I went into the lobby. There were many other taxis around and I could have easily jumped into another one. This would have saved me – and cost the driver – around US$15. Yet, when I asked him to wait he did so without protest. I came out with the necessary information shortly and we drove back to the first hotel where my appointment was. We engage in transactions like these all the time. Yet, if you think about it there was no guarantee for the cab driver that I would come back and pay him. But he trusted my word and waited for me.

In rural areas in many parts of the world, farmers routinely place fresh produce on a table by the side of the road. The table has a box attached to it where people can put money in. The idea is that people driving by can pick up some of the produce and in turn leave money in the box. Here the farmer is essentially trusting people to leave money in return for produce since, with no one watching, someone can just as well pick up the goods and *not* leave any money in the box. Yet most people do leave money. Charities often rely on a similar practice when they leave candy bars (with a price on them) on the counter in gas stations and retail stores. You are supposed to pick up a candy bar and leave the asked for amount in a box next to them.

While we may be convinced that trust plays a crucial role in many transactions, the important question is: How should we go about measuring trust? After all, if we want to engage in any sort of quantitative comparisons between organisations, groups or countries to understand if the members of one group are more trusting than those of another, it is useful to have a handy way of measuring trust.

Joyce Berg, John Dickhaut and Kevin McCabe of the University of Minnesota came up with an elegant game to measure trust. In their game – called the "*Investment Game*" – participants are paired up. One person is called the "sender" and the other person the "receiver".[1] Senders and receivers are placed in different rooms and no one knows who he or she is paired with. Both the sender and the receiver are given US$10. Each sender is then told that she can simply keep all of that money, say "Thank you very much" and leave. The game will end if she does so. In this case the sender will have $10 and the receiver will have $10. But if the sender wishes she can send a part of or all of the $10 to the paired receiver. If the sender sends any money at all then the experimenter will *triple* that amount and give that tripled amount to the receiver. So for instance if the sender sends $5 to the receiver then the experimenter will triple that and give $15 to the receiver. Then the receiver is told the following: he can simply keep the entire amount sent to him and leave. The game will end at that point. Or if he wants he can send some of this amount back to the paired sender in the other room. In any case the game ends with the receiver's decision – regardless of whether he decides to send any money or not – and any money sent back by the receiver is *not* tripled. Figure 3.1 illustrates this game.

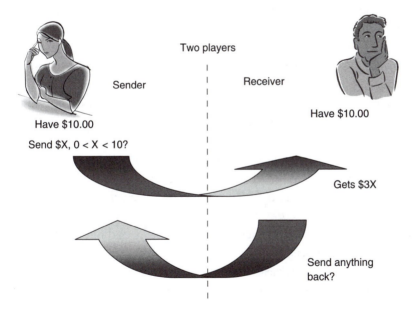

*Figure 3.1* The structure of the trust game.

---

1 Actually they called them players in Room A and players in Room B, respectively. But rather than using the different terms used by different researchers, I am going to use the terms "sender" and "receiver" consistently.

What do you think happens in this game? First, following the principle of backward induction, let us start with the receiver's decision. The receiver has been sent a sum of money – say $15 – by a sender whom he does not know and will most likely never meet again. The receiver knows that the game will end after his decision. A self-interested receiver has no incentive to send any money back. If the receiver is sent any amount then the receiver should simply keep all of it and send nothing back. Now let us put ourselves in the shoes of the sender. If the sender correctly anticipates the receiver's reaction, i.e. the receiver has no incentive to return any money, then it would be foolish to send any money in the first place. By doing so the sender makes herself vulnerable to being exploited by the receiver and would probably be worse off.

But there is an alternative way to think about this situation. Suppose the sender decided to *trust* the receiver and sends him all of the $10. The $10 gets tripled to $30. Now the sender has nothing while the receiver has $40 (remember both senders and receivers get $10 to start with). Suppose the receiver, knowing that he can exploit the sender's trust by returning nothing, decided to *reciprocate* the sender's trust by sending back $20. Then the sender ends up with $20 while the receiver ends up with ($40 – $20) = $20 as well. (Or maybe the receiver sends back $18, in which case the sender ends up with $18 and the receiver ends up with ($40 – $18) = $22.) In both of these cases, both the sender and the receiver are better off than if no money had changed hands. If no money changes hands then both the sender and the receiver make only $10. There are numerous other splits possible. But the noteworthy thing about this second scenario is that in all those cases that the sender *trusts* the receiver and the receiver turns out to be *trustworthy* and *reciprocates* the sender's trust, the sender and the receiver end up with more money than if the sender had not trusted the receiver in the first place.

This game provides an easy way of measuring trust and trustworthiness. Of course this game excludes a number of aspects that would characterise transactions in real-life such as communication, word-of-mouth, face-to-face interaction, handshakes, promises and such. But that is the beauty of this game. It tries to measure trust in a purely abstract way. The factors mentioned above would most likely lead to *increased* trust. But if we can document the existence of trust in this very abstract and context-free situation then we can really claim that trust is a *primitive* in many human transactions. We can always add layers of complexity once we know what happens in the simplest possible (and most abstract) scenario.

The game designed by Berg and her colleagues is a simplified version of another game first studied by Colin Camerer of Caltech and Keith Weigelt of New York University in 1988. Camerer and Weigelt's game is formulated in terms of an entrepreneur who approaches a bank for a loan. The bank is the sender in their game and can choose to lend money or not. If the bank does make a loan then the entrepreneur (who is analogous to the receiver) decides whether to repay the loan with interest or renege. Repaying the loan makes both parties better off compared to the situation where the bank does not make the loan at all. However, in this experiment the entrepreneur can be one of two "types". With some chance he is an "honest" type who prefers to pay back the loan with interest thereby making both parties better off. But with some chance the entrepreneur is "dishonest" and prefers to renege and run off with the money, making him better off at the expense of the bank whose trust is exploited. While the bank does not know for certain which entrepreneur is honest or dishonest, the bank does know the probability of each type. For instance the bank might know that there is a one-third chance that the entrepreneur is honest and two-thirds chance that he is dishonest, etc. The Camerer and Weigelt game and the corresponding analyses are more complex than its simplified version studied by Berg and her colleagues.

In the Berg *et al.* game, if the sender sends any money to start with then we can say that the sender has decided to trust the receiver and the *amount sent* can be used as a measure of the sender's trust. Similarly, if the receiver sends back an amount that makes the sender and the receiver both better off then we can say that the receiver is being trustworthy and use the *amount returned* as a measure of the receiver's reciprocity. Very often rather than using the absolute amount sent back by the receiver, I will use the percentage of the total sent back. This is because, as you will soon see, different receivers receive different amounts. So, for instance, the receiver who receives $15 and sends back $7.50 (i.e. 50% of the amount that he received) is actually being more trustworthy than a receiver who receives $30 but sends back $10 (i.e. 33% of the total amount that he received), even though in absolute amounts the first receiver is sending back less than the second – $7.50 as opposed to $10, respectively.

Berg and her colleagues recruited 64 participants to take part in this game and divided them into 32 pairs of senders and receivers with each participant getting $10. They also implemented a complex double-blind protocol where the experimenter could not observe what individual senders or receivers were doing. Thus, all decisions taken by senders and receivers were completely anonymous with respect to other participants and with respect to the experimenter. What happened? Remember that from the perspective of pure self-interest we expect the sender to send nothing and if the senders do send something then we would expect the receivers to return nothing.

In Figure 3.2A I show the amounts sent by the various senders. The data is arranged in descending order by the amount sent and the senders have been re-labelled accordingly. These participant numbers are different from the actual numbers assigned to them in the original study. Out of the 32 senders, five senders (senders 1 through 5 located at the extreme left of the chart) sent all $10, participant 6 sent $8, senders 7, 8 and 9 sent $7 each, senders 10 through 14 sent $6 each, the next six senders (15 through 20) sent $5 each, senders 21 and 22 sent $4 each, senders 23 through 26 sent $3 each, senders 27 and 28 sent $2 each and senders 29 and 30 sent $1 each. Only two out of 32 senders (senders 31 and 32 located at the extreme right of the chart) sent nothing. Thus, 30 out of 32 senders sent positive amounts and 20 out of 32 senders (63%) sent $5 or more. This seemed to suggest that a majority of the senders were willing to repose substantial amounts of trust in strangers.

Was their trust reciprocated? The answer here is more complicated and the answer is yes and no. In many cases the trust of the senders was reciprocated and both the sender and the receiver of the pair were better off than if the sender had not trusted at all. But this was not always true and in some cases the sender was exploited with the receiver expropriating the entire surplus created, returning little or nothing to the sender.

In Figure 3.2B I show the behaviour of the receivers. Once again, the receivers have been arranged in descending order according to the total amount they received and have been labelled accordingly. Remember that there were five senders who sent all $10 and any amount sent by the sender is tripled by the experimenter. Thus, there were five receivers who received $30. I have labelled these five receivers as receivers 1 through 5. Of these five, receiver 1 sent back $20. This

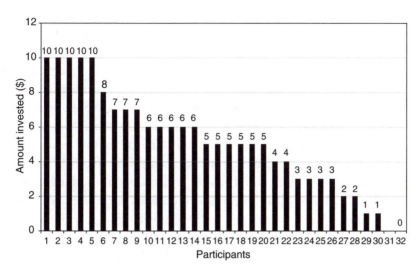

*Figure 3.2* Panel A: amount sent by the 32 senders in Berg *et al.*'s (1995) investment game. Figure created by author on the basis of data provided in the original study.

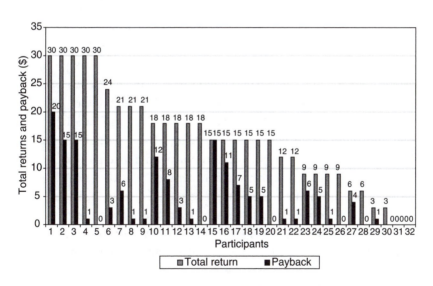

*Figure 3.2* Panel B: total returns and paybacks in Berg *et al.*'s (1995) investment game. Figure created by author on the basis of data provided in the original study.

meant that the sender and the receiver in this pair ended up with exactly $20 each. Receivers 2 and 3 sent back $15. Remember the receiver got $10 at the beginning of the game. This meant that in each case the sender in the pair ended up with $15 while the receiver ended up with $25. The receivers made out better than the sender but the senders still ended up with $5 more – $15 as opposed to $10 – than if they had not trusted the receiver at all. But receivers 4 and 5 were not nice. Receiver 4 sent back a dollar only meaning the sender ended up with a dollar while the receiver ended up with $39. Receiver 5 sent back nothing meaning the paired sender ended up with nothing while receiver 5 ended up with $40. Other receivers sent back various amounts. Thus, while it is true that many receivers did not reciprocate, many others did and the level of reciprocity exhibited exceeded what self-interest based predictions would have held. Senders who sent $5 or more made a profit on the amount sent. Investments of $5 had an average payback of $7.17, while investments of $10 had an average payback of $10.20.

Just as Güth and his colleagues did with the ultimatum game, Berg and her colleagues were aware that the decisions of the participants to trust or reciprocate may be caused by mistakes or lack of comprehension of the instructions. So they decided to run a second experiment called the "*social history*" experiment where the first experiment described above is the "*no history*" experiment. In the "*social history*" experiment they recruited 56 participants (28 pairs) who had *not* participated in the previous "*no history*" experiment and had them take part in the same game with one difference. Each participant in the "*social history*" treatment was given a report summarising the decisions of the 32 pairs in the "*no history*" experiment.

Suppose that in the first experiment senders failed to anticipate that the receivers had no incentive to return any money. Then providing the history of prior plays might make the senders in the second experiment more aware that some of the receivers in the first experiment did not reciprocate and this may make the senders in the second experiment leery of sending money. Alternatively, the senders in the social history treatment may focus on the positive net returns of $5 and $10 investments. This could result in an increase in trust and more decisions to send either $5 or $10. The outcome of the "*social history*" experiment was broadly similar to the "*no history*" one. Only three out of 28 senders sent nothing. Thirteen out of 24 receivers who received more than $1 returned more than what the paired sender sent, resulting in positive net returns for both. Investments of $5 had an average payback of $7.14 while investments of $10 had an average payback of $13.17. In fact, the participants in the social history treatment seemed to exhibit slightly higher levels of trust and reciprocity than the no history participants. Thus history, rather than teaching the participants the folly of being trusting and trustworthy, seemed to have reinforced both of these responses.

So a number of senders seem to believe like Ralph Waldo Emerson *"Trust men and they will be true to you; treat them greatly and they will show themselves great"*.

## 3.2 Is trust nothing but altruism? How about reciprocity?

As with the ultimatum game results, the question arose: Was the decision by the senders to send money in this game motivated by a desire to share rather than based on expectations of reciprocation as would be required if these transfers were motivated by trust? Similarly, was the decision by some of the receivers motivated by generosity rather than reciprocity?

Berg and her colleagues had anticipated and pre-empted this potential criticism by giving $10 to both the sender and the receiver. Think about this for a minute. Suppose senders do care about an equitable distribution. Should they then send money? Not necessarily, because even if they did not send anything, unlike the dictator or ultimatum games, the responder does not go home with nothing. Both have $10 and even in the absence of a transfer from the sender to the receiver, each would still end up with $10 – a perfectly equitable distribution. There is one catch though. In this game each dollar sent gets multiplied. Thus, if a sender cares about *joint* welfare – i.e. the benefit to the sender and the receiver taken together – then she may still send money because each dollar sent will generate three dollars for the receiver. The sender is worse off by a dollar but the receiver is better off by three times that amount and so collectively the two are better off. Thus senders may send money even in the absence of trust if the senders have *"other-regarding preferences"* where they care about the welfare of the receiver (or the joint welfare) rather than only *"self-regarding"* preferences where they care only about their own monetary payoffs.

James Cox of the University of Arizona suggested that the original Berg *et al.* experiments do not allow one to distinguish between transfers resulting from trust and transfers resulting from other-regarding preferences; neither does their design distinguish between receiver reciprocity and returns resulting from other-regarding preferences. Cox designed an experiment which involved each participant taking part in (1) the Berg–Dickhaut–McCabe investment game; (2) the dictator game studied by Forsythe and others earlier in this book[2] and (3) a "*modified dictator*" game. You already know how the Berg-Dickhaut-McCabe investment game and the dictator game works. Cox argues along the following lines: suppose we compare the amounts sent by the senders in the trust game with the amount sent in the dictator game. In the trust game there is the possibility of getting a return from the receiver and, therefore, of making net gains but in the dictator game there is no possibility of getting a return from the receiver. Thus, any transfers made in the dictator game must be motivated by *other-regarding preferences* only, whereas transfers in the investment game can be made either due to trust or due to other-regarding preferences. Thus, if the amounts sent in the investment game exceed those sent in the dictator game then the additional amount must be due to trusting motivations.

Cox's third treatment – the "*modified dictator*" game – is complicated, so I will provide a brief sketch of how this game works. Suppose that in the investment game we have two pairs – (1) Bonnie and Clyde and (2) Thelma and Louise, with Bonnie and Thelma as the senders and Clyde and Louise as the receivers (mnemonic: first person of the pair is the sender while the second person is the receiver). Suppose that in the investment game Bonnie sends Clyde $4 out of $10, while Thelma sends Louise $7 out of $10. This implies that Bonnie has $6 left while Thelma has $3 left. On the other hand, since the amount sent gets tripled, Clyde gets $12 while Louise gets $21. What Cox does at this point is to set up the "*modified dictator game*".

Suppose in this modified dictator game we have two pairs as well – (1) Frankie and Johnny and (2) Butch and Sundance. Then he gives the

---

2   Remember that the dictator game is the one where the proposer is given a sum of money (say $10) and asked to suggest a split of this amount between him and the responder except that the responder has no say in the matter and has to accept any offer that the proposer makes to him which could be zero dollars. In the event that the proposer gives $X to the receiver, the proposer gets $(10 − X) while the responder gets $X.

two senders, Frankie and Butch, the amounts that the two senders, Bonnie and Thelma, kept for themselves. That is Frankie gets $6 (what Bonnie had) while Butch has $3 (the amount that Thelma had). And he gives the two receivers Johnny and Sundance the amounts that Clyde and Louise got which was $12 and $21, respectively.

Then he asks Johnny and Sundance to play a dictator game with these two amounts ($12 and $21, respectively) and asks them if they wish to send any money to Frankie and Butch, respectively. The idea is this: since in this modified dictator game the proposers (or senders), i.e. Frankie or Butch, did not really send anything, the receivers cannot be motivated by positive reciprocity, that is, a need to repay a friendly action by the sender. Thus if the receiver sends any money to the sender in this modified dictator game, that decision must be motivated by other-regarding preferences rather than reciprocity. In contrast, in the investment game, the receiver can be motivated to return positive amounts by reciprocity or by unconditional other-regarding preferences. Thus if the *amount returned* in the investment game exceeds those *sent* in the modified dictator game then *that excess* must be motivated by reciprocity on top of any altruistic tendencies.

Cox finds that participants are motivated by both sets of factors (1) altruistic other-regarding preferences as well as (2) trust and reciprocity. Average transfers in the investment game ($5.97 out of $10.00) are higher than the average transfers in the dictator game ($3.63 out of $10). This shows that participants are motivated by trust over and above any other-regarding preferences. The average amount returned in the investment game ($4.94) is also higher than those transferred in the modified dictator game ($2.06), providing evidence that reciprocity and a desire to reward the sender's trust play a role over and above any altruistic tendencies.

Nava Ashraf, Iris Bohnet and Nikita Piankov at Harvard's Business School also examine this issue of trust and reciprocity in an ambitious project with participants from South Africa, Russia and the US using an approach similar to the one adopted by Cox. They also look at the Berg–Dickhaut–McCabe investment game, the dictator game, but rather than using Cox's modified dictator game, they look at the "*triple dictator game*". In the dictator game if the proposer gives $X to the responder then the proposer gets $(10 − X) while the responder gets $X. The "*triple dictator game*" is similar except in this game the amount ($X) given to the responder is *tripled* by the experimenter so that the proposer gets \$(10 – X), as in the dictator game, but the responder gets \$3X. The responder does not have to make a decision, i.e. the responder does not have to send any money back.

The similarity between the investment game and the triple dictator game is that in both games the amount sent is tripled. The difference is that in the trust game the sender can hold expectations of getting money back and thereby making a profit, while in the triple dictator game there is no possibility of any money being returned. Suppose "S" denotes the amount sent in the investment game and "R" denotes the amount returned by the receiver. Ashraf and her colleagues measure trust by looking at the *amount of money sent* in the investment game (S) and they measure reciprocity by looking at the *proportion of money returned* by the receivers out of the tripled amount received (R/3S). They argue as follows.

First, if senders are motivated by trust then the amount sent (S) should be related to the expected return from the receiver (R/3S). But if the senders are sending money because they have other-regarding preferences and realise that a \$1 sent creates a surplus by generating \$3 for the receiver, then the amount sent in the investment game should be related mostly to the *amount sent in the triple dictator game* rather than the *amount expected back from the receiver* in the investment game.

Second, if receivers are motivated by reciprocity then the proportion of money returned, R/3S, would depend more on 3S (triple the amount sent). But if receivers are motivated by altruism then R/3S would be related more to *money sent in the dictator game* rather than the *money received in the trust game*. As in Cox's study, these researchers also find substantial evidence in support of the trust and reciprocity hypothesis, though they do report that there is some evidence of both senders and receivers being motivated by other-regarding preferences.

## 3.3  The role of expectations in the decision to trust

Because trust is so fundamental to so many transactions – and betrayal of that trust could cause psychological and financial trauma – it is important that we make sure that behaviour in the investment game does indeed reflect a willingness to trust strangers. The two studies discussed above suggest that both trust and other-regarding preferences matter. But what if people are mostly motivated by a desire to share and to a lesser extent by trust? In that case we might be barking up the wrong tree if we put too much emphasis on trust.

Uri Gneezy, Werner Güth and Frank Verboven attempted to understand the behaviour of the senders by having people take part in a trust game where they systematically varied the amount that the responder could return. In this study, amounts sent were only *doubled* rather than tripled. So if the sender sent $10 then the receiver got $20. In one treatment the receiver could return only $2 regardless of the amount that he received from the sender. In the second treatment he could return $10. In this second treatment then, the receiver could at least make a full repayment of any amount sent even if he did not or could not guarantee a positive net return to the sender (in those cases where the sender sent all $10 to the receiver). In the third treatment he could return as much as $18 and could, therefore, give back a positive net return to the sender for any amount sent.

If the senders in this game are motivated purely by a desire to share then the amount that the receiver can repay should not matter and should not have an impact on the amount sent. On the other hand, if senders are motivated by expected reciprocation on the part of the receivers then we would expect them to send more when higher repayments are possible. This conjecture is borne out. The average amount sent when the receiver can repay only $2 is $2. But this amount is significantly higher when the repayment amount is $10 or $18. When receivers can repay up to $10, the average amount sent is $6.50, while for repayments of $18 the average amount sent is $5.63. These two amounts are not statistically different. The reason why the amount sent when the upper bound on repayment is $18 is not different from when the upper bound on repayment is $10 is probably that senders did not expect the receiver to send back much more than $10 even with a higher repayment amount and so the raising of the upper bound from $10 to $18 did not influence decisions much.

Andreas Ortmann, John Fitzgerald and Carl Boeing at Bowdoin College in Maine decided to take a different approach. They start by replicating the findings of the original Berg *et al.* study but then introduce a number of modifications that might help explain whether transfers are in accordance with the trust and reciprocity hypothesis.

They employ five treatments. The *first* is a baseline "*no history*" treatment which is exactly the same as and designed to replicate the "*no history*" treatment in the original Berg *et al.* study.

The *second* is the "*social history*" treatment which again is similar to the "*social history*" treatment in the Berg *et al.* study and replicated the Berg *et al.* "*social history*" treatment by presenting the results from the baseline "*no history*" treatment to the participants.

In the *third* treatment, besides presenting the participants with the values of previous investments and returns in a table (as in the Berg *et al.* study), Ortmann and his colleagues furnished *in addition* a version of the graph shown in Figure 3.2B, i.e. the graph which shows the different amounts received by the receivers and the amounts they returned.

In the *fourth* treatment they use the baseline "*no history*" treatment but then also ask the senders to fill out a questionnaire prior to making a decision about sending money.

The questionnaire is designed with two specific purposes. First, it was to ensure that senders understood the design and considered their decisions carefully before making them. Second, it was to help particip-ants determine how much to invest by having the senders ponder the consequences of their decisions before they made them, thus reducing the potential for confusion. Specifically, the senders were asked the following questions.

a   How much money do you think you will send?
b   How much money will your paired receiver receive if you send this much?
c   How much money do you think will be returned to you?
d   How much money would you return if you were the receiver?

The researchers thought that this fourth treatment (which should prompt strategic reasoning) would lead to significant drops in both the amounts sent and consequently the amounts returned.

In a *fifth* and final treatment they not only have the senders fill out the questionnaire but also present them with a version of Figure 3.2B showing the various amounts returned by the receivers.

Surprisingly none of these manipulations make any difference. Across the different treatments the average amounts sent by the senders are not statistically different. Table 3.1 presents the average amounts sent out of the initial endowment of $10. The authors end by saying that their findings suggest that the original Berg *et al.* results are quite robust. Even a presentation mode which focuses on relative rather than absolute returns coupled with questionnaires designed to

*Table 3.1* Average amount sent across various treatments

| | Number of pairs | Average amount sent (out of $10) |
|---|---|---|
| Berg *et al.* study | | |
| 1  No history treatment | 32 | 5.20 |
| 2  Social history treatment | 28 | 5.40 |
| Ortmann *et al.* study | | |
| 1  No history treatment | 16 | 4.40 |
| 2  Social history treatment | 16 | 4.70 |
| 3  Social history plus graph treatment | 24 | 4.70 |
| 4  No history plus questionnaire treatment | 12 | 5.80 |
| 5  Social history plus graph plus questionnaire treatment | 16 | 5.50 |

Source: Table created by author on the basis of data provided in the original studies.

induce strategic reasoning does not get rid of trust among the senders.

Ananish Chaudhuri at the University of Auckland and Lata Gangadharan at the University of Melbourne also hone in on the role of expectations using 100 participants at the University of Melbourne. In their study participants play both roles – that of the sender and the receiver – in the investment game but with different partners in each role. Participants also play the dictator game. Like the Ortmann, Fitzgerald and Boeing study they also decided to prompt strategic reasoning by (1) asking each sender in their experiment whether she expected anything back from the receiver she is paired with and if she did, how much she expected to get back; (2) but on top of that they also asked the senders to write down (using free-form responses) their motive in sending money to the receiver.

Chaudhuri and Gangadharan find that the amount of money expected back from the receiver plays a major role in influencing the amount of money that is sent. Given that each dollar sent by the sender to the receiver in the trust game gets tripled, the sender is at least as well off or better off if the receiver returns exactly one-third or more of this tripled amount, respectively. For returns of less than a third, the sender is worse off.

There is a significant difference in the behaviour of those who expect less than one-third and those who expect more. There are 44 participants who expect to get back *less than* one-third of what the receiver gets and these participants on average sent $2.14 out of $10.00. The modal amount, sent by 18 out of these 44 participants, is $0. On the other hand, of the 37 participants who expected to get back *more than* one-third, the average amount sent is $6.05. There are 17 participants who expected to get back exactly one-third and these participants on average sent $5.41. Of the 54 participants who expect to get at least one-third or more, the modal amount sent is $10 with 17 out of 54 participants sending all their initial endowment.

The amount that the sender sends to the paired receiver is positively correlated with the sender's expectation about the per cent amount that the receiver will return (i.e. the sender's expectations about the receiver's reciprocity). Chaudhuri and Gangadharan also look at the free responses provided by the senders about what motivated them to send money (or not) to their paired receiver in the trust game and find that a majority of responses exhibit an explicit recognition of the role of trust in generating positive net returns for both the sender and the receiver.

An example of such responses is the following:

> *I want the $10 but we could both make more if we work together and split the $30 and make $15 each. This is a total risk because it would be tempting for the other person to keep the $30. I am hoping that an obvious gesture of generosity will get me some money back, $10 at least.*

This participant sent her entire endowment of $10 to the paired receiver.

Chaudhuri and Gangadharan also find that the amount of money received by the receiver from the paired sender and the proportion of the tripled amount that the receiver sends back are closely related. This implies that when the receiver receives a larger percentage of the initial endowment of the sender, the receiver responds by returning a larger percentage as well. On the face of it then these results suggest – as Ortmann and his colleagues point out – that *"trust may be a primitive that participants use as guiding behavioural instinct in unfamiliar situations."*

## 3.4 Is a trusting decision analogous to a risky one?

Anytime the sender in the investment game decides to repose trust on the receiver, that is whenever someone decides to trust a stranger, she is implicitly taking a chance. There is some chance that the recipient of that trust will turn out to be trustworthy and repay the trust making both parties to the transaction better off. But there is also a chance that the receiver will renege and take the entire amount leaving the trustor worse-off than if she had not trusted at all. Thus the decision to trust *may* be thought of as being similar to buying a lottery ticket. With some chance you will make a lot of money but with some chance you will earn nothing and lose the amount you spent buying the ticket(s). Do people who are confronted with a situation where they have to repose their trust in a stranger behave as if they are essentially buying a lottery ticket? By and large the answer turns out to be in the negative. The mental algorithm that is called upon when asked to repose trust in a stranger seems to be substantially different from the one that is called upon when people buy a lottery ticket.

One of the early attempts to disentangle trust from risk was undertaken by Chris Snijders and Gideon Keren. They look at a simpler version of the Berg–Dickhaut–McCabe investment game. In the Snijders–Keren version of the game the sender has two options – (1) to send all $10 so that the receiver gets $30 or (2) to send nothing.[3] If the sender chooses the second option (which is similar to the sender's decision to send nothing in the investment game) then both the sender and the receiver end up with some default amount. For the sake of convenience let us say this sum is $10. So in the absence of trust each party gets $10. However, if the sender does decide to trust and send money (which means sending all $10) then the receiver is restricted to two options as well. He can *reciprocate* (Snijders and Keren use non-emotive words like "send money" or "send money back" rather than loaded terms like "trust" and "reciprocate") in which case – say – each party gets $20. Or he can *betray* the sender's trust in which case the sender gets $0, and the receiver gets $40.

In this case, the sender's decision to send the $10 to start with essentially implies that there are two possible outcomes – (1) a return of $20

---

3  Snijders and Keren use different amounts. I will use $10 or $20 for the sake of simplicity, convenience and in order to keep parity with my discussion of the investment game above. This will make it easier to follow my arguments.

i.e. a gain of $10 or (2) a return of $0, i.e. a loss of $10. The potential risk associated with the decision to send all $10 can be manipulated by changing the potential amounts that the receiver can send back. For instance, suppose the choices are less stark in that the two options for the receiver are (1) send back $10 out of $30 and keep $20 and (2) send back $20 out of $30 and keep $10. Here the sender is guaranteed that she will *not* lose any money even if she does not make a positive net return. In this case then, the sender is looking at two possible outcomes – (1) a gain of $10 or (2) a loss of $0, i.e. no chance of making a loss. Therefore, a sender may be much more inclined to send money in the second scenario compared to the first. Thus, by changing the amounts that the receiver can send back and consequently the potential gains and losses to the sender, one can see what kinds of changes there are in the sender's decision to send money. Snijders and Keren went on to suggest that the potential gains and losses and *the risks associated with those* seem to matter a lot in the sender's decision to send money.

But a number of studies since then have questioned this finding. Iris Bohnet and Richard Zeckhauser of Harvard's Kennedy School of Government argue that one drawback to the conclusions reached by Snijders and Keren is that they try to evaluate people's attitudes towards risk within the context of the investment game itself whereas a better option would be to evaluate this using a different task. Bohnet and Zeckhauser have participants take part in three different games. First, they play the binary choice version of the investment game where the sender has two options as in Snijders and Keren.

Next, they take part in a second game where the senders are essentially making a lottery choice. They are posed the following: Suppose they send all $10 and there is some chance that they will get back $20 (i.e. gain $10) and some chance that they will get back $0 (i.e. lose $10). *Senders are asked to state under what circumstances they would be willing to send $10.* Would they do it if the chance of getting back $20 is 50% and getting back $0 is 50% (which implies an *expected* return of $10)? How about if the chance of getting back $20 is 60% or 70% and so on?

The researchers had already decided the actual chance of getting back $20 prior to the beginning of the experiment. *Suppose the chance of getting back $10 and thereby making an extra $10 is 50% and the chance of getting back nothing is 50%.* Every participant who states that she is willing to send all $10 as long as there was a 50% chance of getting back $20 then got to play this game. If she stated that she would not send any money unless the chance of getting back $20 was *more than 50%* then she did not have to play the lottery game and simply kept the initial endowment of $10.

However, one issue with the lottery game is that this is an individual decision-making game where there is no receiver, while in the investment game there is a sender and a receiver and we have seen that often the senders do care about what happens to the receiver. Thus, Bohnet and Zeckhauser have their participants take part in a third game – the *"risky dictator game"*. The risky dictator game is similar to the lottery-choice game. But now if the sender sends any money and the chance outcome is such that both the sender and the receiver receive a positive net return then the passive responder of this dictator game also gets some money. So, for example, if the chance outcome is such that the sender gets $20 and the receiver gets $20 then the passive responder in this dictator game will actually be given $20.

Bohnet and Zeckhauser find that sender behaviour is indeed different in the investment game compared to the lottery-choice game or the risky dictator game. People are much less willing to send money and take the chance of being exploited in the investment game while their behaviour in either the lottery-choice game or the risky dictator game are not different. Bohnet and Zeckhauser comment: *"Our results suggest that the decision to trust is influenced by more than just risk.... They behave as though there is a betrayal cost above and beyond any dollar losses"* (emphasis in the original).

Catherine Eckel and Rick Wilson also examine this relationship between trust and risk. Eckel and Wilson recruit participants at two different locations – Virginia Polytechnic and State University and Rice University – to undertake four different tasks.

1   They play the investment game where one member of the pair is in Virginia while the other member is located in Houston. This made it extremely unlikely that members of the pair would ever run into one another.
2   They fill out a 40-question psychological survey called the Zuckerman Sensation Seeking Scale which is designed to elicit participants' preferences about seeking out novel and stimulating activities. The survey asks participants to choose their preferred alternative from a pair of statements about risky activities. For example, one pair of statements is:

Option 1: skiing down a high mountain slope is a good way to end up on crutches; or

Option 2: I think I would enjoy the sensations of skiing very fast down a high mountain slope.

3    They are also asked to choose their preferred option from a series of ten lotteries each offering two alternatives such as:

Option 1: (i) 10% chance of getting $2 and 90% chance of getting $1.60 or (ii) 10% chance of getting $3.85 and 90% chance of getting $0.10;

Option 2: (i) 20% chance of getting $2 and 80% chance of getting $1.60 or (ii) 20% chance of getting $3.85 and 80% chance of getting $0.10 and so on.

4    Then they are asked to make another risky choice where they could choose to get $10 for certain or they could choose a lottery which would pay $0 or $5, or $10 or $15 or $20 with 10%, 20%, 40%, 20% and 10% chance, respectively. The participants get paid $5 for filling out the survey and also get paid depending on their choices in the two lotteries.

What Eckel and Wilson find is that none of the three risk measures (the Zuckerman Sensation Seeking Scale or the two lottery choices) have any significant correlation with the decision to send money in the trust game (i.e. the decision to trust). While it seems to be a logical inference that the decision to trust a stranger may be caused by the same mental processes that allows or induces people to engage in risky gambles, the results presented above seem to suggest that there is little evidence that the decision to trust is perceived in the same way as a risky choice.

Michael Kosfeld, Marcus Heinrichs, Urs Fischbacher and Ernst Fehr at Zürich and Paul Zak at Claremont Graduate University adopt an extremely novel approach towards testing the relation between trust and risk. They look at a slightly modified version of the investment game where both the sender and the receiver have $12 each. (These researchers utilise a fictitious experimental currency which is converted into cash at the end of the session. For the sake of simplicity and convenience I will stick to the dollar notation.) The sender has four options regarding the money he can send. Specifically he can send $0, $4, $8 or $12. This amount is tripled which means that the receiver will get $0, $12, $24 or $36, respectively. The receiver can then send back any amount up to the maximum received. For instance, if the sender sends $8 then the receiver gets $24 and he can return any amount between $0 and $24.

In a second treatment the sender faces the same choices as in the investment game except a random mechanism, rather than a human being, decides how much money the sender will get back. Thus, this second choice is analogous to participating in a lottery with good and bad outcomes both possible. These researchers implement a double-blind protocol where the experimenter is unaware of decisions made by individuals and those decisions could not be traced back to the decision makers.

Here is the novel part of this study. In both the investment game as well as the risky lottery-choice game some of the participants receive a single intranasal dose of oxytocin while the rest receive a placebo. (Participants in the oxytocin group receive three puffs per nostril of Syntocinon spray manufactured by Novartis.) Oxytocin is a neuro-peptide which plays a central role in social interactions. Besides its well-known physiological functions in milk-letdown and during labour, oxytocin receptors are distributed in various brain regions associated with pair-bonding, maternal care, sexual behaviour and the ability to form normal social attachments.

There are 58 senders in the trust game – half of them were adminis-tered oxytocin while the other half received a placebo. The data show that oxytocin increases senders' trust considerably. Out of the 29 participants who received oxytocin 13 senders (45%) showed maximal trust by sending their entire endowment to the paired receiver. However, in the placebo group only six out of 29 (21%) did so. The average transfer in the oxytocin group is $9.60 which is significantly higher than that in the placebo group ($8.10). The median transfer in the oxytocin group is $10 while the median for the placebo group is $8.

There are 61 participants who took part in the risky lottery-choice game: 31 in the oxytocin group and 30 in the placebo group. There are no significant differences in behaviour between these two groups. The average or median amount sent by those in the oxytocin group is not different from those sent by the participants in the placebo group. Thus, administration of oxytocin leads to increased trust in the invest-ment game but does not affect behaviour in the lottery-choice game suggesting, yet again, that the decision to trust is fundamentally differ-ent from the decision to accept a risky gamble.

### 3.5  Do trust and trustworthiness go together?

In most studies of trust there is the implicit assumption that trust and trustworthiness must be similar psychological constructs, i.e. a person who is trusting of another would, when given the opportunity, also reciprocate the trust of others. Surprisingly this turns out not to be true – those who trust do not necessarily reciprocate. Chaudhuri and Gangadharan were well placed to investigate this issue because in their study each participant played once as the sender (which generates a measure of that participant's level of trust) and once as the receiver (generating a measure of that person's trustworthiness).

Chaudhuri and Gangadharan define a participant as "trusting" if she sent *at least 50% or more* of her initial endowment of $10 in the investment game (i.e. $5 or more). If she sent *less than 50%* then this participant is labelled "non-trusting". Then we can see if the participants classified as "trusting" using this definition exhibit greater reciprocity than the "non-trusting" participants. It turns out that the answer is no. Using the 50% cut-off, there are 58 participants who are non-trusting (sent less than 50%) and 42 trusting (sent exactly 50% or more). The non-trusting participants returned on average 18% of the amount they received while the trusting participants returned 16%. This difference is not significant and the result does not change when they try alternative definitions of "trusting".

The people who trust but do not reciprocate seem less motivated by pure trust but rather are interested in exploiting the trust and trustworthiness of others in increasing their own payoff. It appears that this group of participants engages in the following course of action. As the sender they repose trust on the other player hoping for reciprocity from her and consequently a bigger payoff. However, as the receiver (and the recipient of a trusting move from the paired sender) they choose not to reciprocate and choose to appropriate the entire (or most of the) surplus created by the sender's trusting act, thereby grabbing a much larger payoff.

The above evidence suggests that while a large majority of participants in this game exhibit trust, not all of them necessarily reciprocate trust when they have the opportunity to do so. Thus many participants, while trusting, may not be trustworthy. How about those who do reciprocate trust? Do they also trust more? The answer turns out to be an emphatic yes. Suppose a participant is "trustworthy" if he or she returned *at least one-third or more* of any amount offered to them. There are 27 such participants. The remaining 55 who return *less than one-third* are deemed "less trustworthy". It turns out that the 27 "trustworthy" participants, in their role as the sender, send $5.33 out of $10 on average which is higher than the $3.82 on average sent by the remaining 55 "less trustworthy" participants.[4]

One interesting insight arising from the Chaudhuri and Gangadharan study is the dissonance between trust and reciprocity in that those who trust are not necessarily trustworthy but the trustworthy people are more trusting. Chaudhuri and Gangadharan go on to argue that what many prior studies have interpreted as trust has two distinct components. One is being both *trusting* and *trustworthy* in the sense of possessing a general social orientation towards others while the other – a predilection for trust with no associated desire to reciprocate – has an implicit element of *opportunism* associated with it. The former component is definitely a desirable quality but the latter probably not. The noted Harvard sociologist Robert Putnam in his book *Bowling Alone: The Collapse and Revival of American Community* comments:

> *Other things being equal, people who trust their fellow citizens volunteer more often, contribute to charity, participate more often in politics and community organisations, serve more readily on juries, give blood more frequently, comply more fully with their tax obligations, are more tolerant of minority views, and display many other forms of civic virtue.*

But when it comes to the idea of social orientation – as in this quote from Putnam for instance – it is trustworthiness that is more important and relevant rather than trust. If one is trustworthy, then one is definitely trusting but a trusting individual is not necessarily trustworthy. In this particular quote Putnam's use of the word "trust" should be interpreted as "trustworthiness". This insight is summed up very nicely in the following anecdote told by Robyn Dawes and Richard Thaler:

---

4  A sharp reader might notice that 27 and 55 add up to 82 rather than 100, which is the number of participants in this particular study. This is because there were 18 receivers in this study who received nothing from the sender. And, therefore, these 18 receivers had no decision to make regarding how much to send back. These 18 people are excluded from the discussion of amount returned leaving only 82 observations.

*In the rural areas around Ithaca it is common for farmers to put some fresh produce on the table by the road. There is a cash-box on the table, and customers are expected to put money in the box in return for vegetables they take. The box has just a small slit, so money can only be put in, not taken out. Also, the box is attached to the table, so no one can (easily) make off with the money. We think that the farmers have just about the right model of human nature. They feel that enough people will volunteer to pay for the fresh corn to make it worthwhile to put it out there. The farmers also know that if it were easy enough to take the money, someone would do so.*

## 3.6 Implications of trust and reciprocity for economic transactions

The ubiquity of trusting behaviour is a distinguishing feature of the human species. Almost all human social interactions and many economic interactions are characterised by an element of trust. In this part of the chapter I am going to focus on a few of those issues.

A common-place and fundamental issue in economics is what is called an *agency* problem (or in the parlance of the economist a "*principal-agent*" problem). An agency problem arises in many, if not most, employment relationships. Examples abound: an owner of a café or a restaurant hiring a manager to run the place; a landowner hiring a worker to work the land; share-holders of a company hiring a CEO; the state or national government hiring a director to run a state-run enterprise. The crux of the problem is similar in all these cases: the goals of the owner and the worker are often not aligned in the sense that the worker may have very different aims and objectives than the owner does.

Let us take the example of the owner of a café hiring a manager to run the place. The owner obviously wishes the place to do well and sell lots of coffee and pastries so that he can turn a profit. In order for that to happen the manager needs to work hard. But if the manager does not get to share in the profit generated by the business (suppose the manager gets a fixed salary) then the manager may not have much of an incentive to work hard. Hard work requires effort and while the manager's hard work will make more money for the owner, it may not necessarily benefit the manager. Thus, if the manager is paid a fixed wage then he is better off not putting in much effort at all. If business is bad then he can blame it on bad location or hot weather. (Manager to owner: "It's been so hot lately; no one's drinking coffee, Boss. What we really need is a liquor licence so that we can sell beer and mixed drinks."). The problem is that if business is bad, the owner cannot be sure whether that is really due to the location or the weather or whether it is because the manager is lazy or rude to the customers and provides bad service. In order to find that out the owner will have to continually supervise or monitor the manager but in that case the owner might as well run the place on his own. But the owner may have other businesses or other things to do with his time making it impossible for him to spend all his time supervising the manager.

Faced with an agency problem like this, economists suggest that one must provide the proper incentives (carrots and sticks) to the employee in order to get him to perform his duties satisfactorily. The carrots may include wages, salaries, performance based bonuses, commissions and the possibility of promotions while the sticks include rebukes, bad reports (making later promotions more difficult), fines, penalties, demotions and of course, termination. In fact the view that incentives are crucial to achieving optimal outcomes in employment relationships is fundamental to economic thinking. And while economists often dis-agree over a number of issues there is broad agreement about the need for designing proper incentive schemes for employees. So much so that N. Gregory Mankiw, who is the author of one of the most (if not the most) popular textbooks for under-graduates in economics, provides a list of ten fundamental principles that most economists agree on; number four on that list is: *People respond to incentives.*

This in turn leads to the following dictum: employment relationships must be governed by *explicit contracts* which are *incentive compatible*, meaning that they must clearly specify the *incentives* involving the *rewards* of performing well and the *punishments* for performing poorly. In the absence of a well-designed incentive compatible contract provid-ing both carrots and sticks, employees have no incentive to work hard and will inevitably shirk leading to lower profits for the owner. While most economists will readily agree about the importance of incentives, there is mounting evidence now that economists may be over-emphasising the need for *explicit incentives* and that often a system of *implicit contracts* essentially relying on the mutual trust and reciprocity between owners and workers performs as well as a system based on explicit incentives specifying rewards and punishments.

This, however, is not a new idea and has been around for a while; at least since the economist George Akerlof of Berkeley proposed the idea of labour contracts as "gift exchange" in the early 1970s. Akerlof built his arguments on the basis of a study done in the mid-1950s by the sociologist George Homans who focused on the behaviour of "cash posters" at Eastern Utilities located on the east coast of the United States. Homans looked at a group of ten young women whose job it was to record customers' payments on ledger cards at the time of receipt. The company's policy for such cash posting was 300 per hour. Careful records were kept of the speed at which various workers worked and those who fell below the quota received a mild rebuke from the supervisor. What Homans found was that the average number of cash postings per hour was 353, 18% greater than the required number set by the employer.

Standard economic theory has a hard time explaining (1) why the faster cash posters did not reduce their speed to just meet the required standard of 300 and (2) why the firm did not increase the speed expected of the faster workers. All cash posters were paid the same hourly wage rate and it was *not* the case that the faster workers could expect to earn more in the form of performance bonuses. If and when the workers got promoted, it was to a job that brought with it more responsibility but still paid the same wage. Furthermore, workers quit their jobs quite frequently (in most cases to get married) and thus the length of the firm–employee relationship was not particularly long; so the scope for generating long-term feelings of loyalty is limited. Since the hourly wage was fixed and did not depend on effort and the reward of future promotions was rarely a consideration, economic theory suggests that the workers should adjust their work habits to just meet the quality standard set by the company. But it was obvious that the workers were putting in effort far in excess of what was expected of them.

This led George Akerlof to propose a new model of employment relationships based on "gift exchange" between the employer and the employee. According to Akerlof, in their interactions employees acquire sentiments for each other and also for the firm. As a consequence of sentiment for the firm, the workers derive utility (satisfaction) from an exchange of "gifts" with the firm where the level of satisfaction depends on the norm of gift exchange. On the worker's side the "gift" given is work in excess of the minimum work standard;

on the firm's side the "gift" given is wages in excess of what these women could receive if they left their current jobs. When firms pay their workers a wage that exceeds what those workers could earn in an alternative job or a wage which exceeds the wage dictated by the market forces of demand and supply in the market for labour, economists call that an *"efficiency wage"*. Such efficiency wages are used in many industries to (1) create loyalty on the part of the employee; (2) prevent workers from quitting (because the alternative jobs may pay a much lower wage); and (3) attract better skilled workers. Akerlof argues, on the basis of findings in the sociology literature, that workers' efforts are often determined by the prevailing norm in the work group and may not be determined solely by the wage paid.

This in turn has important and somewhat counter-intuitive implications for the market for labour. Classical economic theory assumes that the wage rate in the market for labour is determined by the interaction of the demand for labour coming from businesses and the supply of labour coming from workers.[5] As long as a firm is willing to pay this market-determined wage, it can hire as many workers as it wants. If the firm is unwilling to offer the market wage then it will be unable to hire any workers. But if the gift-exchange model of business-worker interaction is correct then firms may very well find it advantageous to pay a wage *in excess* of *that which they have to pay* in order to hire labour and in return workers may respond by putting in effort that is *in excess* of what they have to provide.

In terms of gift exchanges in the labour market, this means that the worker who does no more than the minimum required to keep his job may at least suffer from a slight loss of reputation; reciprocally, the firm that pays its workers the bare minimum necessary to retain them will also lose some reputation. In the standard economic model a profit-maximising firm *never* chooses to pay more than the market-clearing wage because there is no advantage to doing so. In the gift-exchange model, however, the firm finds it advantageous to pay a wage in excess of the one at which it can acquire labour, because there are benefits from paying a higher wage.

5  For the time being let us pretend that there is one all encompassing labour market. If that does not satisfy you then think of many different markets for labour – one for blue-collar workers, one for white-collar workers, one for CEOs and so on and in each market there is demand for labour and a supply of labour which determines the wages and salaries for the sellers of labour (the workers) in those markets.

Truman Bewley of Yale University has done extensive work in the area of labour contracts and finds that the gift-exchange model does indeed apply to real-life labour management practices. In a study based on interviews with 246 company managers and 19 labour leaders in the north-eastern United States during the early 1990s when unemployment was high due to a recession, Bewley found that the managers of most enterprises were reluctant to enact a reduction in wages *even though, given the extensive unemployment, they could have easily afforded to hire workers at lower wages*. The primary resistance to wage reduction comes from upper management and not from employees. Bewley suggests that the main reason for avoiding pay-cuts is that such pay-cuts hurt morale. Bewley comments:

> *Morale has three components. One is identification with the firm and an internalization of its objectives. Another is trust in an implicit exchange with the firm and with other employees; employees know that aid given to the firm and to co-workers will eventually be reciprocated.... The third component is a mood that is conducive to good work.... Managers are concerned with morale because of its impact on labour turnover, recruitment of new employees and productivity.... The morale of existing employees is hurt by pay cuts because of an insult effect ... Workers are used to receiving regular pay increases as a reward for good work and loyalty and so interpret a pay cut as an affront and a breach of implicit reciprocity.... Resistance to wage reduction and the need for internal pay equity stem from ideas of fairness that usually refer to some reference wage. The reference wage for pay cuts is the previous wage.*

While there seems to be ample evidence to support Akerlof's idea of gift exchange such as the Homans study of cash-posters at Eastern Utilities, still these are non-replicable one-off observations. Ernst Fehr at the University of Zürich along with his collaborators, Simon Gächter, Urs Fischbacher, Georg Kirchsteiger, Arno Riedl, Klaus Schmidt and Alexander Klein among others set off on an ambitious research project to test the validity of the gift-exchange model in employment relationships using a series of well-crafted experiments. Once again the big advantage to these experiments was the fact that Fehr and his associates could change the experimental design in a number of ways to understand what the impact is on behaviour. This allows for teasing out the effects of various factors on the efficacy of employment contracts.

Fehr and his associates examine these issues at length using a variety of different set-ups. In the interests of convenience and simplicity I am going to discuss the findings of their experiments using a uniform language even though the presentation of the actual game varies between different papers. The basic idea is to look at an employment relationship between firms and workers. Participants are assigned to the role of a firm or a worker at the beginning of the session and these roles remain unchanged for the entire time. The worker needs to expend effort to produce an output which is turned over to the firm. Effort imposes costs (possibly psychological) on the worker. The higher the effort the greater is the output produced. But higher effort also imposes a larger cost on the worker. Fehr and his associates impute a monetary value to this cost. The firm sells the output and earns revenue. The worker is paid a wage. The firm's profit is the difference between the revenue it earns minus the wage that it pays the worker. The worker's profit is the difference between the wage and the (monetary) cost of his effort.

Needless to mention the firm is better off the higher is the effort put in by the worker since that generates a higher output and consequently higher sales revenue for the firm. However, since effort is costly, putting in more effort imposes a larger cost on the worker; therefore, if he is paid a fixed amount of money for his effort then the worker is better off putting in low effort. Thus, there is a dichotomy between the goals of the firm and those of the worker. The firm wants the worker to work hard and put in a lot of effort which will create a larger output and more revenue. The worker on the other hand has little incentive to do so if he is paid a fixed amount and should put in the smallest amount of effort that he can get away with (one that will not get him fired from the job).

In most of their settings, for the sake of simplicity, one firm can hire only one worker at a time but usually there are more workers than there are firms implying that some workers will be unemployed in a given round. This gives the firms more market power in the sense that given the competition between workers for jobs the firm can get away with paying a low wage and asking for a large effort in return. Some workers might balk at offers paying a low wage and asking for high effort, but the alternative is to turn down the offer and earn nothing. Faced with the prospect of making no profit and making a small profit some workers might easily prefer the latter option especially if they think that someone else might take the firm up on its offer if they do not. However, firms and workers are randomly re-matched from one round to the next making it extremely unlikely that the same firm and the same worker will interact more than once. This has the effect of making each interaction a one-off encounter. Given that there is little possibility of the same firm and the same worker meeting again in the future, there is an enhanced incentive for both the firm and the workers to behave in a self-interested way and focus narrowly on maximising their earnings on a round-by-round basis without worrying about the possibility of future retaliations by one party or the other.[6]

Ernst Fehr, Georg Kirchsteiger and Arno Riedl undertook one of the first experimental tests of the gift-exchange model. Their starting point was this: if firms and workers all act according to the laws of economics then what we would expect to see in any labour market is that firms will pay their workers the market-wage as determined by the demand and supply of labour. Workers in turn will put in the bare minimum effort that is required in order to keep their jobs. They designed an experiment where in the first stage firms make wage offers to workers. Workers can either accept or reject a particular wage offer. If the worker accepts then the worker can respond with an effort level. In the experiment the workers have no monetary incentive to choose anything greater than the minimum possible effort level and anticipating that, the firms have no incentive to offer anything other than the market-clearing wage as determined by the demand and supply of labour. On the other hand, if the gift-exchange model is a good predictor of actual behaviour then we would expect to see firms routinely offering a wage that is greater than the minimum they need to offer and workers in turn reciprocating with effort levels that are in excess of the minimum required.

Fehr, Kirchsteiger and Riedl's results are strongly supportive of the gift-exchange model. They find that on average firms offer wages which are considerably higher than the market clearing wage even though they do not have to, especially in light of the fact that there are more workers than jobs and, therefore, workers should be willing to work for

---

6   In any case the interactions are anonymous and take place via computerised software. Thus players never learn the identity of those they are interacting with in any round.

relatively low wages. Workers, in turn, respond with effort levels which are four times those of the predicted effort level.

Furthermore, they find that on average worker effort is increasing in the wage offered; that is, when the firms offered the workers a higher wage (which is analogous to a trusting move since the worker can simply take the wage and put in the lowest possible effort in return), the workers reciprocated with higher effort levels. Fehr, Kirchsteiger and Riedl conclude that fairness considerations do prevent wages from declining to the market-clearing level. This is surprising because given that there are fewer jobs than there are workers and, therefore, some workers would be unemployed in any given round, we would expect that workers, in competing against each other for scarce jobs, would put downward pressure on the wage driving it down to the market clearing level. But clearly this is not what happens and firms continue to pay higher wages than they need to in order to attract workers. Firms anticipate worker reciprocity – that offering a higher wage will elicit higher effort.

In a follow-up study Ernst Fehr and Simon Gächter allow the firms to offer two types of contracts:

(1) a *trust* contract; here the firm offers a fixed wage to the worker and asks for a certain amount of effort in return. This is similar to the wage offers in the Fehr, Kirchsteiger and Riedl study. The worker, if he accepts the contract, can take the wage and decide how much effort he wishes to put in. He is under no compulsion to put in the amount of effort requested by the firm since the firm has no opportunity to penalise the worker in any way and cannot retaliate against the worker in a future round since it is extremely unlikely that they will interact more than once. Thus the effort desired by the firm of the worker is more in the nature of a request (or moral suasion) and the worker is under no compulsion whatsoever to abide by this request. Again, following the tenets of classical economic theory, in this scenario where the firm is offering the worker a fixed wage and the worker can provide any effort in return (regardless of the effort that the firm asks for), the worker has no *explicit* incentive to put in anything more than the minimal effort and we would expect that the worker would do exactly that: take the wage and put in the smallest possible effort. Thus the trust contract provides only an *implicit* (or an *intrinsic*) motivation to the worker by reposing trust on the worker and appealing to his reciprocity but does not have any explicit incentives built into it.

(2) Alternatively the firm can offer the worker an *incentive* contract. Here the firm offers the worker a wage and asks for a desired level of effort as in the trust contract; but in addition the firm can choose to monitor the worker and if the worker does not put in the requisite effort level then the firm can penalise the worker by imposing a monetary fine (which could be a salary-deduction) payable to the firm in the event of non-compliance. Monitoring imposes a cost on the firm because the firm has to invest money into installing a monitoring technology (such as closed-circuit cameras or random visits by supervisors to check on the workers). Furthermore, the monitoring is not perfect in the sense that there is a chance that the monitoring technology will pick up when a worker is shirking and penalise him; but there is also a chance that the shirking will go undetected. However, by suitably choosing the values of the wage to be paid to the worker and the penalty imposed, the firm should be able to provide the right incentives to the worker to put in more than the minimum effort. This is the more traditional approach of providing *explicit* carrot-and-stick based incentives and this explicit *incentive* contract is expected to induce the worker to put in more effort than the (implicit) trust-and-reciprocity based contract.

Fehr and Gächter made a series of surprising discoveries. First, on average in the trust-based contracts firms offer higher wages and ask for higher effort from the workers compared to the incentive contract. Second, the effort level put in by the workers under an incentive contract is lower than those put in by the workers in the trust contract. This finding is driven by the fact that even with explicit fines for non-compliance a number of workers shirk given that the monitoring technology is imperfect and does not catch shirking with 100% accuracy. Voluntary cooperation as measured by the excess of effort provided over the amount requested from the worker is higher under a trust contract compared to an incentive contract, meaning that under trust contracts workers routinely provided more than the minimal amount of effort required of them, while under incentive contracts few workers did so. This suggests that the provision of explicit penalties in the contract might have led to a reduction in voluntary cooperation among the workers. Under trust-based contracts an increase in the wage offered elicited much higher effort levels from the workers and overall contracts that relied on mutual trust and reciprocity among firms and workers led to higher earnings for both parties involved compared to incentive contracts.

In another study Fehr, Gächter and Kirchsteiger add a third stage to the employment contract. In the first stage the firm offers a contract to the worker. In the case of a trust contract this consists of a wage offer and a suggested effort level. In the case of an incentive contract this consists of a wage, a suggested effort level and a pre-specified fine payable by the worker to the firm in the event the worker is caught shirking and providing less than the effort asked for. Once again the monitoring is imperfect and the worker may or may not get caught shirking. In the second stage, the worker decides whether to accept the wage offer or not, and if he does accept the wage then he decides what amount of effort to put in. As in the Fehr and Gächter study, the worker has no incentive to provide anything greater than the minimal effort under a trust contract, while with an incentive contract, by appropriately choosing the values of the fine and the chance of getting caught, the firm can guarantee that the worker will provide higher effort.

Fehr, Gächter and Kirchsteiger add a third stage where the firm gets to see the effort level chosen by the worker in the second stage and whether this effort is greater than, equal to or less than the effort level demanded by the firm. After observing the worker's effort the firm can decide to either further punish the worker over and above the fine (in those cases where the effort level is less than the effort demanded) or reward the worker with a bonus (in those cases where the effort level is greater than the effort demanded). However, both the reward and the punishment impose a monetary cost on the firm in the sense that it has to dip into its profit if it wishes to reward or punish the worker. Keep in mind that all of these are one-off interactions with very little possibility of the two parties meeting in the future.

Thus, in the third stage the firm has no incentive to spend money to reward or punish the worker for effort provided. Suppose the worker shirked and caused the firm to lose money. It still does not make sense for the firm to lose more money by punishing the worker because the firm is not going to interact with this particular worker again. So the firm might as well swallow its loss and its pride and move on to the next interaction. Similarly, there is no incentive for the firm to reward the worker even if the worker provided more effort than asked for. The worker has already been paid a wage and the worker has no way of compelling the firm to pay a bonus. The firm does not care if the worker is disgruntled because the firm is not going to interact with this particular worker again and so even if the worker is unhappy it will not affect the firm in future interactions.

Surprisingly (or maybe not so surprisingly) Fehr and his associates find that in about 50% of cases where the worker shirked in stage two, the firm punished those workers in stage three even though this punishment imposed monetary costs on the firm and did not generate any future benefits such as an enhanced reputation for toughness since the same two parties were not going to interact any more. Moreover, in about 50% of cases where the worker simply provides the effort level called for (or in those few cases where the worker provides effort in excess of that demanded) the firm actually rewarded the worker with a bonus even though the firm did not have to do so and the reward was monetarily costly for the firm. While the firms have no incentive to either reward or punish in the third stage and the presence of the reward/punishment opportunities should not make any difference whatsoever, still the mere fact that such an opportunity to reward/punish does exist leads to firms demanding much higher effort in this treatment and workers also responding with high effort in response.

Fehr and his associates go on to argue that such high wage/high effort strategies are better from the point of view of both the firms and workers and that mutual trust and reciprocity between firms and workers lead to better outcomes for them. They suggest that:

> ... exclusive reliance on selfishness and, in particular, the neglect of reciprocity motives may lead to wrong predictions and to wrong normative inferences. We argue that reciprocal behaviour may cause an increase in the set of enforceable contracts and may thus allow the achievement of nonegligible efficiency gains.

The idea of gift exchange between employers and workers might sound great in theory but does it really work as a business practice? Does it reduce employee turnover? Do the firms who implement such a model do better or worse than firms that rely on traditional command-and-control type systems? James Baron and Michael Hannan of Stanford University and Diane Burton of MIT working under the aegis of the Stanford Project on Emerging Companies (SPEC) examine the impact of organisational practices on employee turnover in a sample of high-technology start-ups in California's Silicon Valley. Baron and his colleagues ask the question: Given that different high-tech start-ups in

Silicon Valley seem to have implemented distinctive types of contractual relationships between the owner(s) and the workers, what are the implications of these human resource practices on the propensity of employees to quit?

Baron and his colleagues approached 376 firms founded in the 1990s with at least ten workers or more. Of these, 173 firms agreed to participate in the study. Trained MBA and doctoral students conducted semi-structured interviews with the CEO of the company. The CEO was asked to identify the founder (or member of the founding team) best equipped to provide information about the firm's origins and the best informant regarding human resource management practices in the organisation. The individuals concerned were requested to fill out surveys prior to being interviewed. The researchers found that one aspect of the employment relationship that loomed large in the organisation of many start-ups was *attachment*.

The founders articulated three different bases of employee attachment which the researchers label *love, work* and *money*. Some founders wished to create a strong family-like feeling and an emotional bond between the workers and management on the one hand, and between the workers themselves on the other, that would inspire superior effort and increase retention of highly sought employees, thereby avoiding the frequent quits among workers that plague many of these start-ups. What binds the worker to the company in this framework is a sense of belonging and identification with the company – consistent with the model of gift exchange discussed above. Some founders wished to stimulate their workers by providing the opportunity for interesting and challenging work. Finally, others considered the employment relationship as merely a simple exchange of labour for money. As for coordinating and controlling the actions of workers, there seemed to be two approaches – one involving informal control through peers by creating a particular organisational culture and the other espousing a more traditional view based on formal carrot-and-stick based procedures and systems.

Based on their extensive surveys and interviews, the researchers classify the organisational structures of the high-tech start-ups into five separate models (albeit with some degree of overlap between them):

1  the *engineering model* which involves attachment through challenging work, peer group control and selection based on specific task abilities;

2    the *star model* which creates attachment based on challenging work, reliance on autonomy and professional control and selecting elite personnel based on long-term potential;

3    the *commitment model* which entails reliance on emotional-familial relationships based on mutual trust and reciprocity between management and workers and workers themselves;

4    the *bureaucracy model* which involves attachment based on challenging work, but worker selection based on qualifications for a particular role and formalised control;

5    the *autocracy model* which relies on employment premised on monetary considerations, control and coordination through close personal oversight and selection of employees to perform pre-specified tasks.

In the context of our earlier discussion, the *commitment model* is the one which most closely resembles the gift-exchange model while the *autocracy model* and to a large extent the *bureaucracy model* are the ones that most closely approximate the classical economic approach to employment relationships. If you accept the tenet that it is essential to provide workers with explicit and extrinsic motivations in order for them to put in high effort then the organisations relying on the commitment model should perform worse than the ones using the autocratic or bureaucratic models.

What Baron and his colleagues find is that the main contrast in human resource practices is between the autocracy model, which exhibits the highest rates of employee turnover, and the commitment model which displays the lowest rates. Furthermore, firms whose CEOs rely on either the autocratic or the bureaucratic model experience far greater turnover than the firms which implement the commitment model. Employee turnover is, after all, only one metric of how a firm is doing and possibly more important than employee turnover is the issue of firm profitability, though excessive turnover might have a disruptive influence and reduce profitability. Baron and his colleagues, therefore, decided to look at how these various models perform in terms of "*one compelling indicator of performance*": revenue growth. Given that young high-tech start-ups incur significant set-up costs which might dampen profitability, an ability to increase the revenue flow is a good indicator of later success. Baron and his colleagues find that there is a strong *negative* relationship between employee turnover and revenue growth, implying that firms which experience excessive labour turnover (such as the ones relying on the autocratic or bureaucratic models) also experience much slower revenue growth compared to firms which manage to retain their workers (such as the ones which implement the commitment model).

## 3.7 Concluding remarks

The economist Paul Seabright of the University of Toulouse in his book *The Company of Strangers: A Natural History of Economic Life* points out that the decision to trust strangers and to reciprocate others' trust is crucial to exploiting the benefits of a sophisticated division of labour among large groups of humans; notions of trust and reciprocity are, therefore, fundamental to economic life. A large number of transactions in day-to-day life – particularly more anonymous ones such as those conducted via the Internet – would never take place if people were myopically self-interested and opportunistic. This is because many economic transactions are not simultaneous. Sometimes the buyer pays first and then the seller sends the good; or the seller sends the good first and then bills the buyer later. This in turn requires the more vulnerable party to repose trust in the less vulnerable one. What makes trusting strangers – and thereby making one's own self vulnerable to exploitation – a reasonable thing to do? Seabright argues that this is because we have created structures of social life in which such judgements of trust make sense and these structures work because they fit in well with our natural dispositions.

Trusting actions are not naïve and are predicated upon expectations of reciprocity on the part of the trustee. Neither of these two dispositions – trust or reciprocity – could support cooperation without the other. Those who trust naïvely, without any calculation of expected reciprocity, would be easily exploited. On the other hand, those who engage in calculated and strategic trust without any tendency to reciprocate others' trust would be too opportunistic and it is unlikely that they will be trusted too often.

We have seen in the preceding pages that when it comes to making trusting decisions there seem to be at least two types: (1) a type that typically trusts and reciprocates trust; for whom trust and reciprocity is a general social orientation towards others. But (2) there is also a type of person that tends to trust as a calculated gamble, but also tends not to reciprocate. It is possible that the latter type may benefit in the short-run by exploiting the reciprocity of others, but in the longer term it is probably the former type who will be better able to reap the benefits of complex exchanges and the division of labour among disparate groups of strangers.

I have also adduced evidence to suggest that in the context of many employer–employee relationships, compared to incentive-based contracts that rely on explicit carrots and sticks, implicit contracts relying on mutual trust and reciprocity might do better, or at least no worse, than explicit contracts with regards to employee productivity (or other measures of success). I will return to this theme of explicit/extrinsic versus implicit/intrinsic rewards in the last section of the book.

# Part 4

# Cooperation in social dilemmas

## 4.1 Cooperation in social dilemmas

Now I would like to go back to the example of building the public park that I talked about in the introduction and examine people's motivations in greater detail. Economists refer to a public park as a *"public good"*. A public good is one whose consumption is *"non-rival"* and *"non-excludable"*. A good is *"non-rival"* in consumption when the use of the good by one individual does not prevent other individuals from using (consuming) the same good. *"Non-excludable"* means that once the good (the park) is provided no one can be excluded from the consumption of the public good even if that person did not pay for its provision.

Examples of public goods include: clean environment, national defence, the police, the fire service, highways, public parks, public libraries, public hospitals and so on. Of course some of these are more excludable than others. No one can be prevented from enjoying the benefits of clean air. Similarly if the army goes to war, it does so for every citizen regardless of who paid their taxes or not. If your house is on fire the firemen will show up and fight the fire without asking whether your taxes are up-to-date or whether you contributed when they held a bake-sale at the firehouse last month. But the more drivers there are on the highway that takes you to the beach on a sunny summer weekend, the slower the progress and some people might look at the traffic and decide not to go out at all. In this case the ones who decide to stay home are excluded at the expense of those who are on the road. Thus, highways are more excludable – and in one sense less of a public good – than the environment.

So the questions we are interested in answering are: What motivates people? Who contributes? Who does not? Why do the ones who contribute do and those who do not, do not? Because what we are essentially dealing with here are people's in-built preferences and their beliefs, naturally occurring field data is of not much benefit to us since they do not really allow us to peer inside people's minds. We could certainly use survey questionnaires. We could ask people what motivated them to undertake a particular action. But the problem is that there is no guarantee that they would give you truthful responses. Someone who did not contribute when nobody could see that decision might very easily feel embarrassed to admit that in public.

Economists studying this problem designed an excellent game which simulates this decision-making situation. This is how the game goes. A group of four participants are gathered in a room. They are each given a sum of money (say $5) and they are told that they can allocate this money between a private account and a public account. Money allocated to the private account remains unchanged and is theirs for good. However, any amount contributed to the public account is multiplied by a factor greater than 1 (say 2) by the experimenter. This multiplied amount is then distributed equally between the four group members. Thus, any contribution made by an individual to the public account generates a positive externality in the sense that it yields a return to other members of the group who may not have contributed anything to the public account.

The socially optimal (or socially desirable) outcome in this game is for every player to contribute the entire amount to the public account. Total contributions to the public account are $20 which is doubled to $40 by the experimenter and redistributed back to the group members netting each person $10. Each member then gets a 100% return on her initial investment. However, individual rationality suggests a different course of action. Think about an individual player trying to decide how much to contribute. If this individual contributes $1 and no one else contributes anything, then the $1 is doubled to $2. Distributed equally between the four players, this gives each player $0.50. The player who contributed is worse off (incurs a 50% loss on the investment) while every other player is better off at the expense of the player who contributed. Thus if a player does not contribute, then she is no worse off if no one else contributes, but she is actually better off if some others contribute. This tension between contributing to the public good or free-riding on others' contributions poses a *social dilemma* which has been studied extensively by both economists and psychologists.

John Ledyard of Caltech, who has done extensive work in the area, points out that some of the most fundamental questions about the organisation of society centre around the issues raised by the presence of public goods and the consequent social dilemma posed above. How well do current political institutions perform in the production and funding of public goods? How far can volunteerism take us in attempts to provide efficient levels of public goods? At a more basic level, contributions to public goods raise fundamental questions about whether people are generally selfish or cooperative.

Economic theory, based on the assumption of a rational *homo eco-nomicus*, suggests that faced with a situation like this, every rational self-interested player will engage in strong free-riding behaviour by not contributing any money to the public pool at all, just as Yossarian in *Catch 22*. But now we have access to economic experiments and can see what people do when confronted with this particular situation.

A lot of the early work in this area was undertaken by Mark Isaac at the University of Arizona, James Walker at Indiana and Charles Plott at Caltech along with their collaborators Arlington Williams, Susan Thomas, Oliver Kim and Kenneth McCue. These researchers found that if you get a group of people together – they could be perfect strangers, friends or acquaintances – there is a remarkable regularity to behaviour. Total contributions to the public pool always tend to be between 40 and 60% of the maximum possible. That is, if the maximum total contribution is $20, then contributions usually average between $8 and $12. I should point out that this does not imply that every group member contributes between 40 and 60%. Rather, some contribute 100% while others contribute nothing. And this behaviour seems to be robust in the sense that the behaviour is remarkably similar across various countries and cultures.

What happens if you had the same group of people play the game more than once, i.e. suppose you asked them to continue playing for ten rounds? In each round they have a sum of money (say $2) and they have to make the decision regarding how much to contribute to the public account ten times. (So that if they simply held on to the $2 in each round they would end up making $20). What happens in that case is shown in Figure 4.1. Contributions typically start between 40 and 60% and then decline over time with the average contribution falling lower and lower, even though the contributions never reach zero even if people play for as many as 50 or 60 times. Some people contribute nothing and free-ride for the entire time, while others start by contributing a lot (100% or close to it) and then reduce their contribution over time.

There are a number of puzzles here. Why do some people contribute while others do not? Why do some people cooperate at the beginning and free-ride later? If they are going to free-ride why do they not start to do so immediately? We have already argued that free-riding is the self-interested course of action in this game. So maybe that is easier to understand – why people free-ride. They are self-interested and wish to maximise their own monetary gains at the expense of others. But what can we say about those participants who contribute a lot? Are they

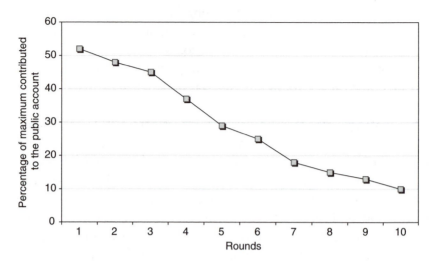

*Figure 4.1* Pattern of decay in contributions to the public account over time. Figure created by author on the basis of data in one of his own studies.

being purely altruistic? That is, do they contribute because they care about the welfare of others? The easy way out would be to say: why is this surprising? Of course there are different types of people in the world. Some of us are generous and care more about cooperating with others, some of us do not (like the Cyclopes in *The Odyssey*):

> *And we come to the land of the Cyclopes, a fierce, lawless people who never lift a hand to plant or plough but just leave everything to the immortal gods.... The Cyclopes have no assemblies for the making of laws, nor any established legal codes, but live in hollow caverns in the mountain heights, where each man is a lawgiver to his own children and women, and nobody has the slightest interest in what his neighbour decides.*

## 4.2 Are contributions caused by confusion on the part of the participants?

One possible explanation for why these contributions decay over time is this: when you bring participants into a laboratory and ask them to play this game for money, the situation confronting those participants is relatively novel. The instructions they are given are often phrased in abstract terms and do not use emotive terms like contributing to charity. Thus it might take people some time to understand what real-life situation this game corresponds to. People might contribute in the beginning before they really understand the incentive structure of the game, but as comprehension dawns they realise that the rational thing to do would be to free-ride and start to do so, which leads to the resulting decay in the contributions to the public account. Different people may come to this realisation at different times which explains the slow decay in contributions rather than a sudden swift drop. We will call this the "*learning*" hypothesis, i.e. participants do not figure out that they should free-ride straight off the bat, but "learn" to do so over time as they gain familiarity with the situation.

A group of economic theorists – David Kreps, Paul Milgrom, John Roberts and Robert Wilson – suggested an alternative hypothesis and a more complex explanation to this phenomenon. They posited the following: suppose there are two types of people – sophisticated ones and unsophisticated ones. The former types all realise that the rational course of action in this game is to free-ride while the latter types do not. Because the unsophisticated players do not understand that they should free-ride, they contribute to the public account. The sophisticated ones realise that they should free-ride but they also realise that if they do so from the very outset then the unsophisticated players will look at what they are doing and figure out the incentives to free-ride as well. Thus, the sophisticated players may decide to mimic the unsophisticated ones at the beginning and contribute to the public pool so as not to alert the unsophisticated players to the possibility of free-riding. Once the unsophisticated players have been lulled into a sense of security that others in the group will also contribute, the sophisticated ones start to free-ride on the contributions made by the unsophisticated ones. This guarantees the sophisticated players a higher monetary return than if they had started to free-ride from the very beginning and induced the unsophisticated players to free-ride as well. Let us call this the "*strategies*" hypothesis.

Are these conjectures correct? How should one test them? This is another example where survey questionnaires or field data are not of much assistance at all. James Andreoni of the University of Wisconsin came up with an ingenious way of putting these conjectures to the test. Andreoni recruited 70 participants to play the public goods game in groups of five for ten rounds. In each round, a participant had 50 tokens. In each round participants could divide their tokens between a private account and a public account. Tokens kept in the private account were worth 1 cent each. Total tokens placed in the public account were multiplied by 2.5 and re-distributed equally among the five participants giving each of them 0.5 cent. This implied that a single token contributed to the public account by any participant generated a return of 0.5 cent for each of the other group members regardless of whether they had contributed anything to the public account or not.

Andreoni looked at the effect of two different treatments. In the "*strangers*" treatment, 40 participants were randomly assigned (by a computer) to one of eight groups containing five participants each. These participants were told that they would play the game exactly ten times, but that after each repetition the composition of the group would change in an unpredictable way with the computer randomly re-assigning participants to groups. While participants knew that they would be re-assigned, they never learn the identity of the other four members of the group in any round. This random re-assignment of participants to groups severely limits the gains from playing strategically. In a second "*partners*" treatment, 30 participants were formed into six groups of five. They played the exact same game as those in the "*strangers*" treatment, except here the composition of the groups remained unchanged for the entire time.

These two treatments are designed to test the strategies hypothesis in the following way: suppose a participant is initially investing a certain amount of tokens to the public account. This participant experiences an epiphany in a particular round $t$ and realises that the rational thing to do would be to free ride in this game. If this participant is in the "*partners*" treatment and is interacting with the same group of participants over and over again, then she might have an incentive to continue to cooperate and contribute to the public account so as not to alert those players who may not have figured out the free-riding strategy. But if this person is in the "*strangers*" treatment then she is interacting with different people in each round and, therefore, each round in this treatment is analogous to a one-off interaction. There is no benefit to engaging in strategic behaviour here – such as mimicking the behaviour of unsophisticated participants or sending signals about one's cooperativeness – because you are not going to interact with them in the future. Thus, once you figure out that the rational course of action is to free-ride, in the "*strangers*" treatment you might as well start engaging in this behaviour from that point onwards because every round you are interacting with a different group of participants. This then implies that we should expect to see greater cooperation – and higher contributions to the public account – in the "*partners*" treatment compared to the "*strangers*" treatment.

In order to isolate the learning hypothesis Andreoni decided to include a surprise "re-start". After the participants had finished interacting for ten rounds, he told them that there was time to play a few more rounds where they could earn additional money. He then had them participate for *three more* rounds. The idea here is this: if the decay in contribution is due primarily to participants gradually figuring out the rational strategy that they should free-ride, then once they learn to free-ride they should continue to do so even after the re-start. Therefore the re-start should not change behaviour in any way. Contributions should continue to exhibit the same pattern of decay even after the re-start. But if not, then this might imply that learning alone cannot explain the pattern of decaying contribution.

The results were surprising and did not provide corroboration for either the "strategies" or the "learning" hypothesis. First, by and large, contributions were higher in the "strangers" treatment compared to the "partners" treatment. Second, the extent of free-riding was greater in the "partners" treatment also. Both of these contradicted the strategies hypothesis. What was even more striking was the fact that following the re-start, contributions jumped up in both the partners and the strangers treatments which contradicted the learning hypothesis. In Figure 4.2, I show the pattern of contributions during the initial ten rounds and then for the three additional rounds after the re-start. For the first ten rounds the contributions show the familiar pattern of decay that we saw in Figure 4.1, but contrary to the strategies hypothesis the contribution by the strangers are almost always greater than those by the partners. After the re-start contributions *increase* in round 11, contradicting the learning hypothesis and this increase is more pronounced for the participants in the partners treatment.

Subsequently, a large number of researchers both in the US and in other countries around the world replicated Andreoni's experiment. Rachel Croson of the University of Pennsylvania and James Andreoni provide a comprehensive overview in a recent paper and discuss nine papers that use this "partners" versus "strangers" paradigm. Out of

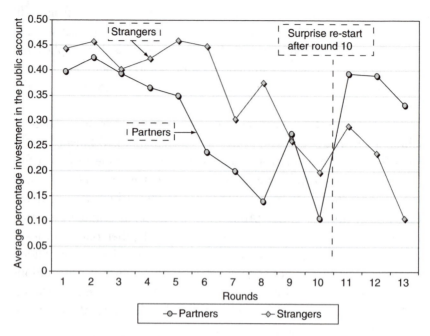

*Figure 4.2* Pattern of contribution in Andreoni's (1988) study before and after re-start. Figure created by author on the basis of data provided in the original study.

those nine studies, two were cross-cultural studies looking at behaviour of participants in more than one country. One of these was an ambitious study carried out by Jordi Brandts, Tatsuyoshi Saijo and Arthur Schram comparing the behaviour of participants in four different countries – Japan, Netherlands, Spain and the US. The other by Roberto Burlando and John Hey compared the behaviour of participants in the UK and Italy. Thus these nine studies analyse differences in behaviour among 13 separate groups of participants. The results are mixed. In five out of 13 groups of participants, partners contribute more than strangers; in four cases the strangers contribute more while in the remaining four cases there is no difference in contributions between partners and strangers.

## 4.3 Looking for alternative explanations

So neither the "strategies" nor the "learning" hypothesis were able to provide a satisfactory explanation to the questions that we posed above.

In 1993, Matthew Rabin of the University of California at Berkeley wrote a paper called "Incorporating Fairness into Game Theory and Economics", where he provided a different explanation behind the behaviour in the public goods game. He suggested that people approach the game differently from what was thought before. He argued that essentially people saw this game as one which required coordinated action on the part of the participants and that there were multiple possible outcomes. In one outcome or in one group, participants may succeed in generating an implicit and virtuous norm where everyone manages to coordinate their actions so that everyone chooses a high contribution to the public account. This is certainly the most desirable outcome from a society's point of view. But it is also possible that at times participants may not be able to coordinate their actions to reach this socially desirable outcome and might end up choosing low contributions. Choosing low contributions becomes a "bad" equilibrium where everyone realises that collectively they have not managed to reach the socially desirable outcome, but once they have all coordinated their actions to choose low contributions no one wants to increase his or her contribution unless everyone else increases their contributions at the same time. For instance, as we discussed in Part 2 earlier, the Lamalera and Ache seemed to have evolved a norm of making generous offers in the ultimatum game while the Machiguenga seemed to have evolved a norm of low offers which are routinely accepted by the responders.

Thus, Rabin suggested that actual behaviour is far more nuanced than it appears at first sight and the motivations behind that behaviour are also quite complex. According to him those who contribute a lot are not being altruistic (at least the majority are not). Rather the majority of people are *conditional co-operators* in the sense that what they contribute depends crucially on what they believe other members of the group will contribute. Those with optimistic beliefs, i.e. those who believe that their peers will be generous and contribute to the public account, start out by contributing a lot as well. These optimists essentially try to coordinate their actions to reach the socially desirable outcome of high contributions. But those who believe that others will contribute little, respond in kind and aim for the outcome where everyone is either free-riding or close to it. Thus, people are neither purely altruistic nor purely free-riders (of course there are some who *are* altruists and some who will *always* free-ride), but rather a majority of people behave according to their perceptions of their group members.

Rabin's paper, however, was theoretical in nature and did not provide actual evidence in support of conditional cooperation. The evidence was provided by three Swiss researchers at the University of Zürich – Urs Fischbacher, Simon Gächter and Ernst Fehr – who designed an ingenious experiment to test this idea. They recruited 44 participants and then divided them into 11 groups of four. Each participant plays only once which generates 44 independent observations. The participants took part in a public goods game very similar to the one described earlier in this chapter. Participants are given an endowment of 20 tokens which could be allocated to a private or a public account. Tokens allocated to the public account are multiplied by 1.6 and re-distributed equally among the group members. The participants were provided with the instructions and ten control questions to practise, so they could understand the mechanics of the game.

Participants were then asked to fill out two separate forms – first, an "unconditional" contribution form where participants had to decide how much to contribute to the public account without knowing anything about the contributions of the others in the group. Following that they were asked to indicate how much they would contribute for each one of 21 possible average contributions (0, 1, 2,..., 20 tokens) of other group members. One member of the group, picked randomly, had to play the game according to the conditional contribution schedule while the other three were free to make unconditional contributions. This induces participants to take the conditional cooperation questionnaire seriously because everyone realises that some of them will have to abide by their responses on this form.

Figure 4.3 summarises their results. These researchers find that: (1) Fifty per cent of the participants are conditional co-operators; as you can see from Figure 4.3, these participants increase their contributions with an increase in the average contribution in the group. If these participants exactly matched the group average then their contribution profile would coincide with the 45° line. That is not the case and the contribution profile of the conditional co-operators lies slightly below the 45° line pretty much for all contribution levels indicating that there is a bit of a self-serving bias among the conditional co-operators. (2) Thirty per cent of the participants are free-riders. (3) Fourteen per cent of the participants have a hump-shaped contribution pattern. The contribution of participants in this last group increases as the group average increases up to an average of ten tokens (50% of the initial

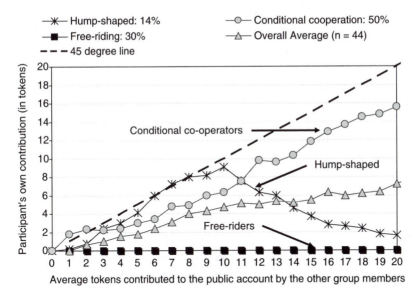

*Figure 4.3* Fischbacher *et al.* (2001): evidence of conditional cooperation; average own contribution level for each average contribution level of other group members. Figure created by author on the basis of data provided in the original study.

endowment), but once the average group contribution exceeds ten tokens, their contributions decline with increasing group average.[1] (4) Finally, 6% of participants behaved in ways that could not be readily categorised. Given that the majority of participants are conditional co-operators, who are willing to contribute more if others do so too, the overall average contribution in the group is also increasing with an increase in the average group contribution. That is as long as others contribute more, the group as a whole will also contribute more *on average*.

Fischbacher and his colleagues go on to provide a rationale for why contributions fall off over time. They suggest that any heterogeneous group of participants consists of conditional co-operators and free-riders. Those conditional co-operators who possess optimistic beliefs about their peers and believe that their peers will contribute to the

1  At this point of time I am not aware of any studies that provide a satisfactory explanation for the behaviour of the participants with a hump-shaped pattern of contributions. But these hump-shaped contributors show up in most studies that examine the phenomenon of conditional cooperation except that they are always a small minority.

public account start out by contributing to the public account as well. But over time they begin to realise that not everyone in the group is like them and that some people in the group are free-riders. In response the conditional co-operators reduce their contributions as well over time leading to the decaying pattern in contributions.

The decay in contributions is also possible even if the majority of participants are conditional co-operators (with a few free-riders) but they differ in their beliefs about their peers. Consider a group of three participants – two conditional co-operators and a free-rider. A conditional co-operator who believes that his peers will contribute a lot – say 80% or more – to the public account will also do the same. Suppose the first contributor contributes 80% of his initial endowment to the public account. But another conditional co-operator might easily possess pessimistic beliefs about fellow citizens and starts out contributing only 20% of his endowment to the public account. The free-rider contributes nothing to the public account. The average contribution in this group then is 50% of the maximum possible. This would then induce the first, optimistic, conditional co-operator to revise his beliefs downwards and reduce his contribution in subsequent rounds. Of course, this should also induce the pessimistic conditional co-operator to revise his beliefs upwards and increase his contribution in future rounds. But it seems to be the case that the disillusionment of the optimist and the consequent reduction in this disgruntled person's contribution far exceeds any increase in contributions from the pessimist leading to a decaying pattern of contributions.[2]

In fact, two researchers at the University of Auckland – Ananish Chaudhuri and Tirnud Paichayontvijit – carry out a public goods game where participants play the game for 24 rounds and do not learn anything about the contributions of others or their own earnings until the very end. They find that in this situation contributions *do not decay* at all. Those who expect their peers to contribute 60% or more to the public account, contribute 60% or more *on average* for the entire set of 24 rounds. Those who expect the members of their group to contribute between 40 and 60%, contribute between 40 and 60% themselves for the entire time and those who expect others to contribute less than

---

2  I am going to side-step the issue of where these beliefs come from in the first place. They could be the product of nature or nurture (upbringing and socialisation). This discussion is beyond the scope of the current volume.

40%, also contribute less than 40% for the whole session. Thus, the phenomenon of decay depends on whether participants can see what their peers are doing. This lends further credence to the arguments by Fischbacher, Fehr and Gächter that the decay in contributions arises from the fact that conditional co-operators reduce their contributions over time as they begin to realise that there are others in the group who are either contributing less or completely free-riding.

Further corroboration of this idea – that decaying contributions result primarily from reduced contributions by co-operators – comes from a study by Anna Gunnthorsdottir (of the Australian Graduate School of Management), Daniel Houser and Kevin McCabe (both of George Mason University).

Here is what Gunnthorsdottir and her colleagues did. They recruited 264 participants at the University of Arizona to take part in a public goods game. There are 12 participants in each session who are formed into groups of four and interact for ten rounds. Participants are assigned to one of two treatments. In the baseline or control condition, the assignment of participants to groups is random. Groups are re-formed at the end of each round but in the control condition this re-grouping is done randomly so that each participant has an equal chance of ending up in a group with any three other participants.

However there is also an experimental "*sorted*" condition. Here, in each round, after participants have made their decisions, the four highest contributors to the public account are placed into one group; the fifth to eighth highest contributors are placed in the second group and so on. Participants are not told the exact mechanism by which the groups are formed, but might be able to deduce this by observing the pattern of contributions to the public account.

It will probably not come as a surprise to you that when the more cooperative types are sorted into the same group they manage to sustain high levels of contribution compared to the randomly formed groups. In the treatment where the groups are formed randomly one observes the usual pattern of decay; but there is considerably less decay in contributions in the "*sorted*" treatment where the like-minded participants are grouped together.

However, the innovative part of this study – and the one that is immediately relevant for our purposes – arises from its analysis of how the behaviour of those with a more cooperative disposition differs from those who are less cooperative. Gunnthorsdottir and her colleagues start from the premise that a person's initial contribution to a public good is a useful and reliable measure of his or her cooperative disposition. Using first-round contributions only, Gunnthorsdottir and her colleagues classify participants into two categories: those who contribute 30% or less of their endowments are labelled "free-riders" while the rest are labelled "co-operators". This classification is done only once and is not changed during the session.

Gunnthorsdottir and her colleagues find that when the co-operators are grouped together with other co-operators in the "*sorted*" treatment, they manage to sustain high contributions throughout. Moreover, the contributions of the co-operators in the "*sorted*" treatment always exceed those in the "*random*" treatment. This is due, in large part, to the nature of the interaction that they encounter. In the sorted treatment the co-operators realise, by observing the average group contribution, that they are interacting with other co-operators and the cooperative nature of their shared history makes them much more inclined to cooperate. However in the control treatment where groups are formed randomly and co-operators interact with free-riders frequently, there is no such shared history of cooperation over time; here the co-operators reduce their contributions over time, sometimes quite rapidly so.

In fact, by comparing separately the contributions of the co-operators and the free-riders in the random treatment (which exhibits the familiar pattern of decaying contributions), Gunnthorsdottir and her colleagues discover that the decay in contributions in this treatment results primarily from a decay in the contributions of the cooperative types. Based on these findings it is likely that the familiar pattern of decay in contributions that we observe in the public goods experiments (where the usual practice is to form groups randomly) arise primarily from a loss of faith on the part of co-operators who start out with high contributions but are disillusioned over time resulting in a reduction in contributions over time.

Subsequently, a number of other researchers have replicated this finding that when it comes to such social dilemmas the majority of the people are neither purely self-interested free-riders nor are they incurable optimists wearing rose-tinted glasses. But rather they are astute individuals who either possess or form beliefs about how their peers will behave and then behave accordingly. If they think their peers will cooperate then so will they; if not, then they will not cooperate either. Claudia Keser and Frans van Winden at the University of Amsterdam also examine this phenomenon and classify participants in their study according to how they responded to the *average group contribution* in the previous round. In keeping with the notion of conditional cooperation, around 80% of their participants respond to the information about group average by changing their own contributions in the next round. Those who are above the average in one round decrease their contributions in the following round and those who are below the average increase their contributions. (Keser and van Winden were probably the first experimental economists to formally use the term "conditional cooperation".)

Ananish Chaudhuri and Tirnud Paichayontvijit analyse the behaviour of 88 participants and find that 62% of these are conditional co-operators while only 16% are free-riders. Around 9% of the participants show the familiar hump-shaped contribution pattern. Furthermore, they find when participants are provided with information about the presence of other conditional co-operators in the group, their contributions to the public account increase, but more importantly, this increase is most pronounced for the conditional co-operators themselves. This in turn suggests that one way of getting people to cooperate more would be to foster more optimistic beliefs because those who think that their peers will cooperate are themselves willing to cooperate. Thus you may have a group of conditional co-operators but they may not necessarily cooperate until they are convinced that others will cooperate as well. Thus, the trick very often is simply to convince these people of the existence of other co-operators in the group in order for cooperation to take root.

Before moving on, I should point out that social psychologists had been writing about the phenomenon, that beliefs about others' actions affect behaviour in social dilemmas, before economists started doing so; even though the psychologists may not have actually used the term "*conditional cooperation*" and typically do not focus on its economic implications. One of the earliest studies on the topic was carried out by Harold Kelley and Anthony Stahelski of the University of California, Los Angeles, in 1970. Kelley and Stahelski look at how participants' beliefs affect cooperation in the prisoner's dilemma game. There is a large literature in social psychology, including this study and a number of others that followed, looking broadly at issues of cooperation and selfishness, often using the prisoner's dilemma game.[3]

---

3  I need to thank Simon Gächter for pointing out to me that research on conditional cooperation in social psychology predates that in economics.

## 4.4 Do participants display a herd mentality?

The concept of conditional cooperation was a radically new one which not only provided a new way of thinking about cooperation in social dilemmas but also, as we will see below, provided ideas about how we could enhance cooperation among humans in such dilemmas. But there was one question mark. There is evidence that people often love to conform because non-conformity is (psychologically) painful. Suppose someone asks you: "*How much will you contribute to the public good out of your 20 tokens, if others in the group contribute 18 tokens (90%)?*" You might very easily respond that you will contribute 90% or close to it also; not because that is what *you want to do* but that is what *you think you ought to do*, so that you can conform with the rest of the group.

One of the most well-known examples of the desire for such conformity in groups comes from the experiments carried out by Solomon Asch. In Figure 4.4, I provide a representation of the cards that Asch used in his study. Asch asked participants to take a "vision test". Participants are shown two cards. The card on the left has the reference line and the one on the right shows the three comparison lines. In reality, all, but one of the participants in any group, were research confederates of the experimenter. The participants – the real one and the confederates – were all seated in a classroom and each in turn was asked which line on the right-hand card was longer than, shorter than or of equal length as the reference line on the left-hand card. The

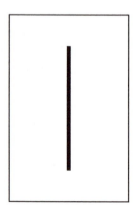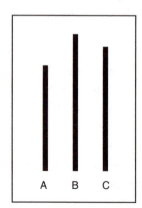

*Figure 4.4* The diagrams used in the experiments by Asch (1955). Figure created by author.

confederates had been instructed to provide incorrect answers. While a number of the real participants answered correctly, a high proportion (32%) conformed to the majority view of the others even when this view was clearly erroneous in that the majority said that two lines were of the same length even though they differed by several inches.

But, by and large, follow-up studies on conditional cooperation suggest that conformity or "herd" mentality is not the primary driving force behind the phenomenon of conditional cooperation. Robert Kurzban at the University of Pennsylvania and Daniel Houser at George Mason explore the heterogeneity in types by having 84 participants take part in a number of public goods games played over a number of rounds. In each game participants are randomly formed into groups of four. Each participant has 50 tokens and all participants simultaneously decide how to allocate those tokens between a private or a public account. In each game this is followed by a number of rounds each of which proceeds as follows: first, one player in each group is provided with the current aggregate contribution to the public account and is afforded an opportunity to change his allocation to the two accounts. Then the next player is given the same opportunity and so on. Each game proceeds round by round with each participant getting at least one chance to change his mind and the game ends at a point unknown to the participants. Payoffs to participants in each game are determined by the final allocation of tokens between the private and public accounts at the point where the game ends. Each experimental session contains at least seven games involving the initial simultaneous contribution decision followed by multiple rounds where the participants are given the chance to change their allocations.

This repeated elicitation of information regarding how much each participant wishes to contribute to the public account guarantees two things: (1) by allowing the participants to think about their answers multiple times it allows participants to learn about the problem and avoids the possibility that contributions are the results of mistakes rather than deliberate acts; (2) the fact that participants are allowed to make their choices anonymously and are provided multiple opportunities of changing their mind reduces the possibility of conformity playing a major role. After all, a participant might choose to conform to what the rest of the group is doing the first time, or the first few times, but it is likely that if a participant does not wish to conform then after the first few attempts he will assert his true preferences especially when participants are told that *they can change their mind if they wish to do so* and when *they can see others doing so.* At the very least, the multiple elicitations of responses should strongly attenuate any latent desire towards conformity.

Kurzban and Houser rely on a procedure similar to the one followed by Fischbacher, Fehr and Gächter discussed above. Like Fischbacher and his colleagues, Kurzban and Houser also look at how contributions vary with a change in the *average* group contribution. They base their inferences about a participant's type by drawing a graph of the participant's contributions against the average contribution to the public account that this participant observes before making his own contribution. Contributions by co-operators lie well above the 45° line on this plot. Contributions by the conditional co-operators cluster around the 45° degree line while contributions by the free-riders are small regardless of the contributions of the others. Using this approach Kurzban and Houser classify 53 out of 84 participants (63%) as conditional co-operators, 17 participants (20%) as free-riders and 11 participants (13%) as co-operators. The remaining three participants could not be classified into any of the above three categories. The authors find that these classifications are stable by having them participate in three additional games and show that those classified as free-riders contribute less on average than their peers, co-operators more and conditional co-operators about the same as their group members. Furthermore, groups that consist of more co-operators, on average generate higher contributions.

## 4.5 Conditional cooperation and the creation of virtuous norms of cooperation

The above suggests that in a variety of social dilemmas people behave as conditional co-operators who decide whether to cooperate or not depending on their beliefs about their peers. Furthermore, conditional co-operators are often able to sustain norms of cooperation sometimes via the use of costly punishments and sometimes via the use of other mechanisms such as communication, expressions of disapproval, assortative matching and advice giving. The noted political scientist Robert Axelrod of the University of Michigan suggests that virtuous social norms can be sustained by (1) deterrence, which relies on punishment of those who deviate from the expected course of action or (2) internalisation, where a norm becomes so entrenched in a society that violating it causes psychological discomfort. This is what I turn to next.

### 4.5.1 *Sustaining social norms by punishing free-riders*

Throughout the 1990s Ernst Fehr and Simon Gächter at the University of Zürich had been thinking and studying the problem of sustaining cooperation in social dilemmas. They had already found that a majority of people were conditional co-operators who behaved in accordance with their beliefs about their peers and were often successful in sustaining cooperation. They now made another startling discovery. They found that conditional co-operators are also "*altruistic punishers*", i.e. conditional co-operators are willing to apply sanctions to those who violate implicit social norms even when such punishments impose a substantial pecuniary cost on those meting out that punishment.

Fehr and Gächter recruited participants to play the public goods game. One set of participants played the game in groups whose composition remained unchanged for the entire 20 rounds. This is the "*partners*" treatment. In another treatment participants are randomly re-matched at the end of each round exactly as in Andreoni's study. This is the "*strangers*" treatment. In each treatment participants play for 20 rounds – the first ten rounds without any punishment possibility and then for the next ten rounds with punishment. Participants are placed into groups of four. In each round a participant has 20 tokens which can be allocated between a private and public account. Total tokens contributed to the public account are multiplied by 1.6 and then re-distributed equally among group members. The participant's earning in each round is the sum of the tokens allocated to the private account plus the returns from the public account. At the end of the experiment tokens are redeemed for cash. In each of the first ten rounds, participants only decide how to allocate 20 tokens between the two accounts.

In the second set of ten rounds there are two stages in each round. In the first stage, participants play the exact same public goods game where they decide how to allocate tokens between a private and public account. In the second stage, participants get to see the contributions of other group members (without learning their identities) and then can choose to punish the other group members. Participants can allocate up to ten punishment points in each round and each punishment point reduces the punished participant's payoff by 10%. However, the punishment is costly to the punisher in that the cost of the punishment points is subtracted from the earnings of the punishing participant, but these punishment points lead to a greater reduction in the monetary payoff of the person being punished.

Fehr and Gächter conjecture – along the lines of Andreoni – that, participants in the "strangers" treatment will not engage in punishment since, with random re-matching at the end of each round, the value of signalling and reputation formation via punishment of free-riders is minimal especially given that such punishment imposes a pecuniary cost on the punisher. Therefore, the *Nash equilibrium* of this game is for no one to punish and anticipating that, for everyone to free-ride. However, in the "partners" treatment there are benefits to building up a reputation by punishing free-riders. A participant who is punished might think that there are punishers in the group and hence might be less inclined to free-ride and thus, in fixed groups the availability of punishment might lead to higher contributions to the public good.

Fehr and Gächter observe significant amounts of punishment under both conditions. The availability of punishment raises contributions significantly in both treatments, but the impact is more pronounced in the "partners" treatment than in the "strangers" treatment. In fact, in the "partners" treatment contributions approach 100% of the maximum in the later rounds. Figure 4.5 provides an overview of average contributions in the two treatments with and without punishments. Across all rounds the average contribution to the public good in the absence of punishment is 19%, while once punishments are allowed contributions average 58%.

Remember that in typical public goods experiments contributions show a familiar pattern of decay over time. However, once participants are allowed to punish one another, in both the "partners" and the "strangers" treatment, contributions exhibit an increasing profile. The average contribution in the last round without punishments is 10% (significantly lower than the average of 19% across all rounds) but with punishments the average last round contribution is 62% which is higher than the average across all rounds of 58%. Fehr and Gächter also found that punishments were primarily aimed at those who contributed less than the group average in any round and the further below the group average the participant's contribution was, the greater the magnitude of the punishment handed out to this participant.

This line of work undertaken by Ernst Fehr and his many collabor-

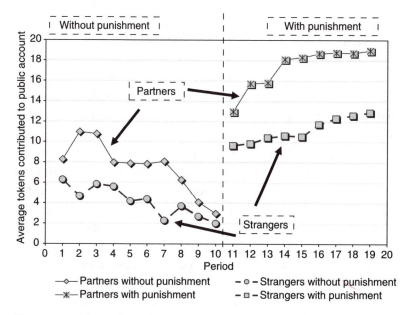

*Figure 4.5* Fehr and Gächter (2000): average contributions without and with punishments. Figure created by author on the basis of data provided in the original study.

ators including Simon Gächter and Urs Fischbacher, has important ramifications for the evolution of cooperation among humans. I will return to this theme below and in the last section of the book.

### 4.5.2 Even non-monetary punishments can be effective in fostering cooperation

A group of researchers that include David Masclet and Marie-Claire Villeval, both of the University of Lyon and Charles Noussair and Steven Tucker, both at Purdue University were intrigued by the Fehr and Gächter results about costly punishment and decided to extend this work by looking at the impact of non-monetary punishments and whether non-monetary punishments, such as expressions of disapproval, can also enhance cooperation. They look at two treatments. The first "*monetary punishment*" treatment works in the same way as in the Fehr and Gächter study. In the "*non-monetary punishment*" treatment, participants are given the opportunity of expressing approval or disapproval of the actions of other group members, but approval or disapproval does not have any pecuniary impact on anyone's payoffs. As in the *monetary punishments* treatment each participant can assign between zero and ten points to another participant where zero indicates no disapproval and ten indicates maximum disapproval.

Each session of this study consisted of 30 periods, divided into three segments of ten periods each. During each ten-period segment, participants did not know whether the experiment would continue beyond that segment or not. However, they knew the segment length and that each period during the segment would proceed in an identical manner. The first ten periods were played without any punishment opportunities. A monetary or non-monetary punishment was introduced at the end of the tenth period and remained in force till period 20. After that participants reverted to the baseline treatment as in the first ten periods and played another ten periods with no punishment opportunities. The authors also compare the performance of fixed groups ("partners") versus randomly re-matched groups ("strangers") in both the monetary and non-monetary punishments environment.

These researchers find that both monetary and non-monetary sanctions initially increase contributions by a similar amount but that over time, monetary sanctions are more effective and lead to higher contributions than non-monetary sanctions. Furthermore, and not surprisingly, they find that non-monetary sanctions are more effective in the "partners" treatment as opposed to the "strangers" treatment. The authors also find that the average earnings of participants are higher with either monetary or non-monetary punishments compared to the situation where no sanctions are available. And again, in keeping with Fehr and Gächter's results, the punishments are primarily aimed at those who contributed below the group average or those who contributed less than what the punishing participant contributed.

## 4.6 Punishments are sufficient to sustain cooperation but are not necessary

The work of Fehr and Gächter and others showed that conditional co-operators are often willing to engage in costly punishment in order to deter free-riding and maintain virtuous norms of cooperation. But as Robert Axelrod points out, the existence of punishment creates a secondary social dilemma. If one member of the group engages in costly punishment of a free-rider then another group member *can free-ride on the first person's punishment.* So I may not necessarily be free-riding but I may not wish to take the time and effort to punish those who are. I am bothered by the litter and the graffiti and the loud music at block parties and drunken brawls at the neighbourhood bar, but I might leave it to my neighbour to go around and knock on doors at the city council or meet the local councillor to do something about it. In this case I am free-riding on the fact that my neighbour is willing to take the time and trouble to tackle these problems. But then, if some people are willing to punish while others are not then *we need a second set of punishments for the non-punishers!* Now we need to punish the non-punishers because unless all conditional co-operators are willing to punish, cooperation will unravel. As Axelrod points out – a norm of cooperation and punishment of free-riders is no longer enough, we now need *meta-norms – punishments of non-punishers* and then *punishments of those who do not punish non-punishers* and so on. Thankfully, however, while such costly punishments are indeed extremely successful at deterring free-riding, it turns out that conditional co-operators do not need to rely on costly punishment exclusively in order to achieve this goal but can resort to various other mechanisms to sustain cooperation as well.

Communication is one such tool for maintaining cooperation. Mark Isaac of the University of Arizona and James Walker of Indiana University look at the role of communication in fostering cooperation. They have participants play the public goods game in groups of four. In one treatment participants play the game for ten rounds without any communication opportunities. Then they play for another ten rounds where they are allowed to engage in free-form communication about all aspects of the problem at hand at the beginning of each of those ten rounds. In a second treatment they are allowed to communicate prior to each round for the first set of ten rounds but then no communication is allowed for the second set of ten rounds. Figure 4.6 illustrates the results.

When the participants start with no communication in the initial set of ten rounds, contributions start at around 45% and show the familiar pattern of decay from then onwards. However, once communication is allowed during the second set of ten rounds contributions jump up to 60% in round 11 and exhibit an increasing profile for the remaining rounds, reaching 100% in round 18 and averaging greater than 90% in the last three rounds. In the treatment where participants start with

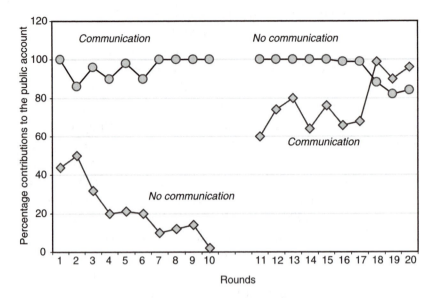

*Figure 4.6* Isaac and Walker (1988a): contributions to the public account with and without communication. Figure created by author on the basis of data provided in the original study.

communication, contributions start at 100% in round 1 and hover around 90% for rounds 2 through 6 before stabilising at 100% for the last four rounds. Surprisingly participants manage to sustain this high level of cooperation even after they are prevented from communicating. Contributions stay at or close to 100% for the next seven rounds, finally dropping down to around 80% for the last three rounds.

One might think that the primary role of communication is to foster a feeling of community and belonging and thus any type of communication might enhance cooperation. But Robyn Dawes, Jean McTavish and Harriet Shaklee showed that in order to be effective such communication must allow participants to talk extensively about the actual dilemma facing them. Irrelevant communication, where participants are allowed to talk about everything else other than the problem facing them, is not as successful in fostering cooperation and deterring free-riding.

Elinor Ostrom, James Walker and Roy Gardner of Indiana University also corroborate this finding vis-à-vis the effectiveness of communication in a common pool resource extraction game. The common pool resource extraction game is similar to the public goods game but rather than contributing to a public account, participants are asked to make withdrawals from a common pool. The optimal outcome is achieved when everyone abides by a pre-assigned quota of extraction, but each individual has an incentive to exceed the quota because if every other participant abides by the quota then the person engaged in over-extracting (analogous to free-riding in the context of the public goods game) is strictly better off. This game simulates a number of real-life dilemmas such as over-fishing in lakes, rivers and oceans, over-grazing on public land as well as environmental pollution.

They look at both communication and costly punishments and find that when participants are allowed to engage in communication at the beginning of each round for multiple rounds, withdrawals decrease and such repeated communication in their study is almost as effective as costly punishments. Though I should point out that in this study the punishment is more benign than in the Fehr and Gächter study since in the study by Ostrom and her colleagues each participant in a particular group can target only one other group member for punishment and cannot punish multiple group members.

Ananish Chaudhuri, Pushkar Maitra (of Monash University) and Sara Graziano (of Wellesley College) were interested in studying how norms of cooperation might be transmitted from parents to their progeny. After all, we are always telling our children to play fair, wait their turn on the playground and to share their toys with others. While we face many social dilemmas in real life, we rarely confront them in a vacuum. When faced with such situations, we often have access to the wisdom of family or friends who may have prior experience with a particular situation and might be able to give us advice regarding how to address a particular issue. In the US, your friends will tell you that you should tip 15% in restaurants and people will think you are a cheapskate if you don't. But in New Zealand or Australia you are not supposed to tip at all and people will get mad if you do. *"You are ruining things for the rest of us"*, they will tell you down under.

Chaudhuri and his colleagues conjecture that playing a public goods game where each group of participants, after their turn is over, can leave advice to the succeeding group, might, over time, lead to the evolution of norms of cooperation, with later generations not only achieving higher levels of contribution but also managing to mitigate problems of free-riding. Norms or conventions of behaviour that arise during one generation may be passed on to the successors.

In this study, participants in one generation leave advice for the succeeding generation via free form messages. Such advice can be *private knowledge* (advice left by one player in one generation is given only to her immediate successor in the next generation), *public knowledge* (advice left by players of one generation is made available to all members of the next generation) and *common knowledge* (where the advice is not only public but also *read aloud* by the experimenter). Contributions in these advice treatments are compared to those in a baseline (no advice) treatment where participants play the usual public goods game without any advice. Participants play in groups of five for ten rounds. Each participant has ten tokens per round and can allocate tokens to a private account or a public account. Tokens contributed to the public account are doubled and re-distributed equally. However, each participant in one generation is connected to another participant in the immediately succeeding generation and each participant in a previous generation earns a second payment which is equal to 50% of the earnings of his successor in the next generation. This second payment provides an incentive to participants to take the advice giving part seriously.

Chaudhuri and his colleagues – using data gathered in Auckland, New Zealand, Calcutta, India and Wellesley, Massachusetts – find that such passing of advice from one generation to the next is indeed successful in enhancing cooperation and reducing free-riding, but only when the advice passed from one generation to the next is *common knowledge* (i.e. the advice left by players of one generation is made available to all members of the next generation and this advice is also *read aloud* by the experimenter). They find that average contributions in the common knowledge of advice treatment are significantly higher than the other treatments including the baseline (no advice) treatment. To a large extent the high contributions in the common knowledge of advice treatment are driven by strongly exhortative advice. In the common knowledge treatment, especially in the later generations, the advice gets very strong with literally every participant exhorting their successors to contribute *"all ten (tokens) all the time!"* This exhortative advice in turn influences behaviour through its impact on the beliefs that participants hold. The authors collected data on the beliefs that participants held about what their peers will do and find that when the advice from a previous generation is common knowledge, subjects are more optimistic about the cooperativeness of their group members.

The above discussion suggests that in *heterogeneous* groups consisting of different types of individuals, cooperation can be sustained by a number of mechanisms such as face to face communication, advice, costly punishments and even, at times, via expressions of disapproval. But in many of the things we do in life we actually *choose* the people we wish to interact with. We decide who to invite to our parties and camping trips; who to watch the Super Bowl or the World Series of baseball or the Rugby World Cup with; we join book clubs and bridge clubs and political parties; we become involved with voluntary associations such as Rotary Club and Amnesty International.

Simon Gächter and Christian Thöni of the University of St Gallen in Switzerland[4] realised that sustaining cooperation among like-minded people may be easier than sustaining cooperation in randomly composed groups. Their aim is to study how like-minded people, i.e. people who know that they share a similar attitude to the cooperation problem, behave when they are confronted with a choice between cooperation and selfishness.

Participants in their study first participate in a public goods game in *randomly formed groups of three*. This game is called the "ranking experiment" and is played only once. Participants do not receive any information about the contribution of other group members or their earnings at this point. Following the ranking experiment, participants take part in the main experiment which consists of playing a ten-period public goods game. Prior to their participation in the ranking experiment, participants are simply told that they would be participating in another experiment immediately afterwards but are not provided any details about the experiment to follow so as not to bias participants' decisions in any way. After the completion of the ranking experiment and prior to the beginning of the main experiment participants are told that the groups from the ranking experiment would be re-arranged in the following way: participants in the ranking experiment would be ranked according to their contribution to the public good. Then for the main experiment, the *three highest* contributors would be put together in one group, the *next three* would form the next group and so on until the *three lowest* contributors would form the last group. Participants

---

4   Gächter had moved from Zürich to St Gallen by this time and at the time of writing this book is at the University of Nottingham in the UK.

are then informed about the contributions of their *new group members* in the ranking experiment.

In order to compare behaviour, as a control treatment, the authors also form *random* (unsorted) groups. Here participants take part in the ranking experiment as above and following that, they are re-arranged into groups of three. But in this latter case the groups are also formed randomly and the formation of these groups has nothing to do with what the participants contributed in the ranking experiment. In another treatment the authors allow participants the opportunity to punish other group members as in the study by Fehr and Gächter which we discussed earlier in this chapter. Here, once again the participants are re-arranged into groups of three following the ranking experiment but in one case the subsequent grouping is *random* and has no connection with what they did in the ranking experiment while in the other case the groups are *sorted* on the basis of their contributions in the ranking experiment. This then gives rise to four separate conditions: (1) Sorted groups with no punishment; (2) Random groups with no punishment; (3) Sorted groups with punishment; and (4) Random groups with punishment.

Gächter and Thöni report that sorting people led to a substantial increase in contributions. Furthermore, the highest co-operators in the *Sorted no punishment* treatment contributed significantly more than the most cooperative third of the participants in the *Random no punishment* treatment. Thus, when "like-minded" co-operators are sorted together, one can expect a substantially higher and more stable cooperation level than in the best case of randomly composed groups. This finding is similar to that reported by Gunnthorsdottir, Houser and McCabe who found that when the co-operators were sorted together into the same group, and were interacting with other co-operators, they were far more cooperative than when they were placed in heterogeneous groups and were interacting with both co-operators as well as free-riders.

Turning to the treatments with punishment the authors find – not surprisingly – that average contributions in the randomly formed groups with punishment (82%) are substantially higher than that in random groups without punishments (48%). But the contributions of the three highest contributors in the *Sorted punishment* treatment are *not significantly different* from those in the *Sorted no punishment* treatment. Thus when participants knew that they were interacting with like-minded people, participants did not need to rely on punishments or the threat thereof to sustain cooperative behaviour. Gächter and Thöni suggest that social norms of cooperation may be easily sustained in *homogeneous* groups of people who are aware that others in the group share their attitudes.

Three American researchers at Brown University – Talbot Page, Louis Putterman and Bulent Unel – also adopt an approach that is quite similar to the one taken by Gächter and Thöni except while Gächter and Thöni do the grouping on the basis of participants' contributions in the ranking experiment, Page and his colleagues allow the participants to choose who they want in a group with them.

These authors look at a number of different conditions of which I will discuss two that are immediately relevant. In the first *baseline* treatment, 64 participants are divided into 16 groups of four and play the public goods game for 20 rounds. The second *regrouping* treatment is similar to the baseline treatment except that at the end of periods 3, 6, 9, 12, 15 and 18 there is a regrouping decision. Each participant is shown a list, without other identifying information and in a random order, of each of the other 15 participants' average contribution to the public account over the experiment until that point. Participants were then given the opportunity to express a preference among possible future partners by ranking them according to the following procedure. If a participant chose to rank others (participants had the choice of *not* providing a ranking), she typed a number in a box next to the information about each other participant. Given that there are 16 participants in a session, potential ranking numbers ran from 1 to 15, with 1 standing for the most preferred prospective partner and 15 for the least preferred one. The same ranking number could be assigned to two or more participants, allowing ties.

When all participants had completed this process, the computer assigned participants to groups by searching, first, for that group of four individuals the sum of whose mutual ranks of one another was the lowest among the universe of potential groups, then repeating this process over the remaining participants, to form the second and third groups, leaving the last four participants in the fourth group. After new groups were formed, participants resumed play without information about who they had been grouped with; though it is conceivable that a participant can draw some conclusions on this matter by observing the contributions of her group members once play had resumed.

Participants were charged 25 experimental cents for the first ranking decision of a period and 5 experimental cents for each additional ranking decision. Page and his colleagues find that regrouping leads to significant increases in contribution to the public good compared to the baseline treatment. Contributions to the public account average 70% in the regrouping treatment and only 38% in the baseline treatment.

These studies show that it is easier to sustain cooperation among like-minded people than among heterogeneous groups and that people's ability to influence who they are grouped with has a demonstrable positive effect on cooperation.

## 4.7 Concluding remarks

I am not going to say a whole lot about the implications of this kind of research for economics for a number of reasons. First, the implications of enhancing cooperation in social dilemmas for economics are probably obvious to most readers. They range from voluntary contributions to charity, to the provision of local and national public goods, to controlling environmental pollution and guaranteeing cleaner air, to protecting over-fishing and over-grazing of public lands. Most readers will be able to think of one or more examples of such social dilemmas that they have first-hand experience with where either they managed to resolve the dilemma by fostering successful cooperation or failed to do so because of free-riding on the part of one or more members of the group.

In the autumn of 2003 New Zealand was faced with an acute shortage of power. The country relies primarily on hydro-electric power and a very dry summer had led to a depletion of the water reservoirs. Faced with this crisis, the government made a public appeal to households and businesses to reduce their power consumption as much as possible. Now, from the point of a view of an economist, an appeal like this is doomed to failure. Because not everyone has to reduce consumption; as long as some do, the power crisis could be averted. Thus, if my neighbour cuts down on his consumption I do not have to do so and I can free-ride on his frugality. Therefore, everyone has an incentive to free-ride by not reducing his own consumption as long as enough others do so. But if everyone reasons along those lines then no one will conserve power and there will certainly be a shortage. To my surprise the crisis was averted. People voluntarily reduced consumption. Restaurants in Auckland turned off their lights and started serving dinners by candle-light. Some restaurants reported that this made the dinners a much more intimate and romantic affair and seemed to have added to the diners' enjoyment.

Second, the issues and findings in this area have implications far beyond economics and go to the heart of the problem of evolution itself. Cooperation or altruistic behaviour is an evolutionary puzzle. In the context of evolution, an organism or individual that does engage in altruistic behaviour effectively reduces its chances of reproductive success at the expense of those who engage in selfish behaviour. If you give up your share of the food or readily share the spoils of your hunt or even put your life on the line for another (members of your clan/tribe/ethnic group/country) then you are making yourself poten-tially worse off, while another person who behaves in a self-interested manner and exploits your altruism gains at your expense. There are many examples of cooperation – not only among humans – but also among other life-forms where some organisms exhibit strategies that favour the reproductive success of others, even at a cost to their own survival and/or reproduction.

Here are some examples: (1) insect colonies, with sterile females acting as workers to assist their mother in the production of additional off-spring; (2) Alarm calls in squirrels or birds; while this may alert group members of the same species to the presence of a predator, they draw attention to the caller and expose it to increased risk of predation. The puzzle here is this: if some individuals are genetically pre-disposed to behave in an altruistic manner to the benefit of others then this behaviour reduces the reproductive fitness of the altruistic individual and such an "altruistic" gene, *if it exists*, will surely die out over time. Therefore, via the process of natural selection, a gene that codes for a particular trait, which increases the fitness of the individual carrying that gene, should increase in frequency within the population over time; and conversely, a gene that lowers the individual fitness of its carriers should be eliminated. The issue of cooperation is one which has received enormous attention from all types of social scientists including economists and is fraught with controversy. The two most popular and well-accepted theories explain-ing cooperation among organisms are (1) the theory of kin selection pro-posed by William Hamilton in 1964 and (2) the theory of reciprocal altruism proposed by Robert Trivers in 1971.

William Hamilton, in two articles published in the same issue of the *Journal of Theoretical Biology* (Volume 7, Issue 1) provided one explanation for the persistence of cooperative behaviour. Hamilton argued that a gene leading to behaviour which increases the fitness of relatives but lowers that of the individual displaying the behaviour, may nonetheless proliferate within the population, because relatives often carry the same gene. This theory came to be known as the theory of "*kin selection*" though the phrase itself was coined by John Maynard Smith. The noted biologist, J. B. S. Haldane is supposed to have said "*I would lay down my life for two brothers or eight cousins*". Haldane's remark alludes to the fact that if an individual loses its life to save two siblings or eight cousins, it is a "fair deal" in evolutionary terms, as siblings share 50% of their genes while cousins share 12.5%.

The theory of reciprocal altruism, proposed by Robert Trivers, suggests that altruistic behaviour can take on a conditional aspect whereby an organism acts generously and provides a benefit to another without expecting any immediate re-payment. However, this initial act of altruism must be reciprocated by the original beneficiary at some point in the future. Failure to reciprocate on the part of the beneficiary will cause the original benefactor to not engage in such altruistic acts in the future. In order for the altruist not to be exploited by non-reciprocators, we would expect that reciprocal altruism can only exist in the presence of mechanisms to identify and punish "cheaters". An example of reciprocal altruism is blood-sharing in vampire bats. Bats, who manage to get enough blood, feed regurgitated blood to those who have not collected much, knowing that they themselves may someday benefit from a similar donation; cheaters are remembered by the colony and ousted from this collaboration.

However, the evidence that I have presented earlier in this part suggests that across a variety of economic transactions humans routinely cooperate with genetically unrelated strangers, often in large groups, with people they will never meet again and when reputation gains are small or even absent. People not only routinely contribute to charity; they also give blood and donate organs – often to complete strangers. Thus sociobiological theories such as kin selection or reciprocal altruism may not be able to explain large patterns of human cooperation.

The extensive work done by Ernst Fehr at the University of Zürich and his many collaborators including Simon Gächter, Urs Fischbacher, Armin Falk, Klaus Schmidt, Herbert Gintis, Samuel Bowles and Robert

Boyd suggest an alternative theory of cooperation which they label "strong reciprocity". This is defined as the predisposition to build virtuous norms of cooperation and to punish (at personal cost, if necessary) those who violate cooperative norms even when it is implausible to expect that those costs will be recouped at a later date. They argue that strong reciprocators are *conditional co-operators* (who behave altruistically as long as they believe that others will do so as well) and *altruistic punishers* (who apply sanctions to those who violate implicit social norms even at a personal cost to themselves).

Furthermore, a group consisting of a majority of co-operators will typically outdo groups consisting predominantly of free-riders and as long as the co-operators engage in assortative matching (i.e. they mate with their own type), the co-operative gene can proliferate in the population. While such group-selectionist arguments have been controversial in biology, given the ability of humans to create culturally evolved norms of cooperation, group selection may be more plausible among humans than in non-human primates.

This line of research on strong reciprocity can provide a new understanding of cooperation and the formation of virtuous norms. What this line of research suggests, then, is that socially connected communities may be able to achieve more cooperation than the standard economic view would suggest. What this also suggests is that in many instances communities may be able to provide local public goods on the basis of their own resources rather than waiting for government intervention. I hasten to add that I am no neo-conservative who believes that government is bad, period. I firmly believe in the virtues of the welfare state and the role of the government in providing a social safety net.

However, we also need to realise the limits on the ability of governments to promote social welfare. Collective action for the common good is not as insurmountable a problem as we (economists) often suppose it to be and communities can adopt innovative approaches – based on networks, communication, punishments or social ostracism – in order to generate norms of cooperation on their own. What seems absolutely crucial to successful cooperation is the creation of optimistic beliefs about the actions of our peers. More importantly, a majority of people are willing to cooperate as long as enough others do; they just need to be made aware of the fact that there are others like them. This seems to be the key to generating the requisite optimistic beliefs that can lead to successful collective action.

# Part 5

# I will if you will

Resolving coordination failures in organisations

## 5.1 I will if you will: examples of coordination failures in real-life

The next time you fly somewhere and you are waiting to board your plane, take a look outside at the waiting aircraft. Most of us do not really appreciate this but there is frenzied activity going on. The pilot and co-pilot are carrying out pre-flight checks; baggage handlers are unloading the baggage from the in-bound flight and loading the baggage for the out-bound passengers; one group is cleaning the cabin and the toilets; another is loading the fuel; yet another is loading the food containers. The only way the plane will get off on time – and the percentage of on-time departures is an important measure of how well an airline is performing – is if all these groups manage to successfully *coordinate* their actions and work at the same pace; if even one group lags behind the others, the plane will be delayed. Delays, even small ones, in one flight taking off – especially at large and busy airports such as Frankfurt, New York or Singapore – often have a ripple effect on flights later in the day with all flights getting progressively more delayed as the day wears on. Thus, on-time departure of a flight requires a disparate number of people to coordinate their actions. It is only when all the people and groups involved do so that the plane takes off on time.

To most of us this seems like a trivial issue – after all planes take off on time more often than they are delayed. But getting a large group of agents to successfully coordinate their actions actually poses a nontrivial challenge for many organisations. Continental Airlines, for instance, ran into trouble in the 1980s due to its failure to resolve such coordination problems in a satisfactory manner. Since de-regulation of the airline industry in the US in 1978, over the next decade or so, Continental typically averaged last among the ten major domestic airlines in on-time arrival, baggage handling and customer complaints, and filed twice for bankruptcy, once in 1983 and then again in 1990. I will have more to say about the experiences of Continental Airlines shortly.

Coordination problems are not restricted to airlines only, but arise in a variety of organisations and across a number of different contexts. Such coordination problems arise in any industry that is engaged in team production along an assembly line such as in steel-mills and automobile factories. The next time you take the kids to McDonald's or Burger King (or even if you sneak in surreptitiously on your own to get your burger fix) take a look behind the counter. There is an immense coordination problem being addressed there. In order to get a burger from the person who is frying them to the person who puts them inside the buns to the person who puts on the cheese, onions and pickles and wraps them to the person at the front of the store who finally hands it over to the customer, a complex coordination problem has just been addressed where success depends on how quickly one can get the burger to the customer and reduce the time people are waiting in line.

A similar coordination problem arises, for instance, in deciding whether to join a protest against an unpopular regime or not. Here, I wish to join the protest if and only if I am convinced that another person or group of people will also join in. The probability of being beaten up by the police or getting arrested is much lower if there are thousands of protesters than if there is only a handful. Thus, I want to join the protest only if enough others join also. The desire on the part of participants in such situations to undertake a course of action only if enough others do the same often means complete lack of coordination and unsuccessful outcomes; but if and when participants do manage to coordinate their actions they can also achieve enormous success.

As the late and unlamented dictator of Romania, Nicolae Ceauşescu found out in December 1989, coordinated actions among protesting citizens can be a very powerful tool in bringing down an unpopular regime. Within a span of about ten days in December 1989, Ceauşescu and his wife Elena went from being absolute rulers of a nation to their execution by a firing squad in Targoviste, Romania, due in large part to massive and coordinated protests across the nation.

Here are a number of other situations where coordination issues are important. If you are sitting next to a computer, look over at the keyboard. The keyboard that the overwhelming majority of us use is called the QWERTY keyboard. It takes its name from the first six letters located to the left of the keyboard's first row of letters. The QWERTY design was patented by Christopher Sholes in 1874 and sold to Remington in the same year, when it first appeared in typewriters. This is in fact the only keyboard that most of us have ever encountered. The original design of the keyboard had the characters arranged alphabetically, set on the end of a metal bar which struck the paper when the appropriate key was pressed. However, when someone typed at speed, the bars attached to letters that lay close together on the keyboard tended to stick to one another, forcing the typist to manually disentangle the bars. This prompted Sholes to split up the keys for letters commonly used together to speed up typing. But this also had the unintended consequence of making the QWERTY keyboard less efficient. There exists another keyboard called the DVORAK keyboard which is simpler and makes for faster typing. But we seldom see these keyboards around. Why? Because to move from the QWERTY keyboard to the DVORAK keyboard would require massive coordination between users and producers of keyboards; people who have already spent time and effort in learning QWERTY will be willing to learn DVORAK if and only if enough others are doing so and these keyboards are available widely; but producers will only produce the keyboard if and only if there are enough users and, therefore, demand for these keyboards. A move to DVORAK then requires a simultaneous switch by users and producers.

Similarly, should an organisation invest in Macs or PCs? I want to be proficient in using PCs if everyone around me is using PCs but if every one used Macs then I am better off with a Mac. But if I have spent an awful amount of time learning how to use a PC and then find everyone around me is using a Mac, then I have a problem and am better off switching to a Mac also, but the switch is costly in terms of time and effort.

These days when we go to the supermarket for groceries we take the barcode on products as given and do not give it a second thought. These barcodes make paying for things a lot easier since it prevents the person at the check-out counter from having to look up the price all the time. But the implementation of these bar-codes required the resolution of a complex coordination problem; it was expensive to install barcode scanners and supermarkets were willing to do so if and only if producers were going to invest in the technology that put barcodes on their products; but producers would be willing to put the barcodes on only if enough supermarkets had barcode scanners.

A similar scenario is being played out right now with the increased use of RFID (radio frequency identification) tags. RFID tags are being increasingly used at toll-booths, subway tokens, credit cards and library books. But once again the use of these tags requires coordinated action between the producers of these tags and their users.

A classic example of a pure coordination problem arises from which side of the road to drive on. Americans and people in Western Europe drive on the right; the British and the people of former British colonies like India, New Zealand and Australia drive on the left; confusion reigns when American tourists visit New Zealand and vice versa.

The city of Auckland provides an excellent example of a coordination problem. Possibly owing to the fact that Auckland has many narrow two way-streets with one-lane in each direction, a convention has emerged where cars (which drive on the left), while making the easier left-hand turn yield to cars coming from the opposite direction which are trying to make the harder right-hand turn. (According to Colin Camerer, this is true of Pittsburgh as well.) (This works well in general except in cases where one of the cars belongs to an American tourist who either does not yield when turning left or sits there with his right-side blinkers on while everyone else waits!) But the success of this system depends on everyone coordinating on this particular convention.

Following the Cultural Revolution of 1966, Chairman Mao of China urged thousands of students, who came to be known as "Red Guards", to change old customs, habits, culture and thinking. It is said that some Red Guards tried to force traffic to *stop* at green lights and *go* on red, red being the colour of the revolution which symbolised progress. This attempt at breaking down the existing convention did not achieve much success!

Along similar lines, while electronic appliances in most parts of the world run on 220 volts, those in the US run on 110 volts. This makes US electronic appliances unusable in other parts of the world. (My wife and I brought over a bunch of electronic goods when we moved from the US to New Zealand and tried to run them using voltage converters for a while; it was not long before they all burned out!)

Here is the point of these stories. First, in most of these cases coordinating to some outcome is more desirable than *not* coordinating at all. So it would be better if we all drove on the left and used 220 volts. This would impose a cost on those who would need to get accustomed to the new system but in the long run this would aid coordination and eliminate the confusion that now exists.

Second, the fundamental strategic problem created by issues of coordination is very different from the social dilemmas that we encountered in earlier chapters. A coordination problem is *not* a social dilemma like the prisoner's dilemma. In deciding whether to work on the officer's club or not, Yossarian is always better off if he shirks and lets Nately do all the work. But when it comes to undertaking coordinated actions this is no longer true. Now it makes sense for Yossarian to work if he thinks Nately will work as well but to shirk if he thinks Nately will shirk; Yossarian would like to join the demonstration if Nately does so and vice versa; Yossarian would like to drive on the left if Nately does so and Yossarian would like to use a PC if Nately is using a PC and so on.

The point is that there is no longer a *unique* strategy for Yossarian as there was in the prisoner's dilemma game; now Yossarian is better off if he does what Nately is doing; but how do they make sure that they both do the same? How do I know for sure that other people will show up at the demonstration? Or in a more general setting, how do the groups at Continental Airlines go about coordinating their actions? Moreover, in many of these cases there is more than one feasible outcome, such as Yossarian and Nately both deciding to work or both deciding to shirk; Yossarian and Nately both showing up with placards at the demonstration and both staying home; the groups at Continental all working quickly to get the plane off the ground at the designated time or all of them taking their own sweet time leading to massive delays and dissatisfied customers.

I have talked about a number of examples above. However, the nature of the underlying problem is not the same in each and every case. There are actually *two different* types of coordination problems that can arise in real life. This is what I turn to next.

## 5.2 Men are from Mars, women are from Venus: battle of the sexes

Pat and Chris are wondering what to get each other on their anniversary. Both Pat and Chris love the 1980s game show *Perfect Match* (a show where couples had to answer questions about each other separately to see how well they knew their partners). Pat and Chris decide to put their knowledge of each other to the test. They decide that for their anniversary evening, each of them is going to buy *one* ticket to an event and see if their choices match! Pat loves the opera and would like to go see Puccini's *La Bohème* at the New York Metropolitan Opera. Chris on the other hand would rather watch the New York Yankees take on the Boston Red Sox at Yankee stadium.

Here is the point. Pat and Chris would like to coordinate their actions and would ideally like to buy tickets to the same event. If they end up at the opera then Pat would be the happier of the two while Chris would enjoy it more if he is sitting behind the home plate at Yankee stadium. But they most certainly want to be together at the same event even if it is the preferred event of the other person. What they do *not* want, under any circumstances, is to mismatch or fail to coordinate; that is they do not want to end up with each holding a ticket to a different event and spending their anniversary evening separately. There are two feasible outcomes (or equilibria) in this game. One, where they both buy tickets to the opera; where Pat is happier and gets greater satisfaction (or payoff) compared to Chris, and the other, where they both go to the Yankees game which makes Chris the happier of the two. But if they fail to coordinate and buy tickets to different events then they both feel wretched and get payoffs of zero each. Thus, a failure to coordinate in this situation results in a bad outcome for both. Game theorists and economists, who are not usually renowned for their sense of humour, often refer to this as the "*battle of the sexes*" game.

In case you are thinking that this is a somewhat contrived example let me assure you that the noted short story writer O. Henry certainly did not think so. O. Henry's short story *The Gift of the Magi* provides an excellent example of coordination failure. It is the day before Christmas and a young couple – James and Della Dillingham – who love each other very much are in despair. Each wants to buy the other a thoughtful gift but neither has much money. There are two possessions in which the couple take great pride. One is Jim's gold watch which is a family heirloom; the other is Della's shining lustrous hair. Suddenly Della has an epiphany; she cuts off and sells her hair for 20 dollars and uses that money to buy a handsome platinum fob chain for Jim's gold watch. Later Jim comes back home with Della's gift, a set of beautiful combs, pure tortoise shell with jewelled rims; just the shade to wear in Della's lustrous (and now vanished) hair. And then Della presents Jim with his gift, the watch chain. At this Jim smiles and says "…*let's put our Christmas presents away and keep 'em a while. They're too nice to use just at present. I sold the watch to get the money to buy your combs.*"

What we have here is a situation where Jim and Della have failed to coordinate their actions. They would be better off if they had managed to coordinate to one of the two outcomes: (1) Della does not cut her hair and does not buy the chain while Jim sells his watch and buys the combs; here Della would be better off; (2) Della cuts off her hair and buys the chain while Jim hangs on to his watch; here Jim is better off. But what they have managed to do is to arrive at an outcome where they are both worse off; a failure to coordinate their actions. I present a theoretic formulation of this game between Della and Jim in Box 5.1.[1]

---

*Box 5.1* Battle of the sexes: the game played by Della and Jim

We can depict the game played by Jim and Della using the payoff-matrix concept we developed in the Appendix to Part 1. Once again we are going to go ahead and assign some arbitrary monetary values to the participants' happiness or satisfaction.

Della has two strategies – (1) *sell hair* (and buy a chain) and (2) *don't sell hair*; while Jim also has two strategies also – (1) *sell watch* (and buy combs) and (2) *don't sell watch*. We can represent their payoffs in the following way (see Figure 5.1).

If Della sells her hair and buys the chain while Jim hangs on to his watch (the intersection of the strategies "*sell hair*" for Della and "*don't sell watch*" for Jim; indicated by a dashed circle in Figure 5.2) then Jim now has a watch *and* the chain and is happy. But Della is happy too at Jim's happiness but a trifle wistful about her lost hair. So her payoff is slightly lower than Jim's.

| Della's strategy | Jim's strategy | |
| --- | --- | --- |
| | Sell watch | Don't sell watch |
| Sell hair | Della's profit = $0<br>Jim's profit = $0 | Della's profit = $3<br>Jim's profit = $5 |
| Don't sell hair | Della's profit = $5<br>Jim's profit = $3 | Della's profit = $0<br>Jim's profit = $0 |

*Figure 5.1* The game played by Della and Jim.

---

1  Of course one can argue, as O. Henry does, that it is the *failure* to coordinate their actions that provides the greatest proof of their love for one another. At the end of the story the author comments: "*But in a last word to the wise of these days let it be said that of all who give gifts these two were the wisest.*"

On the other hand if Della keeps her hair while Jim sells his watch to buy the combs (the intersection of the strategies *"don't sell hair"* for Della and *"sell watch"* for Jim; indicated by a dashed rectangle in Figure 5.2) then Della now has her hair *and* the combs she so desired. Jim is happy at Della's happiness but a little sad about losing the family heirloom (the watch). So his payoff is slightly lower than Della's.

But if Della does not sell her hair and Jim does not sell his watch then they are neither better off nor are they worse off and they both get zero. Finally if Della sells her hair and gets the chain, while Jim sells the watch and gets the combs then neither of them can use his or her gift and they each get zero again.

As we did in Part 1, we need to look for an equilibrium in best responses. If Della chooses *"sell hair"* then Jim's best response is to choose *"don't sell watch"*; and conversely, if Jim chooses *"don't sell watch"* then Della's best response is to *"sell hair"*. This is one equilibrium outcome shown by the dashed circle in Figure 5.2. Alternatively if Della chooses *"don't sell hair"* then Jim's best response is to choose *"sell watch"*, and conversely, if Jim chooses *"sell watch"* then Della's best response is to choose *"don't sell hair"*. This is another equilibrium outcome shown by the dashed rectangle in Figure 5.2. Both of these are perfectly feasible outcomes in this game. However, they both wish to avoid the outcomes where (1) Della sells her hair and Jim sells his watch (as happens in the story) or (2) where neither of them sells anything. In both of these two cases they get a zero payoff.

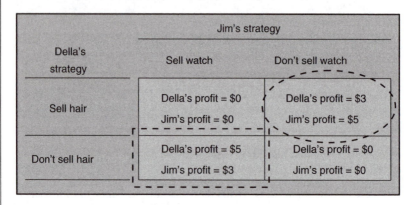

*Figure 5.2* Outcomes in the game played by Della and Jim.

There are a number of real-life situations where this kind of coordination failure happens often. Driving on different sides of the road is an example. There are many other examples of adopting the same or different standards: these include adopting 110 as opposed to 220 volt electrical appliances; Windows versus UNIX operating systems; VHS versus Betamax video recording and playing standards; PAL or SECAM or NTSC colour encoding systems in television broadcasts and so on.

## 5.3  Hunt a stag or a rabbit? The stag hunt game and payoff-ranked equilibria

There is, however, a different type of coordination problem, one that is probably more relevant in every day life and certainly more relevant in economic organisations. In the *"battle of the sexes"* game the trick is to coordinate to one of the two desirable outcomes, rather than fail to coordinate and end up with zero.

However, in many economic transactions the people involved (1) not only need to coordinate to one of the outcomes but (2) at the same time some of these outcomes are more desirable (yield higher payoffs) than the others. Take the example of the plane taking off on time. In this case there are at least two feasible outcomes: (1) where everyone works at speed to ensure that the plane takes off in time; an outcome that is desirable from the point of view of the airline company and in most cases the workers as well; (2) where everyone works at a leisurely pace which often implies delays and problems for the company and consequently for the workers too.

Back in the 1750s the French philosopher Jean Jacques Rousseau alluded to this problem when he talked about two hunters trying to decide whether to hunt a stag or a rabbit. Hunting stag requires coordinated action by both hunters and it is only when they both work together that they can hunt the stag. The payoff to hunting a stag is large with both hunters getting a large amount of meat. However, each hunter has the option of hunting a rabbit. Hunting a rabbit does not require any coordination between the hunters and each can hunt (and catch) a rabbit on his own. But if one hunter is trying to catch a stag (and relying on the other's cooperation in this enterprise) while the other hunter sees a rabbit scurrying by and, abandoning the stag-hunt sets off in hot pursuit of the rabbit, then the second hunter gets the rabbit for sure while the first hunter gets nothing. In that case the first hunter would have been better off hunting a rabbit as well; at least he would have guaranteed himself some meat at the end of the day.

Therefore, the two hunters are *both* better off if they work together and hunt the stag; they both get large quantities of meat. They can alternatively hunt a rabbit in which case they both get some meat but strictly less than what they could have obtained if they had managed to snare a stag. But if one of them hunts the stag while the other hunts a rabbit then the first one ends up going home empty-handed while the second one gets the rabbit. So if there is *any* doubt in the mind of one hunter that the other hunter may not cooperate and might go off on his own to hunt a rabbit then the secure option might be to hunt the rabbit in the first place. In the rest of this part I will refer to games like this one as the "*stag hunt game*". I present a more formal description of this game in Box 5.2.

---

*Box 5.2*  The stag hunt game

Two hunters – let us call them hunter 1 and hunter 2, respectively – can either choose to hunt a stag or hunt a rabbit. They can talk to one another prior to starting the hunt but once they are in the jungle they cannot talk any more – maybe because this might frighten the animals off or because they are too far away. The point is that, even if they have discussed this beforehand and both have promised to hunt the stag, still there is no way to force one or the other to keep his word. So if a hunter sees a rabbit scurrying past, he is perfectly free to break his word and go running off after the rabbit, while the other is blissfully unaware of this defection and keeps looking for the stag.

Once again let us ascribe some monetary payoffs to the various outcomes while preserving the basic incentives of the game. Suppose each hunter hunts the stag, in which case they get it and they both earn $8. If one hunter concentrates on hunting the stag while the other one goes off after the rabbit then the first hunter gets zero while the second one gets $5. Finally, if they both hunt rabbit then they both get $5. Figure 5.3 shows the payoff matrix for this game.

| Hunter 1 | Hunter 2 | |
| --- | --- | --- |
| | Hunt stag | Hunt rabbit |
| Hunt stag | 1's profit = $8<br>2's profit = $8 | 1's profit = $0<br>2's profit = $5 |
| Hunt rabbit | 1's profit = $5<br>2's profit = $0 | 1's profit = $5<br>2's profit = $5 |

*Figure 5.3* The stag hunt game.

Now as before let us look at best responses. Suppose hunter 1 chooses to hunt a stag. What is hunter 2's best response? Hunter 2 gets $8 if he also hunts the stag but only $5 if he hunts a rabbit. Thus hunter 2's best response in this case is to hunt the stag. But by the same argument if hunter 2 is hunting the stag, then hunter 1 is better off hunting the stag as well; getting $8 as opposed to $5 (from hunting a rabbit). Therefore both hunters choosing to hunt the stag is a feasible outcome or equilibrium of this game. This outcome is depicted by the dashed rectangle in Figure 5.4. But suppose hunter 1 decides to hunt the rabbit. In that case hunter 2 has no incentive to hunt a stag since he will certainly not get the stag and end up with zero. In this case, where hunter 1 is hunting a rabbit, hunter 2 is better off hunting a rabbit as well with both getting $5. But by the same argument, if hunter 2 is hunting a rabbit then hunter 1 is better off doing the same. Therefore, both hunters choosing to hunt rabbit is a feasible outcome or equilibrium of this game also. This is shown by the dashed circle in Figure 5.4.

Figure 5.4 demonstrates the two feasible outcomes. Except that both hunters are *strictly better off*, that is they both get a higher payoff, when they work together to hunt the stag as opposed to when they both go in different directions looking for rabbit. Economists usually refer to the outcome where both hunters hunt the stag as the "*payoff-dominant*" outcome simply because this outcome yields a higher payoff ($8 each) to both players compared to the "hunt rabbit" outcome where each gets $5. The outcome where both hunters hunt rabbit is often called the

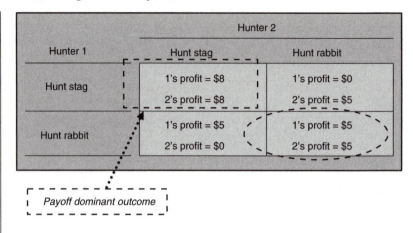

*Figure 5.4* Outcomes in the stag hunt game.

"secure" outcome since by doing so they are both guaranteed $5 each.

In the context of these games, the question often arises as to how to get the two hunters (or a group of participants) to coordinate their actions to hunt the stag, i.e. to achieve the outcome that yields the maximum payoff for everyone involved. Because if there is any doubt in the mind of one of the players that the other might renege on the promise to hunt the stag then that person will most likely go off to hunt rabbit. Thus, both players must be fully convinced and trust that the other player will indeed take part in the stag hunt.

I should point out that Rousseau's description of the stag hunt game is not a stylised example designed to make a point but is a fact of life in many hunter–gatherer societies. The anthropologist Frank Marlowe of Harvard has undertaken extensive field work among the Hadza, a group of nomadic hunter–gatherers who live near Lake Eyasi in northern Tanzania. Here is Marlowe's description of the hunting practices of Hadza men.

> *Men do not do as much cooperative foraging as women ... during the late-dry season, however, men will go hunting at night waiting at the few permanent waterholes to ambush game that come to drink.*

*Because other predators like lions and leopards use the same strategy,*
*night hunting is very dangerous and they always do this in pairs. Men*
*also help each other track game once it has been hit...*

(Emphasis mine)

The difference between the stag hunt game and the battle of the sexes
game is that in the latter game, one person is happier in one outcome
while the other is happier in the other outcome and both get zero if
they fail to coordinate. In the stag hunt game both players not only
need to coordinate to an outcome but more importantly they want to
coordinate to the outcome that yields a higher payoff to both. They are
both better off in one outcome (when they both hunt the stag) compared to the other outcome (where they both hunt rabbit). As a result,
the outcome where both hunters hunt the stag is often referred to as
the *"payoff dominant outcome"* since here both hunters get a strictly
higher payoff compared to the case where they both hunt rabbit. But
the strategy of hunting a stag is risky because if the other hunter goes
off to hunt rabbit then the one hunting the stag will return empty-
handed. The outcome where they both hunt rabbit thereby guaranteeing each a positive, albeit smaller, payoff is often called the *"secure*
*outcome"*.

This kind of coordination problem is actually endemic to many
organisations. I have already talked about the example of airline companies. But this problem arises in any organisation engaged in team
production such as in automobile manufacturing factories or steel mills;
generally, anywhere a group of people have to coordinate their actions
to achieve the most desirable outcome. Another example occurs in
mountain climbing where the climbers are joined to one another and
the progress of the group as a whole is determined by the slowest
climber. As a result, these types of problems are often referred to as a
*"weak-link"* or a *"collaboration"* game.

Stag hunt type problems are not confined to human societies and
show up among other species as well. The hunting practices of orca are
also an example of a stag hunt. Typically orcas cooperatively corral
large schools of fish to the surface of the water and then they use their
tails to hit the fish and stun them. Since this requires that the fish are
not able to escape, it requires the cooperation of many orcas. But each
orca is free to wander off on its own and catch its own fish.

## 5.4 Experimental evidence on coordination failures

So how do people do when confronted with one of the coordination problems described above? How should we go about trying to understand how good or bad people are – and we are going to concentrate on the problem for humans leaving the orca aside for now – in coordinating their actions? One immediate thought that comes to mind is to look at organisations that deal with problems like these on a regular basis. You could go to an automobile manufacturing factory or steel mill and observe how their workers perform along an assembly line. Or you could spend time at an airline hub such as Houston for Continental or Atlanta for Delta or Singapore for Singapore Airlines and see how these companies go about getting their workers to coordinate their actions to ensure smooth landings and take-offs. This would, and certainly does, yield valuable information. But at the end of the day, the data that you get might tell you a lot about the operations of the company in question but it may not be easy to extrapolate from that to the operations of other companies. This is because each organisation has its own culture and its own set of rules and goes about addressing their problems in their own unique ways. It is often difficult to isolate the fundamental problem from the rules and conventions that organisations have evolved in order to solve that problem.

Experiments provide an alternative. It is possible to take the underlying problem and its incentive structure and design a suitable experiment. The sterile atmosphere of the laboratory and the use of neutral context-free language certainly sacrifice a lot of reality but there are some benefits as well. First, it allows us to study the problem in the absence of any intervention whatsoever and thereby gain an understanding of what happens in the absence of any rules or conventions already in place. Because of these conventions and cultures that organisations develop to deal with coordination problems in real-life, operations in these organisations are likely to be much less dysfunctional than suggested by laboratory experiments. But the experiments can establish a lower bound on how bad the problem can be or what a new organisation starting out might expect to encounter.

Second, experiments can also provide valuable pointers regarding how to address these issues. Because you can make small changes to the experimental design in order to tease out differential responses to those changes, you can see which interventions do better than others. Thus you can use the experiments as a "wind-tunnel" where you can test various recommendations and see which ones work well and which don't; it would be very expensive to implement a set of policies at the company level only to find out that they are completely ineffective or worse yet, provide perverse incentives to workers.

Third, the insights gained can complement what you learn via your field studies and, at the same time, might also provide ideas and directions for changes that might lead to greater coordination and efficiency. Experiments not only provide you with a mechanism to get a better handle on the underlying problem but can also provide you with a relatively inexpensive way of figuring out how you might be able to implement policies that help workers coordinate their actions.

At the University of Iowa, in the late 1980s, a group of researchers – Russell Cooper, Douglas DeJong, Robert Forsythe and Thomas Ross – embarked on an ambitious project to understand problems of coordination failure. They decided to look at both the battle of the sexes game as well as the stag hunt game. They essentially ask two questions: (1) How well do people manage to coordinate their actions in these games? (2) If they do not manage to coordinate, then what mechanisms or interventions might help them to achieve greater coordination?

Let me start with the first question. They had 99 advanced undergraduates and MBA students participate in the battle of the sexes game and 275 advanced under-graduates and MBA students participate in two different versions of the stag hunt game. They designed a set of appropriate games which preserved the incentive structure of the two different problems. The games looked similar to the ones I have described in Boxes 5.1 and 5.2 except the strategies for the two players were given non-emotive labels such as "Top" and "Bottom" for one player and "Left" and "Right" for the other. The participants played a number of times and at the end of each round they were randomly rematched so that they usually did not play another player more than once. In any case, all interactions were carried out via computers so that no one ever learned the identity of the player he was paired with.

When Cooper and his colleagues looked at behaviour in the battle of the sexes game, they found, possibly not surprisingly, large-scale coordination failure. The players managed to coordinate to one of the available equilibria in only 48% of the total interactions and failed to coordinate, thereby earning zero for both players, in 52% of interactions. Needless to mention, most of this coordination failure is caused by each player going for his or her most favoured outcome; that is Pat choosing to buy a ticket to the opera while Chris buys a ticket to the ballgame. This suggested that when faced with a problem like this people like Pat and Chris would spend many anniversaries doing something on their own!

But even more surprising was the behaviour in the stag hunt game. In this game the payoffs that players get are common knowledge in that it is immediately apparent to both players that they are both better off if they cooperate (and hunt the stag) rather than act on their own (and hunt rabbit). Yet in the experiments run by Cooper's group there were massive coordination failures. The vast majority of their participants failed to coordinate to the payoff dominant outcome choosing the secure outcome instead. In one version of the stag hunt game where each player had to choose one of two strategies, more than 80% of their participants chose the secure strategy of hunting a rabbit that led to the secure outcome. In another version of the game, where each player had a choice of one of three strategies the lack of coordination was even starker. In the second game, Cooper and his colleagues found that out of 330 choices made by the participants, only five were ones commensurate with the payoff dominant outcome and the remaining 325 were strategies that led to the secure (and lower payoff) outcome.

An even more dramatic example of people's inability to coordinate their actions so as to achieve the maximum payoff came from a group of researchers at Texas A&M University around the same time in the late 1980s. John van Huyck, Raymond Battalio and Richard Beil looked at a more elaborate version of the stag hunt game. Their set-up actually better represents the coordination problems faced by groups in organisations like those working on getting the plane off the ground. Van Huyck and his colleagues called their game "*the minimum effort game*".

In their game, players in a group have to pick numbers between 1 and 7. The choices are made without any communication or interaction of any kind. The money that each person earns depends on two things: (1) the number picked by that person and (2) the *lowest number picked by someone in the group*. If everyone picks 7 each player earns $1.30. If they all pick 6, each player earns $1.20; if they all pick 5, each earns $1.10; and so on down to the case where each player earns $0.70 if everyone picks 1. But here is the catch. Because the payoff depends, not only on your own choice (or your own effort level), but the *lowest number picked by a group member (i.e. the lowest effort exerted in the group)*, even if it is only one person picking that low number (low effort), choosing higher numbers is risky. If you pick a high number while someone in the group picks a low number, then you get next to nothing. For instance, suppose you pick 7 while someone in the group picks 1 then you only get $0.10. This essentially means that being away from (above) the lowest number picked by the group yields little or no money. If everyone but one person in the group picks 7 while that last person picks 1 then the people picking 7 all earn $0.10 each while the person picking 1 earns $0.70. The person picking the lowest number has a lot of power to hurt those who are taking the risk of choosing higher numbers.

This is similar to the example of the plane taking off on time or mountain climbing. In the case of the airplane, even if every group but one works quickly and completes their task in the recommended time while one group dawdles, the plane will not take off on time and the effort put in by the conscientious workers is wasted. Similarly, even if all but one mountain climbers are making steady progress, the one straggler – the weak-link – can hold up progress.

Players in such minimum effort games, therefore, face two challenges. The first is to coordinate their actions to one number between 1 and 7. This is because if everyone else is picking 1 then you don't want to pick anything higher because it will cost you money. But collectively, you want the group to coordinate and pick the highest number possible because that yields the highest payoff to each player. So each player is better off and makes the most money if they all pick 7 (analogous to everyone working hard).

But as I mentioned before, even if every player except one chooses 7 while that one straggler chooses 1, then that person choosing 1 – the lowest number or effort level – can hurt the others badly and slow down progress. So if you are not convinced that every one in the group will choose 7 and if you have even the slightest doubt that someone in the group might actually choose 1, then you might want to be risk averse and choose 1 as well. By choosing 1 you will guarantee that your choice is the minimum in the group. If everyone reasons along the same lines then they will choose 1 as well. And at that outcome you are guaranteed to earn $0.70. Higher choices are more lucrative as long as every one chooses high, but in the absence of any communication with others or commitments from them, higher choices bring with them the risk of a lower payoff; and the further away you are from the person choosing the lowest number, the worse off you are! This then suggests that if you are not certain that others will pick high numbers then the secure course of action would be to choose 1, thereby guaranteeing a payoff of $0.70. So everyone picking one emerges as the secure option in this game. This is not all that different from the stag hunt game. Everyone picking 7 is analogous to the hunters cooperating to hunt the stag, while everyone picking 1 is similar to each hunter going off on his own to hunt rabbit.

Van Huyck and his colleagues recruited 107 participants who took part in seven groups. There were four groups of 16 players each, two groups of 14 each and one group with 15 players. The group members interacted for ten rounds picking a number in each of those ten rounds. At the end of each round, the participants are informed about the lowest number picked by someone in the group but not who picked that number. They also did not learn what the other group members chose. Thus, it is entirely possible that many if not most in a group could have chosen 7 while maybe only one player chose 1. At the end of the round the players only learn that the lowest number picked in the group was 1. Since each player's payoff depends on his choice and the lowest number picked, each player can figure out how much he earned in a particular round once told about the lowest number chosen. The composition of the group remained unchanged for the entire time; so the same group of people interact with one another over and over again; which is probably closer to what happens in real-life.

Remember that each player earns $1.30 if they all choose 7 while each gets $0.70 if they all choose 1. Thus in each round the payoff to coordinating to the payoff dominant outcome is almost twice that of coordinating to the secure outcome. The instructions are read out loud and make this fact common knowledge among the participants. In Table 5.1 I show the minimum number chosen for each of the ten rounds for these seven groups.

The behaviour of the group members – and the failure to coordinate to the payoff dominant outcome – is quite striking! As you can see from Table 5.1, none of the groups managed to coordinate to any number higher than 4. Only two groups – Groups 3 and 4 – managed a minimum of 4 but that too for only the first round. Moreover, none of the seven groups managed to keep the minimum above 1 for more than three rounds. By round 4, at least one person in each and every one of these seven groups chose 1. Furthermore, in most groups by the end of

*Table 5.1* Behaviour of the Group minimum in Van Huyck *et al.*'s (1990) experiment

| Group | Rounds | | | | | | | | | |
|---|---|---|---|---|---|---|---|---|---|---|
| | 1 | 2 | 3 | 4 | 5 | 6 | 7 | 8 | 9 | 10 |
| 1 | 2 | 2 | 2 | 1 | 1 | 1 | 1 | 1 | 1 | 1 |
| 2 | 2 | 1 | 1 | 1 | 1 | 1 | 1 | 1 | 1 | 1 |
| 3 | 4 | 2 | 2 | 1 | 1 | 1 | 1 | 1 | 1 | 1 |
| 4 | 4 | 2 | 3 | 1 | 1 | 1 | 1 | 1 | 1 | 1 |
| 5 | 3 | 2 | 1 | 1 | 1 | 1 | 1 | 1 | 1 | 1 |
| 6 | 1 | 1 | 1 | 1 | 1 | 1 | 1 | 1 | 1 | 1 |
| 7 | 1 | 1 | 1 | 1 | 1 | 1 | 1 | 1 | 1 | 1 |

Source: Table created by author on the basis of data provided in the original study.

round ten, the majority of the group members were choosing 1. In Groups 1 and 2 which had 16 players each, 13 out of 16 players chose 1 in round 10. In Group 4 which had 15 players, 13 of these chose 1 in round 10. Thus, these players were by and large coordinating their actions, no doubt, but they were coordinating to the outcome that was the worst possible in terms of the payoff that they earned! The failure to coordinate to the payoff dominant outcome where everyone chose 7 and earned $1.30 each in round was evident.

To what extent is the lack of successful coordination dependent on the size of the group? The groups that Van Huyck and his colleagues used were relatively large consisting of 14 to 16 people. Would smaller groups do better? Van Huyck and his colleagues repeated the same game but this time with only two players in each group and found that these two participants manage to coordinate to the payoff-dominant outcome of both choosing 7 most of the time. So coordination failure was not a concern in two-person groups. Thus the failure to successfully coordinate seems to be a problem of large groups. But exactly how large is "large"? The answer came from Colin Camerer of Caltech and Marc Knez of the University of Chicago who had participants in their experiment take part in a variant of the minimum effort game in groups of three. The three-player groups were not very successful in achieving coordination to the payoff dominant outcome. Thus groups of three appear to be large enough for coordination to break down and larger groups are expected to do worse.

A number of subsequent studies replicated this inability of groups to coordinate to the payoff dominant outcome and it became clear that these results were robust and not unique to the experiments carried out by Cooper and his colleagues or Van Huyck and his colleagues. Economists have great faith in the rationality of economic agents and their ability to seek out opportunities that yield the most money. Needless to mention the results reported by Cooper and his colleagues or Van Huyck and his colleagues came as an enormous surprise to most economists. Prior to the publication of these results economic theorists had argued that when confronted with a stag hunt type problem, rational economic agents would be able to use their powers of deductive reasoning to figure out that they should coordinate to the payoff dominant outcome; after all that was the outcome that yielded the most money.

These results completely and utterly disproved this conjecture. They suggested that in the absence of any intervention, such as some sort of rules or conventions or the possibility of communication with other group members and the opportunity to make commitments, reasonably intelligent people may find it extremely difficult to coordinate to the payoff dominant outcome. Van Huyck and his colleagues, however, argued that this was not necessarily a failure of deductive reasoning; in the sense that it was not the case that people were unable to figure out that they would make more money if they all chose 7 and coordinated to the payoff dominant outcome. Rather the failure to reach the payoff dominant outcome was caused by *strategic uncertainty*; that is, people are reluctant to choose high numbers because they are not absolutely convinced that every one else in the group will do the same. So in a way, this comes down to a question of trust after all. A particular member of the group is perfectly willing to work hard as long as he knows that he can trust his peers and is convinced that they will work hard as well. But any doubt in the minds of the group members, even if small, that at least one person in the group might end up choosing 1, leads them to choose 1 as well, and thereby destroys the possibility of coordinating to the payoff dominant outcome. The key issue then is to create the appropriately optimistic beliefs in the minds of the participants that fellow group members will all choose the strategy that is commensurate with the payoff dominant outcome.

As I pointed out above, this does not suggest that most groups or organisations are really this bad in coordinating the actions of group members. In fact, most are rather good at addressing such problems. But what these results do suggest unambiguously is that: (1) strategic uncertainty about the actions of other group members loom large in such situations and (2) in the absence of judicious interventions designed to mitigate problems of coordination failure, this strategic uncertainty can lead to massive coordination failures and some seriously sub-optimal outcomes. This, in turn, led to attempts to understand what form those interventions should take and an analysis of interventions that work better than others. That is what I look at next.

But before that I need to point out the following. In discussing interventions that facilitate coordination I am going to focus to a large extent on coordination in stag hunt games. This is for two reasons. First, the kind of problems that are encapsulated by the battle of the sexes game – such as the adoption of standards like keyboards, operating systems, television broadcasting systems, electrical power, which side of the road to drive on, and so on – are often extremely history dependent. That is, a particular standard was adopted due to a historical accident or because somebody invented or discovered something first and that initial incident to a large extent dictated the course of events to follow.

This is like rain falling on one of two sides of a continental divide, a line of elevated terrain. Drops of rain falling on one side of the divide will eventually travel to one ocean or body of water while other drops falling in close proximity but on the other side of the divide will usually travel to another ocean or body of water, generally on the opposite side of the continent. Thus, once one person or a group starts using QWERTY, others start to use it too; movie studios follow the leader and set up around Hollywood; start-up dot-coms congregate around Silicon Valley while other high-tech firms gravitate towards Route 128 in Massachusetts. But this also implies that once players, groups and organisations are locked into one of these choices it is difficult to induce the parties involved to change their strategy and move to a different outcome. As a result, resolving coordination failures in such circumstances is more difficult (and maybe of less immediate relevance).

Second, and quite possibly as a result of the first difficulty, there has been more work trying to understand how to facilitate coordination in stag hunt games rather than battle of the sexes games. Moreover, the stag hunt game is more relevant to the problems faced by many organisations and therefore economists have spent more time trying to understand how to resolve coordination failures in such cases.

## 5.5 Talk is cheap; or is it...? Using communication to resolve coordination failures

So the question is: How do we get people to coordinate their actions to one of the available equilibria in a coordination game? Or put differently: How do we prevent people from failing to coordinate and ending up at a bad outcome? One obvious answer is to allow people to communicate. It is true that in the sterile, context-free environment of the laboratory people are not very successful in using deductive principles to coordinate their actions. But people who confront these problems in their day-to-day lives are colleagues and co-workers who chat with one another over coffee and around the water-cooler. This ability to talk with other members of the group should surely suffice to remove any strategic uncertainty that cause such massive coordination failures in the laboratory.

If you talk to economists, you will often hear the refrain "talk is cheap". What they mean by this is that in a variety of contexts involving strategic decision making people can promise they will behave in a particular way – act fair or be cooperative – but there is nothing to prevent them from reneging on that promise when it comes time to make the actual decision, especially if they will be monetarily better off by doing so. Thus the "talk is cheap" argument essentially inveighs against the possibility of binding commitments because in many situations it is difficult to enforce the promise *ex post*, thereby leaving open the possibility of opportunistic behaviour later on in spite of any promises made earlier. And if someone cannot be held to his promise, then the promise, or the talk, may not be a good indicator of future behaviour. However, as I have argued in previous chapters, in a wide variety of circumstances people's behaviour is far less opportunistic than is suggested by economic theory. Many – if not most people – probably feel an ethical compunction against violating a promise made in good faith and, therefore, we should expect that such promises will have an impact.

Cooper and his colleagues at Iowa were quickly on to this problem. They decided to see what happens when players are allowed to communicate in (1) the battle of the sexes game and (2) in the stag hunt game. One question here was how to structure this communication. After some deliberation Cooper and his colleagues decided that they were going to have their participants make a short announcement rather than engage in unstructured and free-wheeling conversations. This was primarily because it is often difficult to extract the essence of what exactly is said during such free-wheeling conversations. People can often be imprecise and might make different – and even contradictory – statements, so that it is hard to know what course of action a particular participant is really advocating. This can also lead to a loss of experimental control. The advantage of structured statements – such as "I will choose to hunt the stag" – is that they are usually less ambiguous and indicate the participant's desired course of action clearly.

Cooper and his colleagues also decided to look at two different types of communication where: (1) only one of the two players could make an announcement and (2) both players could make announcements. The players also had the option of choosing to remain silent. The results are not surprising; or may be surprising only to economists who are sceptical of "cheap talk" announcements. Cooper and his colleagues first looked at the battle of the sexes game. When only one of the two players could make an announcement, he, of course, almost always announced that he was going to play the strategy that yielded a higher return to him (so Pat says "*Opera*" while Chris says "*Baseball*"); but once that announcement was made, coordination followed in close to 100% of cases. Out of 330 outcomes that Cooper and his colleagues observed there were only 16 times that the players failed to coordinate to one of the equilibria.

However, when they turned to the case when both players could make announcements the result was not as satisfactory. Now there were a lot more disequilibrium outcomes owing in large part due to the fact that each player now tended to announce that he will play the strategy that would yield him the higher payoff. However, what these results clearly demonstrated was that, contrary to the supposition of economists, non-binding "cheap talk" messages can be very effective in fostering coordinated behaviour.

However, as I pointed out before, to economists the more interesting coordination problem is the stag hunt game where players need to coordinate to the payoff dominant outcome. Cooper and his colleagues decided to look at two different stag hunt games: (1) one where players could choose one of two strategies and (2) a more complicated game where players could choose one of three strategies. As before they allowed for (1) "one way" announcements where one of the two players could make a statement regarding his strategy choice and (2) "two way" announcements where both players could make announcements.

When only one of the two players could make an announcement that certainly led to more coordination than in the absence of any announcement, but it did not lead to as much coordination as one would expect. In about 13 % (21 out of 165) of cases the player making the announcement actually chose to say that he would play the secure strategy of hunting rabbit. But even though in the majority of cases (144 out of 165 or 87%) the announcement was "hunt stag" still this led to coordination to the payoff dominant outcome of both players choosing to hunt stag in only about 60% of cases. In 51 cases (35%) players still ended up at one of the disequilibrium outcomes following a promise to hunt stag by one of the players. This was surprising and suggested that one-way announcements are not that effective in removing the strategic uncertainty from the minds of players that both players will indeed choose to hunt stag following the announcement.

However, once Cooper and his colleagues allowed *both* parties to make announcements, coordination improved dramatically. In 95% of cases both players chose to announce that he would hunt the stag and out of 165 cases where both players made this announcement, they managed to coordinate to the payoff dominant outcome in 150 cases (91%). Thus, allowing both players to make an announcement seemed to guarantee two things: (1) both players would overwhelmingly announce playing the strategy that would lead to maximum payoffs and (2) that this in turn would indeed lead to coordination to this outcome.

Van Huyck and his colleagues were also exploring the role of communication in fostering greater coordination among groups and decided to take a slightly different tack. They came up with a deceptively simple idea but one which performed extremely well. They decided that rather than ask *participants* to make public announcements they were going to have an external arbiter make the announcement. The external arbiter's role was simply to point out to the players that they would be far better off monetarily if they managed to coordinate to the payoff dominant outcome, and therefore, it was in their best interest to choose that strategy that led to this outcome. Of course participants were free to completely disregard this announcement and choose whatever strategy they wanted. Van Huyck, working with Ann Gillette and Raymond Battalio, showed that a simple announcement instructing the participants to choose the strategy commensurate with the payoff dominant outcome led to coordination to this outcome in close to 100% of cases.

In case you are wondering about how one goes about making such public announcements to foster coordination, Michael Suk-Young Chwe of UCLA points out that organisations rely on such public announcements all the time. Often this might take the form of relying on television advertisements during widely watched events. In the US, for instance, the event with the highest viewership is the Super Bowl, the championship game of the National Football League. Chwe points out that the most recent trend in television advertising during the Super Bowl is the appearance of advertisements for websites. During the 1999 Super Bowl, HotJobs.com spent nearly half of its yearly revenues on a single advertising spot and Monster.com bought two slots. These are both job listing sites and their growth is essentially a coordination problem. An employee wants to look for a job on one of these websites only if he knows that employers are also looking there and an employer will list his jobs only if he can be sure that enough prospective applicants will be searching this site for jobs.

However, things got murky in a hurry when Cooper and his colleagues looked at more complicated games that allowed people to choose from more than two strategies, that is, games that allowed people more than two choices such as in the minimum effort game studied by Van Huyck and his colleagues, where participants had to choose one of seven available strategies. When Cooper and his colleagues looked at the more complicated game with three strategies for each player they found that players found it more difficult to coordinate to the payoff dominant equilibrium owing in large part to the fact that now players often announced very different strategies. Actually in this case players had an easier time when only one player was allowed to make an announcement. When only one player could make a promise this player chose to announce the strategy "hunt stag" in 118 out of 165 (72%) cases and out of those 118 cases, the players managed to coordinate to the payoff dominant outcome 111 times.

But confusion reigned once both players were allowed to make announcements. *When* both players announced their desire to "hunt stag", this was generally followed by both players coordinating to the payoff dominant outcome. But the problem was that in over one half of the cases the players announced their desire to choose a strategy that was different from "hunt stag". In fact, a whopping 25% of the announcements were that the player concerned was going to "hunt rabbit". Needless to mention the fact that players often announced their desire to play strategies other than "hunt stag" meant that coordination to the payoff dominant outcome was harder to achieve in this more complicated game.

The result obtained by Cooper and his colleagues that announcements did not work so well in those games where players could choose one of three strategies, was corroborated by Jordi Brandts of the Centre for Economic Analysis in Barcelona and Bentley McLeod of the University of Montreal. They also found that recommending a particular strategy to the players (along the lines of Van Huyck, Gillette and Battalio) did not do all that well in getting players to coordinate their actions in more complicated games where the payoff dominant outcome was also risky, in the sense that failure to coordinate to the outcome could result in a bad outcome (little money) for the players.

Andreas Blume of Pittsburgh and Andreas Ortmann of Charles University in Prague looked at the impact of communication in the minimum effort game where players are asked to choose a number between 1 and 7. They had 12 groups play the game. Each group had nine players each and played for eight rounds with the composition of the group remaining unchanged for the entire time. Four of these groups played the minimum effort game without any communication opportunities while the other eight groups could communicate. Following the lead of Cooper and his colleagues, Blume and Ortmann had participants make a single public announcement rather than engage in unstructured conversation. In each of the eight rounds there are two stages. In the first stage players can send messages to one another indicating what number they are going to choose in the second stage. Thus, in stage 1 a player might say "I will choose 7" and this message is conveyed to the other members of the group via their computer screens. Once all players have had an opportunity to send a message, the experiment moved on to the second stage where the participants made actual number choices. These messages are "cheap talk" because the players are not making binding commitments. A player can say he will choose 7 in stage 1 but then he is free to change his mind and choose a different number in stage 2 and no one can force him in the second stage to choose the number he said he would choose.

Blume and Ortmann found two things. First, and not surprisingly, the ability to send messages helps coordination. Thus, groups who can send messages to one another manage to coordinate much better than the groups who have no such opportunity. But second, and surprisingly, groups still find it difficult to coordinate to the payoff dominant outcome consistently. Out of the eight groups that had the opportunity to communicate, there was only one group where the participants consistently chose 7 for all eight rounds. The other groups achieved various degrees of success but none of them could manage to sustain the all-7 outcome for the entire eight rounds.

These results suggest that:

1   Coordination problems in real-life need not pose as much of a challenge as suggested by the early laboratory experiments which used context-free language and did not allow the participants any opportunity to communicate.
2   In real-life subjects might be able to resolve such coordination issues by simply talking to their group members in some form or other.
3   But, at the same time, these experiments also suggest that getting participants to consistently coordinate to the payoff dominant outcome is harder than one would suppose.

Bilateral or multi-lateral communication, while certainly useful and enabling greater coordination than would be possible in the absence of any communication, still does not seem to succeed in getting participants to coordinate to the payoff dominant outcome consistently, especially if (1) the game is complex, allowing players more than two strategy choices and (2) if the game involves a large number of players, where "large" means three or more group members.

In a way, the fact that participants did not manage to do well with multi-lateral messages may not be that surprising. The primary point here is to reduce the amount of strategic uncertainty so that everyone is convinced that everyone else will choose to hunt a stag. So when only one person can make an announcement and says "*I am off to hunt a stag*" it may be easier for others to coordinate their actions than when everyone can talk all at once. If everyone can send a message that might effectively create a *two-tiered* coordination problem. Now everyone must first coordinate to the *same message* and having successfully done so – which is not guaranteed by any means – they must then go on to successfully coordinate on the *same action*. Too many message options do not seem conducive to greater coordination.

This in turn led researchers to start thinking of other ways besides communication to foster coordination in organisations. In what follows I examine these different approaches. I would like to remind you once more that below I will confine my attention to stag hunt type games for reasons I outlined earlier.

## 5.6  Money talks: the role of incentives

Most economists believe that a wide variety of economic problems can be resolved by providing the right incentives. So the obvious question is: Could we improve coordination in organisations by providing an incentive to the workers to efficiently coordinate their actions? And if so what form should those incentives take?

Jordi Brandts of the Institute of Economic Analysis at Barcelona and David Cooper of Case Western's Weatherhead School of Management set out to understand coordination problems, particularly in the context of economic organisations, and designed a set of experiments that simulated the inner workings of a firm. In order to add more reality to their set-up they moved away from the standard economic practice of using non-emotive and context-free language and chose to provide instructions using more realistic language. They took the minimum effort game studied by Van Huyck and his colleagues and changed it into a *"corporate turnaround game"*. In this game participants were referred to as "employees" who work for a "firm". Each firm has four workers and one manager. The workers can choose one of five numbers – 0, 10, 20, 30 or 40 – which is tantamount to choosing how many hours to work during the week. Choosing "0" means not doing any work at all while choosing "40" means putting in a 40-hour work week. The payoff dominant outcome is the one where all the workers choose to work for 40 hours a week while the secure outcome is the one where they all slack off and choose 0. There are a total of 60 firms with 240 workers over two locations – Barcelona and Cleveland.

The manager's aim is to get the workers to coordinate to the payoff dominant outcome by choosing appropriate incentive bonuses. Workers' salaries depend on a fixed wage *and* an incentive bonus rate which pays them an amount that depends on what the minimum hours of work chosen (by someone in the group) is. The total bonus that the workers can earn is obtained by taking the minimum hours worked by a member of the firm and multiplying it by a constant amount, the bonus rate. Thus, the corporate turnaround game preserves the features of the minimum effort game because one worker choosing to loaf around can lower the minimum effort for the group as a whole and lead to a lower bonus amount for everyone involved, including those who are working much harder. This also implies that if even one person in the group chooses to put in zero effort then the effective bonus for the group as a whole is zero. But if the minimum number of hours is greater than zero then the workers all get an appropriate bonus depending on the minimum hours and the bonus rate.

The participants play the game for 30 rounds in three blocks of ten rounds each. The composition of the firm remains unchanged for the entire 30 rounds. This implies that the same four workers interact with each other for the entire duration allowing them to build trust and develop a feeling of community. Furthermore, in real-life it is often the case that most groups facing such coordination problems are fixed in nature in that it is the same people interacting with each other for long periods of time. But at the same time the fixed nature of the grouping might also exacerbate problems of history dependence, that is once a group has fallen into the low or no coordination trap they may find it more difficult to climb out of that if they are interacting with the same people over and over again.

In the first study that Brandts and Cooper carry out, the manager plays a passive role and the magnitude of the incentive bonus is actually predetermined for each ten round block. In each case, the bonus is set at a very low level for the first set of ten blocks. Brandts and Cooper do so deliberately because they *want* the workers to be unsuccessful in their attempts to coordinate. That is, they want the workers in each firm to end the first block of ten rounds choosing low numbers close to zero so that each firm is experiencing serious coordination failures at the end of those ten rounds. The reason they do so is this: if the firms do not experience coordination failure then there really is no problem left to solve. It is only when firms are experiencing coordination failures that one can study whether changing the incentives has an impact in enabling workers to achieve greater coordination. So Brandts and Cooper essentially want to establish a history of coordination failure during the first block of ten rounds and then see if increasing the incentive bonus rate can get people to break out of this and achieve greater coordination.

By setting the bonus rate quite low, Brandts and Cooper do successfully trap these firms into pervasive coordination failures. During the first block of ten rounds the minimum effort chosen is indeed quite low and is zero for 71% of effort choices. The average minimum across all firms and aggregated over all rounds is only 5.71 during the first block of ten rounds. That is, averaged across all firms and over the first ten rounds, the minimum amount of work put in by the workers is about 5.71 hours per week. Most firms are experiencing serious coordination failures with multiple workers choosing to shirk completely and put in zero hours per week. Out of 45 firms with a minimum effort of zero in round 10, 43 have more than one employee choosing zero and 26 have all four employees choosing zero.

The question is: can increments in the bonus rate induce the workers to break out of this coordination failure trap and move them towards working harder? The answer turns out to be a resounding yes, but with a twist. Brandts and Cooper look at three possible increments in the bonus rate: (1) where the bonus rate is increased by 33%; (2) where it is increased by 67%; and (3) where it is raised by 133%. What Brandts and Cooper find is that increasing the bonus rate has a large positive impact on coordination. The average effort levels forthcoming are much higher when the bonus rate is raised, but strangely enough the actual increase in the bonus rate does not seem to matter. While all three increments led to higher effort, the 133% increase does not improve performance any more than the 33% increment does! So employees seem to react to a higher bonus but beyond a point the actual increment becomes secondary as long as they *are* rewarded for working harder. Of course, given that there is an upper bound on work effort, there is a limit to how much of an improvement a bonus can elicit no matter how high that bonus is.

There are a number of other interesting findings. Once the bonus rate is increased and the employees were being rewarded for working harder, most workers did increase their effort up from zero. But a bifurcation emerges over time. In some groups the employees who have moved to higher effort levels drag their more recalcitrant compatriots up with them, but in other groups the laggards, who do not increase their work effort, ultimately discourage the others who are trying and the hard workers in turn eventually respond by lowering their work effort also. Thus at the micro-level the impact of higher bonuses is not the same for every firm – for some it works better than others.

To an extent, whether the bonus works well or not depends on the presence of "strong leaders" – workers who respond to an increase in the bonus by sharply increasing their work effort. The more strong leaders there are in a particular group, that is, the more people there are who increase their work effort significantly following an increment, the better the firm does in raising its average productivity. I will come back to this point shortly below.

Brandts and Cooper also find that once the firm has managed to break out of the low effort trap, reducing the bonus rate does not hurt. This is good news for the firm because paying the bonus is costly and has implications for the firm's bottom-line. So it seems that all the workers need is a temporary crutch. Once the higher bonus reduces strategic uncertainty and enables them to improve their productivity, they can manage to remain coordinated even if the bonus is reduced later on.

Finally Brandts and Cooper ask: does it matter how long a firm has experienced lack of productivity and low morale? Is it more difficult to turn around firms that have been mired in a low productivity trap for a much longer time? The answer, not surprisingly, turns out to be yes. When the coordination problems have persisted for a longer time the effectiveness of a bonus is less. When the bonus is introduced earlier, a number of employees – the leaders – increase their effort and persist there and eventually they drag the laggards up to higher effort levels as well. But when the coordination failure problems have been allowed to fester for a longer time and the bonus is introduced later, the leaders do increase their effort levels in response but give up soon and reduce their effort when others do not follow suit quickly. It appears that a long history of coordination failures breeds much greater pessimism even among the more dynamic leaders who do respond positively to the increased incentives.

In a follow-up study Brandts and Cooper bring in a fifth participant into each firm – the manager. While in the previous study the bonus rate was pre-determined for each block of ten rounds at a time, now the manager has discretion from round to round as to what bonus he wants to pay the workers. Furthermore, the manager can also send messages in an attempt to exhort those workers to expend greater effort. A "firm" now consists of four workers and one manager who interact for 30 rounds with the composition of the firm remaining unchanged for the entire duration. For the first ten rounds the manager is purely passive and does not take any part in the proceedings. Once again the aim here was to get the workers in the firm to fall into a low (or no) coordination trap and then have the manager come in and try to improve coordination by the judicious use of messages and/or bonuses. So the manager plays an active role for the last 20 rounds. In each round the employees choose an effort level between zero and 40, as in the previous study. The manager gets to see only the *minimum* effort put in and not the effort put in by individual workers; so in a sense the manager cannot distinguish who is working hard and who is not but can make out if the assembly line is moving along quickly or not. (The participants in this second study are actually getting less feedback than the former, which makes resolving coordination problems more difficult.) Once the manager takes over he can use a mixture of performance bonuses based on increased effort as well as exhortative messages in an attempt to foster greater coordination.

Brandts and Cooper find, again not surprisingly, that the use of a mixture of exhortative messages and appropriate performance bonuses are indeed successful in improving coordination and productivity. But the surprising result is that communication – the ability to send messages – seems to be a more effective tool than the payment of performance bonuses alone. Here is how Brandts and Cooper see it:

> *Our results emphasize the importance of communication. As the available avenues of communication increase, both employees' effort and managers' profits increase. Communication is a more effective tool for increasing manager profits than financial incentives.... This is the central result of our paper – for managers attempting to overcome a history of coordination failure, it's what you say, not what you pay, that largely determines your success. While managers try a wide variety of communication strategies, including complex multi-round plans, the most successful communication strategy is quite simple: explicitly request that all employees choose a high effort level, emphasize the mutual benefits of coordinating at a high effort level, and assure the employees that they are being paid well (although it is not necessary to actually pay them well). In other words, managers succeed in this environment by acting as good coordination devices.*

The reason why good communication is a more profitable strategy is not hard to see. Messages cost far less than incentive bonuses! Therefore, if you can improve performance using suitably exhortative messages then that improves your profitability far more than when you actually have to pay your workers more in order to motivate them. Does this mean incentive bonuses are not important and simple "cheap talk" messages (a deft "attaboy" here or a pat on the back there) are good enough to improve performance in firms mired in low productivity? Not so, suggest Brandts and Cooper. They go on to add that financial incentives are important but *in conjunction* with appropriately exhortative messages. Simply raising incentives is poor managerial strategy; it is essential to reinforce the financial incentives with messages providing the insight that everyone is better off when everyone works harder. In that sense, Brandts and Cooper's findings add weight to the results of Van Huyck, Gillette and Battalio who also looked at the efficacy of messages announced by an external arbiter. The combination of incentive bonuses and messages together seems to be a better coordination device and is better able to reduce strategic uncertainty among the participants.

The previous study looks at whether managers can make a difference; but the "manager" in this study is after all an under-graduate student who has little, if any, real managerial experience. The way to see if managers can really make a difference in getting their workers to coordinate would be to look at real-life managers. If getting employees to work in a coordinated manner is a central issue in many organisations then successful managers should be good at figuring out how to resolve such coordination failures. This could be for two reasons. First, it is those who are better at motivating their workers that eventually beat out others and rise to top management positions. Second, the fact that they are in managerial positions also implies that they have greater experience dealing with problems of coordination failures and this in turn gives them valuable perspective and knowledge into what policies work better than others.

This is what David Cooper proceeded to study next. (This is another example of how experimental economists are increasingly drawing their participants from outside the usual pool of students.) But how do you get real managers to come to a laboratory and take part in this game? The Executive MBA programme at the Weatherhead School provided a solution. The participants in the Executive MBA programme are all experienced and successful mangers, with at least ten years of work experience, including five years in a managerial role. Cooper finds that the experience of managers does matter in that when the members of the Executive MBA programme are placed in the role of the manager in the corporate turnaround game, they are able to overcome a history of coordination failure much faster than students playing the role of the manager. This superior performance is not driven by paying more money to the workers but by sending more effective messages that work better in motivating workers.

In order to understand which communication strategies work better, Cooper takes the various messages sent and puts them into appropriate categories: for instance, there is a category for "ask for effort". Under this category there are three sub-categories: "polite", "rude" and "specific" effort level. What Cooper finds is that professional managers are far more communicative than student managers and have a better intuitive feel for what kinds of messages would do better in reducing strategic uncertainty among employees. It is not so much that the "real" managers say things that are different from what the "student" managers say; rather the "real" managers say the right things more frequently. For example, professional managers are far more likely to ask for a specific effort level and more likely to offer encouragement to workers. One striking difference is that professional managers are six times more likely than student managers to make explicit references to *trusting* one's fellow workers.

Cooper adds:

> To understand why this particular communication strategy works, recall that coordination is largely a problem of beliefs. Communication correlates beliefs, leading to the correlation in actions.... With a good communication strategy, the manager creates common beliefs that most employees will be choosing high effort levels. This is most obvious when a manager asks employees for a specific effort level.... More subtly, pointing out the mutual benefits of successful coordination ... creates expectations that all employees will select high effort levels in order to enjoy higher payoffs, making it safer for any one employee to increase his effort level.

## 5.7 When in Rome ... creating culture in the laboratory

Two themes emerge from our discussion so far. First, in the absence of any communication or other interventions and in the stark context-free laboratory settings participants often find it difficult to coordinate their actions. Second, a number of interventions such as various types of communication mechanisms or performance bonuses can help alleviate this problem to a large extent if not completely. Turning towards the real-world, while large scale coordination failures are a reality in many organisations, yet many others do seem to address these issues adequately. At the very least many organisations are not as dysfunctional as the laboratory worst case scenario and many of them do manage to do well in resolving these issues.

How do they do it? It is very likely that they rely on a combination of approaches like the ones suggested above, but there may be yet another option for fostering coordination: a process of acculturation of new workers. Corporations engage in a wide variety of exercises in an attempt to build trust and promote teamwork among workers. These include mentoring of junior recruits by more senior members of the firm; sometimes they involve going on retreats including rock-climbing or white-water rafting in teams which force team members to rely upon and support one another and build trust among team-mates.

Roberto Weber of Carnegie Mellon University decided to see if a process of acculturation can help workers learn to coordinate their actions better. We already know that typically a small group (say two players) finds it easier to coordinate actions. It is when the groups start to get large that the problems creep in. Yet, in real life many large firms and organisations do manage to get their workers to coordinate their actions. Weber conjectures that this might be due to the fact that the founding members of a firm, who are a small group to start with, manage to resolve coordination problems and in doing so they manage to establish a set of rules or norms of self-governance. As the group grows, new entrants are exposed to and acculturated into these "good" norms and manage to sustain the norms of coordination that are already established. So the idea is to start small, establish a norm of coordination early on (which is easier in small groups), grow slowly while exposing new members to the already established norm and expecting them to adhere to it. This should allow organisations to grow but still remain coordinated.

Weber uses the minimum effort game originally studied by John Van Huyck and his colleagues in order to see if he could indeed get small groups to first manage to coordinate their actions and then grow larger while maintaining that coordination. I would like to remind you that in the minimum effort game each participant picks a number between 1 and 7 and the payoff he gets depends on the number he picks and the smallest number picked by someone in the group. However, everyone is better off and gets the maximum payoff if all group members manage to coordinate their actions to choose 7.

Weber looks at three treatments:

1   A control treatment where a group of 12 players play the minimum effort game for 12 periods.

2   A "history" treatment where each group starts out with two players; the rest of the group initially do not participate but only observe what the initial players are doing; every few rounds one person is added to the group and start to play the game with the ones who were playing before so that all 12 players are participating for the last few rounds. (On a few occasions Weber added more than one person at the same time, but that was the exception rather than the rule.) Weber comments that this history condition serves as a "*simple metaphor for the extensive training, socialization and acculturation often required of new entrants to a firm or country*".

3   There is also a "no history" treatment which is similar to the "history" treatment in that players are added, usually one at a time, except unlike the "history" treatment these new entrants do not get to see what happened prior to their entry into the game and therefore have no history to fall back upon.

There were five "control" groups with 12 players in each for a total of 60 participants; nine groups in the "history" treatment each with 12 players for a total of 108 participants and there are three groups of 12 each (36 players) in the "no history" treatment. The composition of these groups remains unchanged for the duration of the session.

Weber demonstrates a strong regularity that this process of slow organisational growth while exposing the workers to "history" – a shared norm of coordination – does often lead to large groups of 12 efficiently coordinating their actions; that is all members of the group manage to choose 7 for multiple periods at a stretch. In three of 12 groups the minimum remains at 7 throughout the growth process even when all 12 players are participating. In another group players choose 5 throughout the growth process and in five out of nine groups, the full group of 12 manages to sustain coordination to a minimum higher than 1. This is in sharp contrast to what happened in Van Huyck, Battalio and Beil's study where by round 4 in any group the minimum had dropped down to 1.

Not all groups that get to see the prior history do well in that in four groups, by the time the group reaches its full size of 12, the minimum had dwindled down to 1. However, it is equally true that the groups that play with history do manage much better coordination than either the control groups or the groups that do not get to see history. Weber's results suggest that efficient coordination can be achieved if groups start out small, grow slowly and expose new members to the already established norm of coordination during this growth process. If this history is not available then efficient coordination is not possible.

Ananish Chaudhuri at the University of Auckland, Andrew Schotter at New York University and Barry Sopher at Rutgers University take Weber's idea of acculturation further by designing an elaborate experiment where new entrants can not only observe the history of what happened before their arrival, but can also receive advice from their predecessors. Andrew Schotter and Barry Sopher were already engaged in an elaborate research project trying to understand the evolution of norms and conventions in various economic transactions. They argued that socialisation and cultural influences have enormous impact on all aspects of human behaviour, including economic interactions. Norms or conventions of behaviour that arise during one generation may be passed on to the successors in following generations. Such norm-driven behaviour may help sustain higher levels of cooperation in many social dilemmas than is predicted by gene-based economic or evolutionary theory such as the theory of reciprocal altruism or the theory of kin selection that I discussed at the end of Part 4.

In order to examine the evolution of social norms, Schotter and Sopher had designed an innovative *"inter-generational framework"*. Here a sequence of participants play a variety of games (such as a battle of the sexes game or an ultimatum game) for a number of periods and are then replaced by new players, who continue the game in their role for a similar length of time. Players in one generation can communicate with their successors in the next generation and advise them on how to play the game. Norms developed during one generation can be passed on in the history of human societies via word-of-mouth transmission of knowledge and experiences. In addition, players in each generation care about the succeeding generation in the sense that each player's payoff depends on not only the payoffs achieved during his own generation, but also on the payoffs of his children in the next generation. Thus, each generation has a direct monetary stake in what happens in the next generation.

The idea is to study how such advice left by people who have experience with the problem at hand creates norms of behaviour which help resolve social dilemmas or problems of coordination. After all, we ask for advice in so many things that we do: when we choose a doctor or a dentist or an auto-mechanic or a school for our child; or when we buy a house or a car or pick a mutual fund. Therefore, it stands to reason that when we encounter a problem for the first time, we may not be in a complete vacuum; there may be, and usually are, others around who already have some experience and can advise us regarding the appropriate course of action. This is Weber's idea of acculturation of new entrants into the mores and culture of the new organisation or country.

Chaudhuri, Schotter and Sopher decided to apply this idea of generations of players leaving advice for their successors in order to see if that could help resolve problems of pervasive coordination failure. Like Weber, they also look at the minimum effort game of Van Huyck and his colleagues but their design is more elaborate than Weber's. In the experiments carried out by Chaudhuri and his colleagues there are eight players in a group and each group constitutes a generation. Each group plays the minimum effort game for ten rounds and the composition of the group remains unchanged for the entire duration.

Chaudhuri and his colleagues look at the impact of both history and advice. In one treatment subjects in each generation leave advice "privately" in the sense that a player in one generation leaves advice to only his *own* successor in the next generation; here members of each generation get one piece of advice from their immediate predecessor. In a second treatment advice is combined with history, in that members of each generation not only get a piece of advice from their immediate predecessors but they can also get to see the history of prior interactions, that is, they can see what happened in their parents' generation and their grand-parents' generation etc. In a third treatment the advice is "public"; here the advice from the members of one generation is made available to *all* the members of the next generation. But the public advice is provided in two different ways:

1   For some participants the advice from a previous generation is typed up on a sheet of paper and given to members of the current generation; each member of the current generation knows that each of them is looking at a sheet with the exact same information on it, eight pieces of advice written by their immediate predecessors.

2   But for some others this advice is not only distributed on sheets of paper but they are also *read aloud* by the experimenter (or an assistant) prior to the beginning of the session.

In these public advice treatments participants are not shown the history of prior plays. As always the behaviour of the participants who get advice and/or get to see the history of prior interactions is compared to the behaviour of a control group of participants who play the same game with no advice or history.

Chaudhuri and his colleagues conjecture that allowing participants to leave advice to their successors using such an inter-generational design might over time enable future generations to achieve efficient coordination. A generation that failed to resolve the underlying coordination problem might advise the next generation accordingly by writing advice that suggested *"do as we are telling you to do, not as we did"*, and such advice, if followed, might lead to a convention selecting the payoff-dominant outcome.

Chaudhuri and his colleagues, however, go one step further and also collect data on the beliefs that people hold. Remember I said at the outset that often the fundamental reason behind the lack of coordination success is *strategic uncertainty*; uncertainty regarding the actions to be taken by others. Mechanisms or processes that create more optimistic beliefs will be more successful in resolving coordination problems. It is likely that the interventions that succeed do so by creating appropriate beliefs but it is still important and instructive to actually look at those beliefs and how they are affected by different institutions.

Chaudhuri and his colleagues find that while the availability of advice does help considerably in resolving coordination failures, the manner in which this advice is distributed is of crucial importance. When advice from one generation to the next is private, so that a parent advises his or her offspring alone, this advice does not help coordination at all, mostly because the advice here tends to be pessimistic suggesting that participants stick to the strategy that leads to the secure outcome. A lot of the advice here takes the following form: *"Pick 1 in all the rounds. You could bet that everyone may pick 7 but they will not. Always pick 1."* Or words to that effect.

Contrary to Weber's finding that history helps if the group starts small and grows slowly, Chaudhuri and his colleagues find that history is not very helpful for groups that are already large. In fact, they find that advice is more useful and facilitates greater coordination than history does. Strangely enough, if participants receive pessimistic advice, then they are most likely to end up at the "bad" secure outcome even if they can see that their predecessors were relatively successful in achieving coordination via the history of prior plays. In this sense "good" history does not help if the advice left is "bad" and "good" advice (even if coupled with "bad" history) works better than "good" history.

In order for advice to help people coordinate their actions, this advice must, first, be distributed publicly in the sense that the advice from all members of one generation must be made available to all the members of the next generation and, second, must also be *read out loud*. Thus, each and every member of a group must know that everyone else is receiving the exact same information (message) and, furthermore, each person must be convinced that each of them has heard this message being read out loud. Therefore, it must be common knowledge that everyone has received the same message. It is only when the message is made public and also read out loud, making it common knowledge, that the participants consistently choose 7 in the minimum effort game and manage to coordinate to the payoff dominant outcome. The nature of the advice when it is public is also qualitatively different from when it is private. A typical example is: "*Pick 7 every time, EVERY TIME. If everyone picks 7 every time, everyone will make the max per round $1.30 \times 10 = \$13.00) \ldots Don't be stupid. Pick 7.*"

There is one twist to this finding. If the message being given to the subjects is very strong in that every member of one generation urges their successors to choose 7 all the time, as in the strongly exhortative message quoted above, then the message will foster coordination even if it is *not* read out loud as long as it is distributed in a public manner so that everyone knows that everyone else is reading the same message. But if there is even a small amount of equivocation in one or more of the pieces of advice given then in order for efficient coordination to occur, these messages must be public and also read out loud.

Why does advice – particularly strongly exhortative advice – have such a positive impact on behaviour? One way advice can foster coordination is via the creation of more optimistic beliefs. I have argued above that the problem here is essentially one of trust. In order to choose the strategy that leads to the payoff dominant outcome, each and every subject must be convinced that their group members are also going to choose the same strategy. Even a small modicum of doubt regarding the choices of others is often enough to destroy any possibility of successful coordination. The role advice plays or can play then, is to remove or reduce that doubt about the strategy choice of other players. Does it do so? Chaudhuri and his colleagues were uniquely placed to answer this question because they had actually collected data on those beliefs.

At the beginning of the experiment Chaudhuri and his colleagues provided their participants with the instructions to the experiment. Then the participants were provided the advice, and depending on the treatment, the history, from the previous generation. This advice could be private or public. After this, and before commencing the actual game, these researchers asked the participants to state what they expected each and every member of the group to choose in the first round of the ten-round session. Participants are actually paid on the basis of how accurate their predictions are. Therefore, they have an incentive to think about their predictions carefully and to make accurate predictions. Chaudhuri and his colleagues found that most of their treatments involving history and/or advice did *not* completely remove the doubt that someone would choose 1. In all these treatments participants thought there was a positive, albeit small, chance that someone in the group will choose 1. This very small amount of doubt was enough to destroy successful coordination and made certain that in short order participants fell into the coordination failure trap of the majority, if not all, choosing 1. The one treatment where this doubt was removed was when the advice was public and read out loud. Here, finally, participants were convinced that no one in the group would choose 1. These optimistic beliefs led participants to choose 7 consistently in this treatment.

Why does reading aloud the messages make such a difference? Michael Chwe in his book "*Rational Ritual: Culture, Coordination and Common Knowledge*" comments:

*Because each individual wants to participate only if others do, each person must also know that others received a message. For that matter, because each person knows that other people need to be confident that others will participate, each person must know that other people know that other people have received a message, and so forth.*

*In other words, knowledge of the message is not enough; what is also required is knowledge of others' knowledge, knowledge of others' knowledge of others' knowledge and so on – that is "common knowledge". To understand how people solve coordination problems, we should thus look at social processes that generate common knowledge.*

In order to successfully coordinate their actions, players need to possess appropriately optimistic beliefs about each other's actions and their beliefs about others' beliefs and so on. When advice is private or less than common knowledge, players' beliefs are not sufficiently optimistic. But when the advice is made common knowledge by making it public and also read aloud, each subject reads and hears the same information and knows that everyone else is also reading and hearing the same message. This finally succeeds in creating an atmosphere where players feel sufficiently bold to start by choosing 7 and then go on to establish a norm of coordination based on that auspicious start.

## 5.8 From the laboratory to the real world: do these interventions work? The story of Continental Airlines

Our discussion up to this point should have convinced you of two things: first, in stag hunt type coordination problems participants often find it difficult to coordinate to the payoff dominant outcome; but second, a number of relatively easy interventions such as communication among participants, advice from people who have prior experience in the matter, acculturation into the norms of the relevant group or incentive bonuses, seem to be quite successful in facilitating coordination. The big question is: these interventions seem to work well in the relatively sterile atmosphere of the laboratory, but will they still work out there in the real world?

Marc Knez and Duncan Simester (of MIT) decided to see if the interventions work by looking at how Continental Airlines managed to turn things around in the mid- to late-1990s. I mentioned before that the operations of an airline require extensive coordination and have a "weak-link" structure in that the performance of the organisation as a whole is crucially dependent on the performance of component units. One slow worker or group can slow things down and hurt the organisation even if everyone else is working at speed. Therefore, the overall performance of the organisation is determined to a large extent by the performance of the slowest or worst-performing entity within the organisation. This in turn implies that the benefits to the organisation from getting all the groups and workers involved to coordinate their activities are immense. The operations of an airline company can tell us a lot about the success, or lack thereof, of various interventions in facilitating successful coordination.

Prior to 1995 Continental was one of the worst performing airlines in the industry. Following de-regulation of the airline industry in the US in 1978, Continental had declared bankruptcy twice, once in 1983 and again in 1990, and on average was ranked last among the ten major domestic airlines in important measures of performance such as on-time arrival, baggage handling and customer satisfaction. At the end of 1994 a new senior management team was brought in to address the myriad problems Continental was facing. The new team introduced the "Go Forward Plan". This plan had three important components: (1) changing airport managers; (2) improving the flight schedule; and (3) introduction of a *group incentive scheme* that paid a *monthly bonus* if a firm-wide on-time performance goal was met. The bonus scheme announced on January 15, 1995 promised $65 to every hourly paid employee, including part-time employees, in every month that Continental's on-time performance ranked within the top five in the industry. In 1996 the scheme was modified paying $65 per month in months when Continental ranked second or third in on-time performance and $100 if it ranked first.

After reporting net losses of $125 million in 1992, $199 million in 1993 and $613 million in 1994, Continental reported a net profit of $224 million in 1995. This grew to $319 million in 1996 and $385 million in 1997. These profit increases were accompanied by improvements in other measures of performance such as on-time arrival and departure. Continental's senior management attributed much of the success to the new bonus scheme which resulted in an increase in employee effort as well as mutual monitoring of co-workers and a reduction in employee turnover and the number of people taking days off due to sickness. Furthermore, the bonus scheme was self-funding. After the introduction of the scheme fewer Continental customers missed connections and fewer had to be re-accommodated on other flights while other airlines now increasingly used Continental to re-assign their customers with missed flights.

But in addition to the financial incentives provided for improvements in performance, the new management also adopted other new policies which included the introduction of bulletin boards and a quarterly employee magazine, regular voice-mail and video statements from the CEO and increasing visibility and accountability of senior managers. These additional steps also contributed significantly to the turnaround.

At the time Continental had approximately 35,000 employees who individually had a negligible influence on overall performance. Moreover, the employees were geographically dispersed, restricting (or preventing) direct interaction between workers and direct observations of each other's actions. How and why did the policies implemented by the new management team – including the bonus and other devices such as the use of bulletin-boards and public announcements from the CEO – impact performance? Knez and Simester argue that to a large extent the interventions improved performance by increasing the level of *mutual monitoring* among the workers. Continental's adoption of the incentive schemes raised *expectations* that other groups – whether at the same airport or different ones – were improving their on-time performance as well, and this enhanced expectation enabled workers to coordinate their actions.

The performance bonus was not targeted towards particular employees but was based on coordinated actions by many workers. Therefore, the choice of low effort by any one worker or group not only reduces the chances of that group getting the bonus, but also reduces the chances of all other groups whose performance depends on the one group lagging behind. This creates an incentive for employees to monitor each other's efforts and to encourage lagging colleagues to work harder. This can take two forms: (1) peer pressure on those who are not putting in the required effort coupled with (probable) feelings of shame on the part of the laggard; (2) reporting low effort on the part of some workers to management. Because workers in many groups work closely with one another in pushing out or waving in aircrafts, loading and unloading baggage etc., they are well placed to see how hard someone is working.

Such mutual monitoring took a variety of forms and included employees being summoned from the break-room by colleagues or employees being chastised for leaving their stations. Employees also began to contact colleagues who had called in sick to ask if assistance was needed and also to monitor if the absences were legitimate or not. When Knez and Simester asked Continental's CEO why the bonus was offered to all workers and not merely the ones who did improve their performance, he responded that this was done to impress upon all workers that improvements would require effort and commitment from everyone, not just a key few. Thus, the focus was squarely on creating more optimistic expectations and on changing overall employee behaviour.

Thus, Continental used a judicious mix of financial incentives as well as good communication strategies and exhortative messages to turn things around; exactly as suggested by some of the papers I have cited above.

## 5.9 From the real world, back to the laboratory: are you partners or strangers?

Many of the coordination problems that arise in real-life involve peoples and groups who interact with one another repeatedly. The people who work at Continental or at a steel-mill or work along the assembly line of a car manufacturing company are essentially interacting with the same group of people over and over again. They, therefore, usually know each other well. This also makes it easier to monitor the work of others and figure out when someone is not putting in the requisite work, spending too much time in the break-room or calling in sick under false pretences. We have already seen that even among people who interact with each other on a daily basis the problems of coordination failure can be severe. The majority of the studies that I have discussed above (with the exception of the work done by Russell Cooper and his colleagues at Iowa), and especially all the ones that looked at how to improve coordination in large groups using the minimum effort game, have done so using groups whose composition remains fixed over time. This focus on fixed groups is understandable given that many of these problems are essentially problems faced by groups whose members interact repeatedly over time.

But it is not the case that all coordination problems are faced by groups whose composition remains relatively stable over time. There are a number of instances where group membership changes frequently. The Internal Revenue Service in the US or tax agencies in other countries routinely hire additional temporary workers right around the deadline for filing taxes. Similarly immigration agencies in many countries will take on additional temporary workers when faced with a sudden influx of applications. The Post Office will hire additional workers to bide them over the rush of the holiday season. The turnover rate of workers at most fast-food outlets is very high meaning that there are workers coming and going frequently. All these enterprises are also called upon to resolve demanding coordination problems.

But the nature of their problem differs in that members of these groups are not as close-knit as those working for companies where the group composition is relatively stable over time. If we think of the group members at Continental as *"partners"* (people who have known each other for extended periods of time), the workers at McDonald's or the IRS are often *"strangers"* to one another – people who work together for relatively short periods of time and then disperse with not enough time to build lasting relationships. So how do these strangers perform when it comes to taking coordinated actions?

There are two ways this can go:

1 The ability to interact repeatedly with the same people and the possibility of forming long-term relationships can make it easier to establish trust; this in turn can help coordination by creating optimistic beliefs about the actions of fellow group members. If this is true then fixed groups should be better able to coordinate their actions compared to groups which are short-lived.

2 However, one cannot rule out the possibility that fixed groups may encounter more problems. In groups where the composition is fixed, initial acts of bad faith such as providing low effort may tend to fester and the group might end up in a cycle of recriminations like a bad marriage, where the group gets caught in a low-effort outcome and with no new blood coming in, no one can quite find the energy to break out of this cycle. In this case, short-lived groups may actually do better. With the composition of the group changing frequently, new people with no baggage or ill-feelings from previous interactions come in and bring new optimism and expectations. This might enable these groups to do better in coordinating their actions.

It turns out that it is the former conjecture that is proved correct. One of the first studies to explicitly look at this issue was Kenneth Clark of Manchester and Martin Sefton of the University of Newcastle upon Tyne in the late 1990s. They had 160 participants take part in a simple stag hunt game. Participants are formed into pairs and play a game where each player can choose one of two strategies. The game has two equilibria – one payoff dominant and the other secure.

Each session consists of 20 participants. Ten of these are sent to one room while the other ten are sent to a different room. People in one room are always paired with the people in the other room. In one treatment subjects are in "fixed" groups. Here the same two participants (located in separate rooms) play against one another ten times in a row. In a "re-matching" treatment each participant plays ten times but each time with a different participant who is always in the other room. Thus, in the first treatment, since the participants are interacting repeatedly, they have greater opportunity to build trust and establish a reputation for behaving in a particular way. They have the option of using conditional strategies of the following type: *I am going to start by putting in high effort because I expect you to do the same; if you do not then I will stop working hard as well and we will both be worse off.* These types of conditional strategies, using the early rounds to build a relationship, might encourage people to choose the more risky strategy of hunting stag early on and then go on to build on that early cooperation. Participants who do not have this opportunity and are continually being thrown into new relationships would have a hard time establishing trust.

Clark and Sefton find that more participants choose the riskier stag hunt strategy in fixed groups. They have 200 observations for the game played in each treatment: fixed pairings and re-matched pairings. Participants in fixed pairings manage to attain the payoff dominant outcome 116 out of those 200 times, while in re-matched pairings this happens only four out of 200 times. People in the fixed pairings also managed to coordinate their actions, either to the payoff dominant outcome or the secure option, more often. These participants ended up at a disequilibrium outcome in only 17% of cases while the participants who were re-matched at the end of each round found it more difficult to coordinate and ended up at disequilibrium outcomes in 30% of cases.

If participants playing as partners in fixed pairings do better in this game then it is conceivable that the same would be true for the more complex minimum effort game which captures the nature of the interaction in many corporations. That is exactly how it turns out. Ananish Chaudhuri and Tirnud Paichayontvijit at the University of Auckland have 210 participants take part in a slightly modified version of the minimum effort game. They ask the following questions: Do groups which experience greater turnover fare worse in coordinating their actions? And if that is the case then what kinds of interventions work for these groups? Do the ones that work for fixed groups also work for groups whose composition changes frequently?

Participants are formed into groups of five and play for a number of rounds. There are two matching protocols: in the *first* treatment, this grouping is "fixed" in that the composition of the group remains unchanged and the same five participants interact with one another for the entire time. In a *second* treatment, participants are re-matched at the end of each round. Here each session typically has 20 participants and at the beginning of each round these participants are randomly formed into groups of five using a computer program which makes it unlikely that the same group of five will interact more than once. Remember that in this game the best outcome is when all members of the group choose 7 which yields the maximum money to each participant and corresponds to the payoff dominant outcome.

In each matching protocol groups first play five rounds without any intervention. There are five players in each group and one play of the game in any particular round is generated once all five members of a group have made an effort choice. This gives Chaudhuri and Paichayontvijit 120 observations in the random matching protocol and 75 observations in the fixed matching protocol. Exactly as in the Clark and Sefton study, groups whose composition remains unchanged over time are far better at taking coordinated actions compared to groups whose members are re-matched at the end of each round. When these researchers look at the proportion of cases where the smallest number chosen in the group was 1, i.e. at least one person in the group chose 1 so that the group minimum was 1, they find that for the fixed groups the proportion of cases where the group minimum is 1 is relatively stable and hovers around 10%. The situation is radically different among the randomly re-matched groups. Here the proportion of groups ending up at the minimum possible effort level increases from 27% in round 1 to 50% in both rounds 4 and 5.

Given this lack of coordination success on the part of the re-matched groups the next question was: What kinds of intervention work better for these groups? Chaudhuri and Paichayontvijit look at two different kinds of interventions: (1) a public announcement along the lines of Van Huyck, Gillette and Battalio and (2) an incentive bonus along the lines of Brandts and Cooper. In the case of the public announcement, an assistant reads out a public announcement which points out that all players are better off in monetary terms if they choose 7 all the time. The bonus works a little differently than in Brandts and Cooper. In Brandts and Cooper the bonus depends on the minimum amount of work hours chosen and workers get a bonus as long as the minimum is higher than zero; of course the highest bonus is received when they choose to work the maximum of 40 hours (analogous to choosing 7 in the minimum effort game). In Chaudhuri and Paichayontvijit the bonus is given in every round that the group manages to coordinate to 7, i.e. all group members choose 7. There is no bonus for coordinating to anything less than 7 unlike in the Brandts and Cooper study. This is similar to Continental's policy of paying a $100 bonus for coming first, or paying $65 for coming second or third; but a fourth place finish or worse yields no bonus at all.

Chaudhuri and Paichayontvijit find that when the composition of the group remains fixed over time, a public announcement exhorting everyone to choose 7 and pointing out the benefits of doing so is enough to get consistent coordination to the payoff dominant all-7 outcome. However, the same announcement enjoys limited success when the groups are short-lived and participants are randomly re-matched at the end of each round. Here the intervention that ultimately gets players to coordinate to the payoff dominant outcome is the payment of an incentive bonus and a public announcement of that bonus; short of that public announcement and the payment of a performance bonus these groups are not very successful in coordinating their actions. This suggests that groups that experience frequent turnover are much more prone to pervasive coordination failures; communication alone may no longer suffice in resolving these failures but needs to be accompanied by financial carrots in the form of performance bonuses.

## 5.10 Concluding remarks

Michael Kremer, an economist at Harvard University points out a dramatic and ultimately heart-rending story of coordination failure. On January 28, 1986 the space shuttle Challenger exploded 73 seconds into its flight after an O-ring seal in its right solid rocket booster failed at lift-off. This in turn led to structural failures and eventually aerodynamic forces broke up the shuttle. The shuttle was destroyed and all seven crew members were killed. While the thousands of components of the space shuttle were fine, the shuttle blew up because an O-ring, a relatively minor component did not work properly.

Kremer uses this example to argue that in a variety of economic contexts coordinated action is prevented by seemingly minor glitches or small degrees of uncertainty. He goes on to use the experience of the space shuttle Challenger and the failure of the O-ring to propose that extensive coordination failures might be at the heart of underdevelopment in many countries. Here countries may be caught in a low-level equilibrium "trap" when development requires the simultaneous industrialisation of many sectors of the economy but no sector can break-even industrialising alone. Successful development then might require a "big push" needing coordinated action by different sectors of the economy. Similarly, in a macroeconomic context, an economy can get trapped in an under-employment equilibrium. In such instances no firm wishes to expand production unless it can be assured that others will do so, yet not doing so leads to an outcome that is worse for everyone concerned.

The available evidence suggests that in most of these cases of coordination failure, the primary source of the problem is strategic uncertainty about others' actions. I do not wish to adopt the risky strategy that could lead to the payoff dominant outcome until and unless I am convinced that others in my group will do the same. And until I acquire that trust in my peers, we might be doomed to be caught in a low (or no) coordination trap. To a large extent, resolving such coordination failure problems boils down to the creation of appropriately optimistic beliefs that others in the group will choose the more risky stag hunt strategy as well.

The exact mechanism of creating those beliefs will depend on the particular problem at hand and could involve the use of either good communication strategies such as exhortative messages via bulletin boards or television advertisements; sometimes they might require monetary incentives; at times the monetary incentives might need to be reinforced by congratulatory messages; other times one might need extensive acculturation and socialisation of new entrants. Whatever the nature of the intervention, it will almost always require social processes that generate common knowledge by putting the information in the *public* domain so that everyone is convinced that everyone else is getting the exact same message and feels emboldened to act so as to coordinate their actions. A shared comprehension of the message is crucial to achieving successful coordination.

**Part 6**

# Epilogue

Further economic implications of
fairness and trust

## 6.1 Further economic implications of fairness and trust

I would like to end by reflecting upon some further implications of the issues that I talked about previously, especially the role of trust and reciprocity in economic interactions. I provide a few more examples of why such emotional dispositions matter for economics; and discuss why economists and policy makers should pay attention to such issues.

At the end of the day, a fundamental pre-occupation of economists is the betterment of people's lives, which involves addressing issues of economic development. Economists usually stress the importance of markets, legal and political institutions and a system of formal rules and laws governing economic activity for successful economic development. This traditional approach does not make allowances for the role of fairness or social norms in the process of development. But over the last few parts I have shown that informal social rules or norms of behaviour, embodied in things such as the decision to trust strangers or reciprocate others' trust, willingness to punish violations of cooperative norms, even if such punishments impose non-trivial pecuniary costs on those meting out that punishment, are equally, or more, important. At the very least economists and policy makers need to be aware of the roles that such social norms play because ignoring them can often lead to unintended consequences causing more harm than good.

In his book *Globalization and its Discontents* the 2001 Economics Nobel Laureate Joseph Stiglitz points out that one reason policies espoused by international agencies, such as the International Monetary Fund (IMF), have often been controversial is due to an excessive emphasis on "market fundamentalism", the view that open and free markets are the panacea for all the ills of less-developed economies. No serious economist will ever suggest that free markets are undesirable, but what needs to be understood is that the success of reforms are often dependent upon the sequencing of such reforms and also on local norms and conditions. External regulations imposed by central governments or international agencies which completely disregard local community-based initiatives might exacerbate problems rather than alleviate them. I end this part with some relevant examples.

## 6.2 The Grameen Bank experience

A pervasive problem in third-world countries (or even for the less well-off in some first-world countries) is the lack of credit; that is, an inability to borrow money to finance entrepreneurial activities. Let me stick with the problems of the third world for now. In rural areas of these countries there are people who are engaged in agriculture or handicrafts and often work for others for a pittance. Some of them might be able to work on their own – till their own land or start their own basket-weaving or wood-carving enterprise. Most such activities, however, require some start-up money, typically amounts that would be considered embarrassingly small by those of us who are used to a first-world lifestyle. Yet, even these very small amounts of money pose an insurmountable barrier to these people. Formal banks are unwilling to lend money to them because they rarely have any collateral that they can pledge against that loan.

The recourse is often to borrow money from local money-lenders who typically charge exorbitant interest rates, sometimes 100% or more. This, in turn, often forces the borrower into life-long debt that they struggle to pay off year after year. It is not difficult to understand the reluctance of banks to lend money to the rural poor because it is difficult for the banks to monitor these loans. For instance, when a debtor comes in and says that he is unable to repay the loan because of reasons beyond his control such as floods, droughts or pestilence, the bank manager often is not well-placed to corroborate this story. As a result default rates are high and many rural credit schemes have a poor track-record of loan recovery. Economists had been aware of this problem faced by the rural poor but the first truly innovative solution was offered by an enterprising economist from Bangladesh named Muhammad Yunus, who in the early 1980s started an enterprise named *"Grameen Bank"* (literally *"rural bank"* in Bangla, the language spoken in Bangladesh).

The Grameen Bank makes small loans to the rural poor without requiring any collateral. Borrowers must belong to a "solidarity group" typically consisting of five members. One member of the group receives a loan and must re-pay it before another member can receive a loan. The group is not required to give any guarantees for a loan to one of its members. Repayment responsibility rests solely on the individual borrower, while the group's job is to ensure that the borrower behaves in a responsible way. The vast majority of Grameen Bank loans are given to women on the basis of prior evidence that money lent to women is used more effectively. The system essentially relies on two principles: (1) *peer monitoring*, where members of the group who live in the same village monitor the debtor and make sure that the money is spent on productive activities and not on alcohol or cigarettes; and (2) *mutual trust and reciprocity* between the bank and the borrowers on the one hand and between the group members on the other hand. Prior to getting a loan group members have to pledge to uphold a number of values and principles which include:

*(1) We shall not inflict any injustice on anyone; neither shall we allow anyone to do so. (2) We shall collectively undertake bigger investments for higher incomes. (3) We shall always be ready to help each other. If anyone is in difficulty, we shall all help him or her. (4) We shall take part in all social activities collectively.*

Grameen Bank's track record has been notable, with loan repayment rates of close to 100%. More than half of its borrowers in Bangladesh (close to 50 million) have risen out of acute poverty thanks to these loans, as measured by standards such as having all children of school age in school, all household members eating three meals a day, a sanitary toilet, a rainproof house, clean drinking water and the ability to repay a loan of 300 taka (around US$4.50 at the exchange rate prevailing in mid-2008) per week. In 2006 Muhammad Yunus and the Grameen Bank together were the recipient of a Nobel Prize *"for their efforts to create economic and social development from below"*. But, probably reflecting the fact that Yunus's ideas are radical and not entirely commensurate with mainstream economics, the award given was the Nobel Peace Prize rather than the Nobel Prize in Economics.

Dean Karlan of Yale University provides an excellent illustration of the role that economic experiments can play in policy making. In the early 2000s, while working on his doctoral dissertation at MIT, Karlan travelled to Peru to look at participation in a micro-credit association called FINCA (Foundation for International Community Assistance). He had 397 pairs of participants take part in a slightly modified version of the Berg–Dickhaut–McCabe investment game and then also looked at the behaviour of these participants in terms of their involvement in the credit association. He finds that participants who behave in a trustworthy manner in their role as the receiver in the investment game (that is, those who returned at least as much as they were sent by the sender so that the sender did not lose money) are also *more likely* to repay loans, *more likely* to engage in greater voluntary saving and *less likely* to drop out of the credit programme.

## 6.3  Extrinsic incentives can crowd-out intrinsic motivations

In Part 3, while discussing the role of trust and trustworthiness in economic transactions, I mentioned that economists typically emphasise the need and importance of explicit and extrinsic incentives, in order to motivate people to take the appropriate course of action (such as inducing workers to put in the desired level of effort). But I also pointed out that at times mechanisms that rely on mutual trust and reciprocity and moral suasion among socially-connected groups of people can do at least as well as, if not better than, mechanisms that rely on explicit carrots-and-sticks. Here I provide some more examples of situations where externally provided carrots and/or sticks achieve inferior outcomes compared to approaches that appeal to people's sense of fair play and civic mindedness.

Bruno Frey and Felix Oberholzer-Gee at the University of Zürich look at people's responses to what are called "*NIMBY*" ("*Not in My Backyard*") problems. This refers to a community's willingness, or lack thereof, to accept the location of noxious or undesirable facilities (such as nuclear power plants, prisons, airports, electrical pylons, chemical factories etc.) in their neighbourhoods. One response by governmental agencies in such cases is to offer financial compensation to communities in return for their willingness to accept such facilities. Frey and Oberholzer-Gee argue that in some cases offering an external incentive, such as monetary payments, may actually be counter-productive because such incentives partially destroy or "*crowd out*" any intrinsic motivation that the community may have felt in accepting the facility. Consequently such monetary incentives may become less effective and in some instances may lead to a *lower* willingness to accept the facility in question. If a person derives intrinsic benefits by behaving in an altruistic manner or doing her civic-duty, then paying her for this service may reduce her intrinsic motivation to do so.[1]

Frey and Oberholzer-Gee conjecture that if local residents perceive it as their civic duty to accept a NIMBY project, introducing monetary compensation may reduce support for the noxious facility. In early 1993 the researchers hired a professional survey institute to approach 305 residents of two communities in central Switzerland to inquire about their willingness to accept the placement of a nuclear waste repository in their locality. The first question asked of all respondents was:

> *Suppose that the National Cooperative for the Storage of Nuclear Waste (NAGRA), after completing exploratory drilling, proposes to build the repository for low- and mid-level radioactive waste in your hometown. Federal experts examine this proposition, and the federal parliament decides to build the repository in your community. In a town hall meeting, do you accept this proposition or do you reject this proposition?*

Fifty-one per cent of respondents said that they would vote in favour of having the nuclear waste repository in their community, 45% opposed the facility while 4% did not care.

Next, the researchers repeated the exact same question asking the respondents whether they would be willing to accept the construction of a nuclear waste repository if the Swiss parliament offered to compensate all the residents of the community that accepted the nuclear storage facility. The initial amounts offered to respondents were (i) $2,175 per individual per year or (ii) $4,350 per individual per year or (iii) $6,525 per individual per year. Surprisingly, while 51% of the respondents agreed to accept the nuclear waste repository when no compensation was offered, the level of acceptance *dropped* to 25% when compensation was offered. However the exact amount of the compensation did not appear to have a significant effect on people's acceptance levels. Everyone who rejected the first compensation was then made a better offer, thereby raising the amount of compensation from $2,175 to $3,263, from $4,350 to $6,525, and from $6,525 to $8,700. Despite this marked increase, only a single respondent who

---

1 In the early 1970s Richard Titmuss claimed that while a lot of people are willing to donate blood voluntarily, paying people to donate blood actually leads to reduced blood-donation. Many voluntary donors are turned-off by such payments since these payments (possibly) reduce the donor's option of indulging in the "warm-glow" of altruistic feelings. When an external motivation is seen to be controlling, it might destroy or reduce an internal motivation to do something out of a sense of altruism.

declined the first compensation was now prepared to accept the higher offer.

To further test the *"crowding-out"* effect, Frey and Oberholzer-Gee conducted an identical survey in six communities in north-eastern Switzerland designated as potential sites for a second Swiss repository, a facility for long-lived, highly radioactive waste. Two hundred and six interviews were conducted in these communities using procedures identical to the first survey. Here 41% respondents stated they would vote for the high-level radioactive waste facility, 56% would have voted against it, and 3% did not care. When community members were offered compensation, the level of acceptance *dropped* to 27%. As before, offering higher amounts did not lead to significant changes in the level of support. These findings are not unique to Switzerland. Howard Kunreuther and Douglas Easterling carry out a similar survey regarding the location of a nuclear waste facility in Nevada in the US and find that increased tax rebates failed to elicit increased support for such a facility. Other researchers have reported similar findings that support for noxious facilities often decline when people are offered compensation.

One possibility, as to why citizens' acceptance levels decline when offered compensation, is that the offer of a generous compensation might be taken as an indication that the facility is more hazardous than they previously thought. A higher compensation then might indicate higher risk associated with the facility, which in turn leads to a lower level of acceptance. Frey and Oberholzer-Gee test this by directly asking respondents whether they perceived a link between the size of the compensation and the level of risk. Only 6% agreed with this connection which indicates that it is not the perception of higher risk with higher compensation that is driving these responses.

Frey and Oberholzer-Gee conclude by commenting

> ...*where public spirit prevails, using price incentives to muster support for the construction of a socially desirable, but locally unwanted, facility comes at a higher price than suggested by standard economic theory because these incentives tend to crowd out civic duty.... These conclusions are of general relevance for economic theory and policy because they identify a particular limit of monetary compensation to rally support for a socially desired enterprise. The relative price effect of monetary compensation is not questioned in*

*any way, but this measure becomes less effective when crowding-out is considered.*

While Frey and Oberholzer-Gee use surveys, Juan Camilo Cardenas (of the Universidad Javeriana) and John Stranlund and Cleve Willis (of the University of Massachusetts, Amherst) provide experimental evidence of the same phenomenon. Cardenas and his colleagues carry out their experiments in the three rural villages of Circasia, Encino and Finlandia in Colombia. Of these, Encino is located in the eastern Andean region while Circasia and Finlandia are located in the Quindio coffee region of the mid-Andes. These locations were chosen because they each have predominantly rural populations with significant interest in local natural resources and environmental quality. Their experiments are designed to approximate an environmental quality problem that villagers in developing countries routinely face.

Specifically, participants were asked to decide how much time they would spend collecting firewood from a surrounding forest, given that the collection of firewood has an adverse effect on the water quality of the region due to soil erosion. Next, the researchers confront their participants with a government-imposed quota on the amount of time that can be spent collecting firewood. The quota, however, is enforced imperfectly; in the sense that there is only a small chance that someone exceeding the quota would be detected and punished, which is typical of such command-and-control environmental problems in rural areas of third-world countries. Thus the participants are essentially confronted by a social dilemma which is very similar to the ones that they face in their day-to-day lives. What Cardenas and his colleagues find is that the outcome, in terms of time spent collecting firewood, was *worse* in the presence of the imperfectly enforced government-imposed regulation because when confronted with the external regulation the behaviour of the participants became significantly more self-interested, while in the absence of any regulatory control their choices were more group-oriented.

Cardenas and his colleagues have their participants take part in two treatments of their experiments whose design is very similar to the public goods games that I talked about in Part 4. One hundred and twelve participants are divided into 14 groups with eight members in each group. All groups play a number of initial rounds of the game without any regulation and without being able to engage in any communication with fellow-group members. Seventy-two of those 112 participants (nine groups) then play additional rounds of the game in which they are allowed to communicate with their group members between each round. The remaining 40 participants (five groups) go on to play additional rounds, where they do not have any communication opportunities but instead face a regulation, which stipulates that they should not spend more than a particular amount of time collecting firewood. They are told that once each group member had made a choice regarding how much time to spend in this activity, there was a small chance that one group member would be selected for an audit to verify compliance with the rule. Specifically, after each group member had decided, a die would be rolled and an audit would take place only if an even number, i.e. 2, 4 or 6, came up. If an audit was to take place then a number between 1 and 8 would be drawn from a hat to indicate which particular member out of the eight group members would be audited. There was thus a 1 in 16 (approximately 6%) chance of being detected and penalised in the event of non-compliance.

Cardenas and his colleagues find that when participants do not face any external restrictions and cannot communicate with each other, their decisions tend to be neither purely self-interested nor commensurate with what would maximise the group interest. This is in keeping with other studies that look at behaviour in social dilemmas. When there is no regulation but participants are allowed to communicate with group members between rounds, individuals make more efficient choices, i.e. choices generate more social welfare. But, surprisingly, regulatory control caused subjects to tend, on average, to make choices that were much more self-interested than in the other two cases. Consequently, average individual earnings under regulation were lower than in the absence of such regulation, and much lower than the earnings of those subjects who were simply allowed to communicate with each other, in spite of the fact that the regulatory institution was designed to induce more efficient choices.

Cardenas, Stranlund and Willis conclude:

> *Economic theory will be a poor guide for designing environmental policies if it does not allow for other-regarding motivations, or if it fails to recognize that these motivations are not fixed with respect to institutional arrangements. Recognizing ... the balance between self-interested and group-regarding behaviour when it occurs will have*

*profound implications for nearly every aspect of environmental policy design and evaluation.*

Further experimental evidence about the downside of external incentives comes from the work of Ernst Fehr and Bettina Rockenbach. Fehr and Rockenbach had 238 participants take part in the Berg–Dickhaut–McCabe investment game that we discussed in Part 3. The sender and the receiver have $10 each. The sender can send any or all of this $10 to the receiver. Any amount sent to the receiver is *tripled* by the experimenter. The receiver then is given the option of keeping all the money given to him or sending some back to the sender. The game ends at that point.

Fehr and Rockenbach look at two treatments. (1) The first treatment is the *trust* treatment; this is almost identical to the original investment game and works mostly in the way described above, except, if the sender does transfer any money to the receiver then the sender is asked to specify a "back-transfer"; that is the sender is asked to specify an amount she would like the receiver to return. For instance, suppose the sender sends $5. In that case the receiver would be given $15. Then the sender can specify a "back-transfer" of any amount between $0 and $15 (that is any amount less than or equal to the maximum amount received by the receiver). In the trust treatment the receiver is under no compulsion to adhere to this desired back-transfer and can return any amount which can be less than what the sender asked for.

(2) The second treatment is the *incentive* treatment. This is similar to the trust treatment except, here, in addition to specifying a desired "back-transfer", the sender can also *choose* to impose a fine of $4 on the receiver if the receiver returns an amount which is less than what the sender asked for. However, the sender can, if she chooses, decide *not* to impose the fine.

Fehr and Rockenbach find, in keeping with prior studies, that senders choose to trust the receivers and transfer non-trivial amounts and receivers reciprocate that trust by returning money. But surprisingly, across all transfers by the sender, the receivers return *more* money when the sender had the option of imposing a fine but chose not to do so and the receivers return *much less* when the sender imposes the fine at the outset. On average, the receivers return 41% of the tripled amount received in the trust treatment (where no fine is available to the sender), 30% of the tripled amount in the incentive treatment where the sender chooses to impose the fine and 48% of the tripled amount in the case where the sender could have imposed the fine but chose *not* to do so.

If we look at the amount of money returned by the receivers as a proportion of the "back-transfer" that the sender specified, then we find that on average the receivers return 74% of the desired "back-transfer" in the trust treatment (where no fine is available to the sender), 55% of the desired "back-transfer" in the incentive treatment where the sender chooses to impose the fine and 74% of the desired "back-transfer" in the case where the sender could have imposed the fine but chose *not* to do so.

Once again, the above suggests that there is considerable experimental, as well as survey based, evidence that external incentives may crowd-out intrinsic motivations and, therefore, may be detrimental to successful collective action. Does this work in real life? Elinor Ostrom and her colleagues associated with the "*Workshop in Political Theory and Policy Analysis*" at Indiana University have been collecting thousands of written cases about resources managed by local users of fisheries, irrigation systems and grazing lands. In Nepal, they have collected data about the rules and general management strategies used to manage over 200 irrigation systems. Some of these are managed by government agencies (agency-managed irrigation systems or AMIS) while some are managed by the farmers (farmer-managed irrigation systems or FMIS). Ostrom and her colleagues find that compared to AMIS, FMIS are able to achieve a higher agricultural yield, a more equitable distribution of water and better maintenance of the irrigation systems. There are striking differences in the way the two systems are managed. Under AMIS infractions are recorded by government officials while under FMIS they are recorded by the farmer-monitors. Furthermore, the AMIS tends to rely more on fines for infractions than FMIS. Rules and quotas are followed 65% of the time in FMIS compared to only 35% of the time in AMIS. Thus rules and sanctions designed by the farmers themselves tend to be more effective than those imposed by government officials.

Another example of the detrimental effects of external intervention comes from Uri Gneezy and Aldo Rustichini's study of ten private day-care centres in Haifa, Israel. The day-care centres are all located in the same part of town and there are no obvious locational or other differences among them. The owner of the day-care also acts as the principal.

These day-care centres operate between 7:30 AM and 4:00 PM during week days. If a parent does not pick up his or her child by 4:00 PM then a teacher has to stay back with the child. This is inconvenient for the teacher who does not get any additional financial remuneration for staying beyond the usual operating hours. Teachers typically rotate this task which is considered part of their duties, a fact that is clearly explained at the time a teacher is hired.

Gneezy and Rustichini had their research assistants approach the principal of each of these ten day-care centres. The principals were requested to participate in an academic study about the influence of fines. Each principal was promised that at the end of the study she would receive coupons with a value of 500 New Israeli shekels for buying books.[2] The study lasted 20 weeks between January and June 1998. In the first four weeks Gneezy and Rustichini simply recorded the number of parents who arrived late each week. At the beginning of the fifth week, they introduced a fine in six of the ten day-care centres. The announcement of the fine was made with a note posted on the day-care centre's bulletin board, which is usually the means via which important information and announcements are conveyed to the parents. The announcement specified that the fine would be 10 shekels for a delay of ten minutes or more. The fine was per child. Thus, if a parent had two children in the centre and arrived late to pick them up, then that parent had to pay 20 shekels. These fines would be added to the usual monthly payments made by the parents. At the beginning of the seventeenth week, the fine was removed with no explanation. Notice of the cancellation was posted on the same bulletin board. If parents asked about the removal of the fine, the principals were instructed to inform them that the fine had been a trial for a limited time and that the results of this trial were being evaluated.

Figure 6.1 indicates the rather dramatic impact of the fine. The solid line with stars shows the average number of parents coming late per week, before and after the introduction of the fine, at the six day-care centres where the fine was introduced. The broken line with circles shows the average number of parents coming late per week at the remaining four day-care centres where no fines were in place.

---

2 At the time of this study during the first half of 1998, one US dollar was approximately equal to 3.7 shekels.

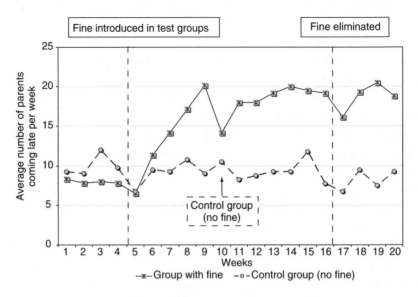

*Figure 6.1* Gneezy and Rustichini (2000): average number of parents coming late per week. Figure created by author on the basis of data provided in the original study.

Two things are obvious from this figure. (1) In the six day-care centres where the fine is introduced there is a dramatic *increase* in the number of parents arriving late in the first three to four weeks after the fine is put in place. The rate finally settled at a level that was higher than (around 20 late arrivals per week) and almost twice as large as the initial one. There is no noticeable change in the number of parents arriving late at the other four day-care centres where no fine is imposed. (2) In the six day-care centres where the fine is introduced, the number of parents arriving late continues to be high and remains considerably above their pre-fine levels *even after the fine is withdrawn* at the beginning of the seventeenth week.

Thus, the introduction of an explicit incentive in the form of a fine imposed on parents arriving late seems to have exacerbated the problem of late arrivals rather than alleviating the problem. How can we explain this rather counter-intuitive phenomenon? Here is how Gneezy and Rustichini interpret the behaviour of the parents. Prior to the introduction of the fine, parents probably regarded the action of a teacher who stayed behind with a child as an act of generosity.

*They may have thought: "The contract with the day-care centre only covers the period until four in the afternoon. After that time, the teacher is just a nice and generous person. I should not take advantage of her patience." The introduction of the fine changes the perception into the following: "The teacher is taking care of the child in much the same way as she did earlier in the day. In fact this activity has a price (which is called a 'fine'). Therefore, I can buy this service as much as needed." Parents feel justified in their behavior by a social norm that states, approximately: "When help is offered for no compensation in a moment of need, accept it with restraint. When a service is offered for a price, buy as much as you find convenient." No guilt or shame ... can be attached to the act of buying a commodity at will.*

## 6.4 Trust and growth

In previous chapters I have discussed how mutual trust and reciprocity among members of a community can create social connections that might enable those communities to achieve successful collective action which would be difficult to attain in the absence of such social ties. The all-encompassing phrase that is often attached to such social networks based on mutual trust and reciprocity among citizens is "*social capital*". Traditionally economists have tended to emphasise the importance of physical and human capital as pre-requisites for successful economic development.[3] But more and more economists are beginning to realise that such intangible things as the degree of trust exhibited by a country's citizenry – trust in their governments, in the country's legal and political institutions, indeed trust among themselves – also play a crucial role. In fact, in the absence of such mutual trust and reciprocity, economic development may falter even with adequate supplies of physical and human capital.

Stephen Knack and Phillip Keefer of the World Bank and Paul Zak of Claremont Graduate University have undertaken extensive work looking at the relationship between a country's level of trust and that country's economic performance for 29 market-based economies

---

3 The phrase "physical capital" refers to investments in entities such as machines, factories and infrastructure, such as roads, bridges and highways. "Human capital" refers to investments in health, education and skills of citizens.

surveyed during the early 1980s and the early 1990s.[4] They report that social capital matters for economic performance. These researchers focus on the role of trust and that of civic cooperation among citizens. The question used to assess the level of trust in a society is: *"Generally speaking, would you say that most people can be trusted, or that you can't be too careful in dealing with people?"* They use as their indicator of trust, the percentage of people in each country who say that "people can be trusted".

To get a measure regarding norms of civic cooperation they use responses to questions about whether each of the following behaviour *"can always be justified, never be justified or something in between"*: (1) *claiming government benefits which someone is not entitled to*; (2) *avoiding a fare on public transport*; (3) *cheating on taxes given the chance*; (4) *keeping money that someone has found*; and finally (5) *failing to report damage one has done accidentally to a parked car*. Suppose respondents answer these five questions by choosing numbers on a numeric scale such as 1 (*always justifiable*) to 10 (*never justifiable*). These numerical responses can then be used to construct a quantitative measure of the degree of civic cooperation that exists in that society with higher numbers (closer to 10) indicating greater degrees of civic cooperation.

For the 29 countries mentioned above, Knack and his colleagues look at the relationship between rates of growth in per capita income on the one hand and their measures of trust and civic cooperation on the other. They find that trust and norms of civic cooperation have a strong influence on the rates of growth of per capita income. Countries whose citizens exhibit higher levels of trust and civic cooperation, experience faster economic growth and this effect of trust and cooperation on growth is more pronounced for poorer countries than richer countries.

Knack and his colleagues explain their findings by suggesting that this is mostly because individuals in higher-trust societies spend less to protect themselves from being exploited in economic transactions. Written contracts are less likely to be needed and litigation may be less frequent. Individuals in high-trust societies are also likely to divert fewer resources to protecting themselves – through arbitrary tax pay-

---

4   The countries included are Argentina, Australia, Austria, Belgium, Brazil, Canada, Chile, Denmark, Finland, France, Germany, Iceland, India, Ireland, Italy, Japan, Mexico, Netherlands, Nigeria, Norway, Portugal, South Africa, South Korea, Spain, Sweden, Switzerland, Turkey, the UK and the US.

ments, bribes, or private security services and equipment – from unlawful or criminal violations of their property.

Low trust can also discourage investments and innovation. If entrepreneurs must devote more time to monitoring possible malfeasance they have less time to devote to innovations in new products and processes. Societies characterised by high levels of trust are also less dependent on formal institutions to enforce agreements. Thus, informal credit markets based on strong inter-personal trust (such as the one implemented by the Grameen Bank) can facilitate investments in situations where bank loans are unavailable. Government officials in higher-trust societies are perceived as more trustworthy and their policy pronouncements as more credible. This, in turn, often triggers greater investment and other economic activities. Finally, trusting societies not only have stronger incentives to innovate and to accumulate capital, investments in citizens' health, education and welfare are more likely to yield higher returns in these countries.

## 6.5 Concluding remarks

In the preceding pages I have provided evidence that social norms and such norm driven behaviour, as embodied in a sense of fairness or a disposition to trust strangers and to reciprocate others' trust, have a profound influence across a wide range of economic transactions. Such norms have enormous ramifications including an impact on the growth and development of societies as a whole.

It would be a mistake to think that this book argues against the use of game-theoretic tools in the context of strategic decision making. Game theory is a powerful tool which allows us to model succinctly a wide variety of economic behaviour. Even if our game theoretic models, that rely heavily on the rational self-interest assumption, sometimes make inaccurate predictions, nevertheless, having a formal model of behaviour and its predictions is useful because that prediction can serve as a benchmark for trying to understand how actual behaviour deviates from that benchmark. This allows us to organise our data and results in a more coherent way than if we had started with no model at all. Having a map with incomplete directions is better than starting out without any map whatsoever.

What the book does argue, however, is that our reliance on game theoretic tools should be *tempered* by an appreciation of the fact that our models of human behaviour need to take account of the powerful role played by social norms and such norm driven behaviour. At times that might mean building more elaborate models of human behaviour that incorporate such norms. And economists have already made or are making steady progress in that direction. I have already referred to the seminal work done by Matthew Rabin of Berkeley, which explicitly incorporates notions of fairness in his theoretical model. There are many others doing similar work including Ernst Fehr of Zürich, Klaus Schmidt of Vienna, Gary Bolton of Penn State, Axel Ockenfels of Cologne and David Levine of UCLA.

One immediate outcome of the reliance on game theoretic models and the assumption of rational self-interest in economic thinking is the emphasis on the use of explicit/extrinsic motivations in employment contracts. As I have argued above, and as Bruno Frey of the University of Zürich points out in his book *Not Just for the Money*, there are many cases where such explicit carrots and sticks are useful, and indeed necessary, to elicit effort from workers or ensure compliance with the desired course of action. But in many cases – and I have identified quite a few above including Frey's own results on the location of noxious facilities – this reliance on explicit incentives can be counter-productive and detrimental because they "crowd out" intrinsic motivations and one's latent desire to do the right thing even without any financial incentives to do so. It is important to bear in mind the results of this line of research when designing economic policies because ignoring them may lead to large welfare losses.

At the risk of being panglossian, the fact is that the world today faces myriad economic problems ranging from extreme poverty (with large parts of the world subsisting on less than a dollar a day), to genocide, to global warming. Many of the problems we face are economic in nature and/or call for economic solutions. In his book *Collapse: How Societies Choose to Fail or Succeed* Jared Diamond points out that very often genocidal wars, such as the ones in Somalia or Rwanda in the 1990s, are the inevitable outcome of rapidly increasing population pressures leading to deforestation, habitat destruction, soil problems and increasing pressures on fast dwindling resources. All I want to emphasise is that in tackling these complex and multi-faceted problems it is essential that we do not apply textbook theories based on game theoretic models or market fundamentalism blindly; rather we need to be aware of local norms and customs that may play an important role and influence behaviour in ways not predicted by our theoretical models. Sometimes we can incorporate such norms in designing innovative solutions, as in the case of the Grameen Bank. But this in turn also means that solutions to problems will often have to be de-centralised relying on local community initiatives; and they would almost certainly need to take a more multi-disciplinary approach. Experimental economics provides a new and novel way of incorporating these insights from economics as well as other disciplines.

# Bibliography

Akerlof, G. A. (1982) "Labor contracts as partial gift exchange", *Quarterly Journal of Economics*, 97: 543–569.

Andreoni, J. (1988) "Why free ride? Strategies and learning in public goods experiments", *Journal of Public Economics*, 37: 291–304.

—— (1990) "Impure altruism and donations to public goods: a theory of warm-glow giving?", *Economic Journal*, 100: 464–477.

—— (1995a) "Cooperation in public-goods experiments: kindness or confusion?", *American Economic Review*, 85: 891–904.

—— (1995b) "Warm-glow versus cold-prickle: the effects of positive and negative framing on cooperation in experiments", *Quarterly Journal of Economics*, 110: 1–21.

Andreoni, J. and Croson, R. (forthcoming) "Partners versus strangers: the effect of random rematching in public goods experiments", in V. Smith and C. Plott (eds), *Handbook of Experimental Economics Results*, New York: Elsevier.

Andreoni, J. and Petrie, R. (2004) "Public goods experiments without confidentiality: a glimpse into fund-raising", *Journal of Public Economics*, 88: 1605–1623.

—— (2008) "Beauty, gender and stereotypes: evidence from laboratory experiments", *Journal of Economic Psychology*, 29(1): 73–93.

Armendáriz de Aghion, B. and Morduch, J. (2005) *The Economics of Microfinance*, Cambridge, MA: The MIT Press.

Asch, S. E. (1951) "Effects of group pressure upon the modification and distortion of judgment", in H. Guetzkow (ed.) *Groups, Leadership and Men*. Pittsburgh, PA: Carnegie Press.

Asch, S. E. (1955) "Opinions and social pressure", *Scientific American*, 193: 31–35.

Asch, S. E. (1956) "Studies of independence and conformity: a minority of one against a unanimous majority", *Psychological Monographs*, 70 (Whole no. 416).

Ashraf, N., Bohnet, I. and Piankov, N. (2006) "Decomposing trust and trustworthiness", *Experimental Economics*, 9: 193–208.

Axelrod, R. (1984) *The Evolution of Cooperation*, New York: Basic Books.

—— (1986) "An evolutionary approach to norms", *American Political Science Review*, 80: 1095–1111.

—— (1997) *The Complexity of Cooperation: Agent-Based Models of Competition and Collaboration*, Princeton, NJ: Princeton University Press.

Axelrod, R. and Hamilton, W. D. (1981) "The evolution of cooperation", *Science*, 211: 1390–1398.

Baron, J., Hannan, M., and Burton, D. (1996) "Inertia and change in the early years: employment relations in young, high technology firms", *Industrial and Corporate Change*, 5: 503–536.

Baron, J., Hannan, M. and Burton, D. (2001) "Labor pains: organizational change and employee turnover in young, high-tech firms", *American Journal of Sociology*, 106(4): 960–1012.

Berg, J., Dickhaut, J. and McCabe, K. (1995) "Trust, reciprocity, and social history", *Games and Economic Behavior*, 10: 122–142.

Bewley, T. (2005) "Fairness, reciprocity and wage rigidity", in H. Gintis, S. Bowles, R. Boyd and E. Fehr (eds), *Moral Sentiments and Material Interests: The Foundations of Cooperation in Economic Life*, Cambridge, MA: MIT Press.

Blount, S. (1995) "When social outcomes aren't fair: the effect of causal attributions on preferences", *Organizational Behavior and Human Decision Processes*, 63: 131–144.

Blume, A. and Ortmann, A. (2007) "The effects of costless pre-play communication: experimental evidence from games with Pareto-ranked equilibria", *Journal of Economic Theory*, 132: 274–290.

Bohnet, I. and Zeckhauser, R. (2004a) "Social comparisons in ultimatum bargaining", *Scandinavian Journal of Economics*, 106: 495–510.

—— (2004b) "Trust, risk and betrayal", *Journal of Economic Behavior and Organization*, 55: 467–484.

Bolton, G. E. and Zwick, R. (1995) "Anonymity versus punishment in ultimatum bargaining", *Games and Economic Behavior*, 10: 95–121.

Bolton, G. E., Brandts, J. and Ockenfels, A. (2005) "Fair procedures: evidence from games involving lotteries", *Economic Journal*, 115: 1054–1076.

Bolton, G. E., Katok, E. and Zwick, R. (1998) "Dictator game giving: rules of fairness versus acts of kindness", *International Journal of Game Theory*, 27: 269–299.

Bolton, G. E. and Ockenfels, A. (2000) "ERC: a theory of equity, reciprocity, and competition", *American Economic Review*, 90: 166–193.

Bowles, S. and Gintis, H. (2002) "Homo reciprocans", *Nature*, 415: 125–128.

Boyd, R. and Richerson, P. J. (1985) *Culture and the Evolutionary Process*, Chicago, IL: University of Chicago Press.

Brandts, J. and Cooper, D. J. (2006) "A change would do you good ... an experimental study on how to overcome coordination failure in organizations", *American Economic Review*, 96: 667–693.

—— (2007) "It's what you say and not what you pay: an experimental study of manager employee relationships in overcoming coordination failure", *Journal of the European Economic Association*, 5(6): 1223–1268.

Brandts, J. and MacLeod, W. B. (1995) "Equilibrium selection in experimental games with recommended play", *Games and Economic Behavior*, 11: 36–63.

Brandts, J., Saijo, T. and Schram, A. (2004) "How universal is behavior? A four country comparison of spite and cooperation in voluntary contribution mechanisms", *Public Choice*, 119: 381–424.

Burks, S., Carpenter, J. and Verhoogen, E. (2003) "Playing both roles in the trust game: the golden rule and Machiavellian behavior", *Journal of Economic Behavior and Organization*, 51: 195–216.

Burlando, R. and Guala, F. (2005) "Heterogeneous agents in public goods experiments", *Experimental Economics*, 8(1): 35–54.

Burlando, R. and Hey, J. (1997) "Do Anglo-Saxons free-ride more?", *Journal of Public Economics*, 64: 41–60.

Burton, A. and Sefton, M. (2004) "Risk, pre-play communication and equilibrium", *Games and Economic Behavior*, 46: 23–40.

Cachon, G. P. and Camerer, C. (1996) "Loss-avoidance and forward induction in experimental coordination games", *Quarterly Journal of Economics*, 111: 165–194.

Camerer, C. (2003) *Behavioral Game Theory*, Princeton, NJ: Princeton University Press.

Camerer, C. and Knez, M. (1994) "Creating expectational assets in the laboratory: coordination in 'weak link' games", *Strategic Management Journal*, 15: 101–119.

Camerer, C. and Weber, R. (forthcoming) "Growing organizational culture in the laboratory", in V. Smith and C. Plott (eds), *Handbook of Experimental Economics Results*, New York: Elsevier.

Camerer, C. and Weigelt, K. (1988) "Experimental tests of a sequential equilibrium reputation model", *Econometrica*, 56: 1–36.

Cameron, L. A. (1999) "Raising the stakes in the ultimatum game: experimental evidence from Indonesia", *Economic Inquiry*, 37: 47–59.

Cardenas, J., Stranlund, J. and Willis, C. (2002) "Economic inequality and burden-sharing in the provision of local environmental quality", *Ecological Economics*, 40: 379–395.

Carpenter, J., Harrison, G. and List, J. (2005) *Field Experiments in Economics*, Greenwich and London: JAI Press.

Cavalli-Sforza, L. L. and Feldman, M. W. (1981) *Cultural Transmission and Evolution: A Quantitative Approach*, Princeton, NJ: Princeton University Press.

Chamberlin, E. H. (1948) "An experimental imperfect market", *Journal of Political Economy*, 56: 95–108.

Charness, G. (2000) "Self-serving cheap talk: a test of Aumann's conjecture", *Games and Economic Behavior*, 33: 177–194.

Chaudhuri, A. and Gangadharan, L. (2007) "An experimental analysis of trust and trustworthiness", *Southern Economic Journal*, 73: 959–985.

Chaudhuri, A. and Paichayontvijit, T. (2006) "Conditional cooperation and voluntary contributions to a public good", *Economics Bulletin*, 3: 1–14.

—— (2008a) "Credible assignments and performance bonuses in the minimum effort coordination game", Working Paper, University of Auckland.

—— (2008b) "Social learning and conditional cooperation in a laboratory public goods game", Working Paper, University of Auckland.

Chaudhuri, A., Ali Khan, S., Lakshmiratan, A., Py, A. L. and Shah, L. (2003) "Trust and trustworthiness in a sequential bargaining game", *Journal of Behavioral Decision Making*, 16: 331–340.

Chaudhuri, A., Graziano, S. and Maitra, P. (2006) "Social learning and norms in a public goods experiment with inter-generational advice", *Review of Economic Studies*, 73: 357–380.

Chaudhuri, A., Schotter, A. and Sopher, B. (2008) "Talking ourselves to efficiency: coordination conventions in inter-generational minimum effort games with private, almost common and common knowledge of advice", *Economic Journal*, forthcoming.

Chaudhuri, A., Sopher, B. and Strand, P. (2002) "Cooperation in social dilemmas, trust and reciprocity", *Journal of Economic Psychology*, 23: 231–249.

Chwe, M. S. (2001) *Rational Ritual: Culture, Coordination and Common Knowledge*, Princeton, NJ: Princeton University Press.

Clark, K. and Sefton, M. (2001) "Repetition and signalling: experimental evidence from games with efficient equilibria", *Economics Letters*, 70: 357–362.

Conway, M. A. and Gathercole, S. E. (1990) "Writing and long-term memory: evidence for a 'translation hypothesis'", *Quarterly Journal of Experimental Psychology*, 42A: 513–527.

Cooper, D. J. (2006) "Are experienced managers experts at overcoming coordination failure?", *Advances in Economic Analysis and Policy*: 6(2), Article 6. Available at: http://www.bepress.com/bejeap/advances/vol6/iss2/art6.

Cooper, R. (1999) *Coordination Games: Complementarities and Macroeconomics*, Cambridge: Cambridge University Press.

Cooper, R., DeJong, D. V., Forsythe, R. and Ross, T. W. (1989) "Communication in the battle of the sexes game: some experimental results", *RAND Journal of Economics*, 20: 568–587.

—— (1990) "Selection criteria in coordination games: experimental results", *American Economic Review*, 80(1): 218–233.

—— (1992) "Communication in coordination games", *Quarterly Journal of Economics*, 107: 739–771.

Cox, J. C. (2004) "How to identify trust and reciprocity", *Games and Economic Behavior*, 46: 260–281.

Croson, R. (2000) "Thinking like a game theorist: factors affecting the frequency of equilibrium play", *Journal of Economic Behavior and Organization*, 41: 299–314.

Dawes, R. and Thaler, R. (1988) "Anomalies: cooperation", *Journal of Economic Perspectives*, 2: 187–197.

Dawes, R., McTavish, J. and Shaklee, H. (1977) "Behavior, communication, and assumptions about other people's behavior in a commons dilemma situation", *Journal of Personality and Social Psychology*, 35: 1–11.

Dawkins, R. (1976) *The Selfish Gene*, Oxford: Oxford University Press.

DeHaan, E. H., Appels, B., Aleman, A. and Postma, A. (2000) "Inter- and intra-modal encoding of auditory and visual presentation of material: effects of memory performance", *Psychological Record*, 50(3): 577–587.

De Palma, B. (director) (1983) *Scarface*, M. Bregman (producer), USA: Universal Studios.

Diamond, D. and Dybvig, P. (1983) "Bank runs, deposit insurance, and liquidity", *Journal of Political Economy*, 91: 401–419.

Diamond, J. M. (2005) *Collapse: How Societies Choose to Fail or Succeed*, New York: Viking.

Eckel, C. and Wilson, R. (2004) "Is trust a risky decision?", *Journal of Economic Behavior and Organization*, 55: 447–465.

Emerson, R. W. (1911) *Essays (First, Second and Third Series)*, London: Ward Lock & Co.

Ephron, N. (director) (1993) *Sleepless in Seattle*, G. Foster (producer), USA: TriStar Pictures.

Falk, A. and Fischbacher, U. (2006) "A theory of reciprocity", *Games and Economic Behavior*, 54: 293–315.

Falk, A., Fehr, E. and Fischbacher, U. (2002) "Appropriating the commons: a theoretical explanation", in E. Ostrom, T. Dietz, N. Dolsak, P. C. Stern, S. Stonich and E. U. Weber (eds), *The Drama of the Commons*, Washington: National Academy Press.

—— (2003a) "On the nature of fair behavior", *Economic Inquiry*, 41: 20–26.

—— (2003b) "Reasons for conflict: lessons from bargaining experiments", *Journal of Institutional and Theoretical Economics*, 159: 171–187.

—— (2005) "Driving forces behind informal sanctions", *Econometrica*, 73: 2017–2030.

Fehr, E. and Fischbacher, U. (2002) "Why social preferences matter: the impact of non-selfish motives on competition, cooperation and incentives", *Economic Journal*, 112: C1–C33.

Fehr, E. and Gächter, S. (1998) "Reciprocity and economics: the economic implications of homo reciprocans", *European Economic Review*, 42: 845–859.

—— (2000) "Cooperation and punishment in public goods experiments", *American Economic Review*, 90: 980–994.

—— (2002a) "Altruistic punishment in humans", *Nature*, 415: 137–140.

—— (2002b) "Do incentive contracts undermine voluntary cooperation?", Working Paper No. 34, Institute for Empirical Research in Economics, University of Zürich.

Fehr, E. and List, J. (2004) "The hidden costs and returns of incentives – trust and trustworthiness among CEOs", *Journal of the European Economic Association*, 2(5): 743–771.

Fehr, E. and Rockenbach, B. (2004) "Human altruism: economic, neural, and evolutionary perspectives", *Current Opinion in Neurobiology*, 14: 784–790.

—— (2003) "Detrimental effects of sanctions on human altruism", *Nature*, 422: 137–140, (March 13, 2003).

Fehr, E. and Schmidt, K. (1999) "A theory of fairness, competition and cooperation", *Quarterly Journal of Economics*, 114: 817–868.

Fehr, E., Fischbacher, U. and Gächter, S. (2002) "Strong reciprocity, human cooperation and the enforcement of social norms", *Human Nature*, 13: 1–24.

Fehr, E., Gächter, S. and Kirchsteiger, G. (1997) "Reciprocity as a contract enforcement device: experimental evidence", *Econometrica*, 65: 833–860.

Fehr, E., Kirchler, E., Weichbold, A. and Gächter, S. (1998) "When social norms overpower competition: gift exchange in experimental labor markets", *Journal of Labor Economics*, 16: 324–351.

Fehr, E., Kirchsteiger, G. and Riedle, A. (1993) "Does fairness prevent market clearing? An experimental investigation", *Quarterly Journal of Economics*, 108(2): 437–459.

—— (1996) "Involuntary unemployment and non-compensating wage differentials in an experimental labour market", *Economic Journal*, 106: 106–121.

—— (1998) "Gift exchange and reciprocity in competitive experimental markets", *European Economic Review*, 42: 1–34.

Fehr, E., Klein, A. and Schmidt, K. (2007) "Fairness and contract design, incentives and contractual incompleteness", *Econometrica*, 75(1): 121–154.

Fischbacher, U., Gächter, S. and Fehr, E. (2001) "Are people conditionally cooperative? Evidence from a public goods experiment", *Economics Letters*, 71: 397–404.

Flood, M. M. (1958) "Some experimental games", *Management Science*, 5: 5–26.

Forsythe, R., Horowitz, J. L., Savin, N. E. and Sefton, M. (1994) "Fairness in simple bargaining experiments", *Games and Economic Behavior*, 6: 347–369.

Frank, R. H. (1985) *Choosing the Right Pond: Human Behavior and the Quest for Status*, New York: Oxford University Press.

—— (1999) *Luxury Fever: Money and Happiness in an Era of Excess*, New York: The Free Press.

—— (2005) "Does absolute income matter?", in P. L. Porta and L. Bruni (eds), *Economics and Happiness*, Oxford: Oxford University Press.

Frey, B. S. (1997) *Not Just for the Money: An Economic Theory of Personal Motivation*, Cheltenham, UK and Brookfield, VT: Edward Elgar Publishing.

Frey, B. S. and Oberholzer-Gee, F. (1997) "The cost of price incentives: an empirical analysis of motivation crowding-out", *American Economic Review*, 87: 746–755.

Friedman, D. and Sunder, S. (1994) *Experimental Methods: A Primer for Economists*, Cambridge, UK and New York: Cambridge University Press.

Fukuyama, F. (1995) *Trust: The Social Virtues and the Creation of Prosperity*, New York: The Free Press.

Gächter, S. and Fehr, E. (1999) "Collective action as a social exchange", *Journal of Economic Behavior and Organization*, 39: 341–369.

Gächter, S. and Thöni, C. (2005) "Social learning and voluntary cooperation among like-minded people", *Journal of the European Economic Association*, 3: 303–314.

Gächter, S., Hermann, B. and Thöni, C. (2004) "Trust, voluntary cooperation, and socio-economic background: survey and experimental evidence", *Journal of Economic Behavior and Organization*, 55(4): 505–531.

Geanakoplos, J., Pearce, D. and Stacchetti, E. (1989) "Psychological games and sequential rationality", *Games and Economic Behavior*, 1: 60–79.

Gintis, H., Bowles, S., Boyd, R. and Fehr, E. (2005) *Moral Sentiments and Material Interests: The Foundations of Cooperation in Economic Life*, Cambridge, MA and London: MIT Press.

Gneezy, U. and Rustichini, A. (2000) "A fine is a price", *Journal of Legal Studies*, 29:1–17.

Gneezy, U., Güth, W. and Verboven, F. (2000) "Presents or investment? An experimental analysis", *Journal of Economic Psychology*, 21: 481–493.

Gunnthorsdottir, A., Houser, D. and McCabe, K. (2007) "Disposition, history and contributions in public goods experiments", *Journal of Economic Behavior and Organization*, 62: 304–315.

Güth, W., Schmittberger, R. and Schwarze, B. (1982) "An experimental analysis of ultimatum bargaining", *Journal of Economic Behavior and Organization*, 3: 367–388.

Hamilton, W. D. (1964a) "The genetical evolution of social behaviour – I", *Journal of Theoretical Biology*, 7: 1–16.

—— (1964b) "The genetical evolution of social behaviour – II", *Journal of Theoretical Biology*, 7: 17–52.

Heller, J. (1961) *Catch 22*, 1994 ed., London: Vintage.

Henrich, J. P., Boyd, R., Bowles, S., Camerer, C., Fehr, E. and Gintis, H. (2004) "Introduction and guide to the volume", in J. P. Henrich, R. Boyd, S. Bowles, C. Camerer, E. Fehr and H. Gintis (eds), *Foundations of Human Sociality: Economic Experiments and Ethnographic Evidence from Fifteen Small-scale Societies*, Oxford: Oxford University Press.

Henrich, J. P., Boyd, R., Bowles, S., Camerer, C., Fehr, E. and Gintis, H. (eds) (2004) *Foundations of Human Sociality: Economic Experiments and Ethnographic Evidence from Fifteen Small-scale Societies*, Oxford: Oxford University Press.

Henry, O. (1992) *The Gift of the Magi and Other Short Stories*, New York: Dover Publications Inc.

Hoffman, E., McCabe, K., Shachat, K. and Smith, V. (1994) "Preferences, property rights, and anonymity in bargaining games", *Games and Economic Behavior*, 7: 346–380.

Hoffman, E., McCabe, K. and Smith, V. (1996) "On expectations and the monetary stakes in ultimatum games", *International Journal of Game Theory*, 25: 289–301.

Hoffman, E., McCabe, K. and Smith, V. L. (1996) "Social distance and other-regarding behavior in dictator games", *American Economic Review*, 86: 653–660.

Homans, G. C. (1954) "The cash posters: a study of a group of working girls", *American Sociological Review*, 19: 724–733.

Homer (1996) *The Odyssey*, trans. R. Fagles, New York: Penguin Classics.

Houser, D. and Kurzban, R. (2002) "Revisiting kindness and confusion in public goods experiments", *American Economic Review*, 92: 1062–1069.

Howard, R. (director) (2001) *A Beautiful Mind*, B. Grazer and R. Howard (producers), USA: Universal Pictures (Domestic), DreamWorks SKG (International).

Hugo, V. (1862) *Les Misérables*, trans. L. Fahnestock and N. MacAfee, 1987 ed., New York: Signet Classics.

Ichniowski, C., Shaw, K. and Prennushi, G. (1997) "The effects of human resource management practices on productivity: a study of steel finishing lines", *American Economic Review*, 87: 291–313.

Isaac, R. M. and Walker, J. M. (1988a) "Communication and free-riding behavior: the voluntary contributions mechanism", *Economic Inquiry*, 26: 585–608.

—— (1988b) "Group size effects in public goods provision: the voluntary contributions mechanism", *Quarterly Journal of Economics*, 103: 179–199.

Isaac, R. M., McCue, K. F. and Plott, C. R. (1985) "Public goods provision in an experimental environment", *Journal of Public Economics*, 26: 51–74.

Isaac, R. M., Walker, J. M. and Thomas, S. H. (1984) "Divergent evidence on free riding: an experimental examination of possible explanations", *Public Choice*, 43: 113–149.

Jackson, M. O. and Kalai, E. (1997) "Social learning in recurring games", *Games and Economic Behavior*, 21: 102–134.

Jensen, K., Call, J. and Tomasello, M. (2007) "Chimpanzees are rational maximizers in an ultimatum game", *Science*, 318: 107–109.

Jerome, J. K. (1889) *Three Men in a Boat*, 1993 ed., Hertfordshire: Wordsworth Editions Ltd.

Kagel, J. H. and Roth, A. E. (eds) (1995) *The Handbook of Experimental Economics*, Princeton, NJ: Princeton University Press.

Kahneman, D., Knetsch, J. L. and Thaler, R. H. (1986a) "Fairness and the assumptions of economics", *Journal of Business*, 59: S285–S300.

—— (1986b) "Fairness as a constraint on profit seeking: entitlements in the market", *American Economic Review*, 76: 728–741.

Karlan, D. (2005) "Using experimental economics to measure social capital and predict real financial decisions", *American Economic Review*, 95(5): 1688–1699.

Kelley, H. H. and Stahelski, A. J. (1970) "Social interaction basis of cooperators' and competitors' beliefs about others", *Journal of Personality and Social Psychology*, 16: 66–91.

Keser, C. and van Winden, F. (2000) "Conditional cooperation and voluntary contributions to public goods", *Scandinavian Journal of Economics*, 102: 23–39.

Kim, O. and Walker, J. (1984) "The free rider problem: experimental evidence", *Public Choice*, 43: 2–34.

Knack, S. and Keefer, P. (1997) "Does social capital have an economic payoff? A cross-country investigation", *Quarterly Journal of Economics*, 112: 1251–1288.

Knez, M. and Simester, D. (2001) "Firm-wide incentives and mutual monitoring at Continental Airlines", *Journal of Labor Economics*, 19: 743–772.

Kosfeld, M., Heinrichs, M., Zak, P., Fischbacher, U. and Fehr, E. (2005) "Oxytocin increases trust in humans", *Nature*, 435: 673–676.

Kramer, R. M. (1999) "Trust and distrust in organizations: emerging perspectives, enduring questions", *Annual Review of Psychology*, 50: 569–598.

Kremer, M. (1993) "The O-ring theory of economic development", *Quarterly Journal of Economics*, 108: 551–575.

Kreps, D. M., Milgrom, P., Roberts, J. and Wilson, R. (1982) "Rational cooperation in the finitely repeated prisoners' dilemma", *Journal of Economic Theory*, 27: 245–252.

Kunreuther, H. and Easterling, D. V. (1990) "Are risk-benefit trade-offs possible in siting hazardous facilities?", *American Economic Review: Papers and Proceedings*, 80: 252–256.

—— (1996) "The role of compensation in siting hazardous facilities", *Journal of Policy Analysis and Management*, 15: 601–622.

Kunreuther, H., Easterling, D. V., Desvousges, W. and Slovic, P. (1990) "Public attitudes toward siting a high-level nuclear waste repository in Nevada", *Risk Analysis*, 10: 469–484.

Kurzban, R. and Houser, D. (2005) "An experimental investigation of cooperative types in human groups: a complement to evolutionary theory and simulations", *Proceedings of the National Academy of Sciences*, 102(5), 1803–1807.

LaPierre, R. T. and Farnsworth, P. R. (1936) *Social Psychology*, New York: McGraw-Hill.

LaPorta R., Lopez-de-Silanes, F., Shleifer, A., and Vishny, R. (1997) "Trust in large organizations", *American Economic Review Papers and Proceedings*, 87: 333–338.

Ledyard, J. O. (1995) "Public goods: some experimental results", in J. Kagel and A. Roth (eds), *Handbook of Experimental Economics*, Princeton, NJ: Princeton University Press.

Levine, D. K. (1998) "Modeling altruism and spitefulness in experiments", *Review of Economic Dynamics*, 1: 593–622.

McCarey, L. (director) (1957) *An Affair to Remember*, L. McCarey and J. Wald (producers), USA: 20th Century Fox.

Mankiw, N. G. (2007) *Principles of Economics*, Mason, OH: Thomson South-Western.

Marlowe, F. W. (2004) "Dictators and ultimatums in an egalitarian society of hunter-gatherers: the Hadza of Tanzania", in J. P. Henrich, R. Boyd, S. Bowles, C. Camerer, E. Fehr and H. Gintis (eds), *Foundations of Human Sociality: Economic Experiments and Ethnographic Evidence from Fifteen Small-scale Societies*, Oxford: Oxford University Press.

Marwell, G. and Ames, R. (1981) "Economists free ride, does anyone else?", *Journal of Public Economics*, 15: 295–310.

Masclet, D., Noussair, C., Tucker, S. and Villeval, M. C. (2003) "Monetary and nonmonetary punishment in the voluntary contributions mechanism", *American Economic Review*, 93: 366–380.

Maynard Smith, J. (1964) "Group selection and kin selection", *Nature*, 201: 1145–1147.

Miller, J. H. and Andreoni, J. (1991) "Can evolutionary dynamics explain free riding in experiments?", *Economics Letters*, 36: 9–15.

Murdock, B. B. and Walker, K. D. (1969), "Modality effects in free recall", *Journal of Verbal Learning and Verbal Behavior*, 8: 665–676.

Murphy, K., Shleifer, A. and Vishny, R. (1989) "Industrialization and the big push", *Journal of Political Economy*, 97: 1003–1026.

Nasar, S. (1998) *A Beautiful Mind: A Biography of John Forbes Nash*, New York: Simon & Schuster.

Nash, J. F. (1950a) "Equilibrium points in n-person games", *Proceedings of the National Academy of Sciences*, 36: 48–49.

—— (1950b) "The bargaining problem", *Econometrica*, 18: 155–162.

—— (1951) "Non-cooperative games", *Annals of Mathematics*, 54: 286–295.

Noussair, C. and Tucker, S. (2005) "Combining Monetary and Social Sanctions to Promote Cooperation", *Economic Inquiry*, 43(3), 649–660.

Orbell, J. and Dawes, R. (1981) "Social dilemmas", in G. Stephenson and J. H. Davis (eds), *Progress in Applied Social Psychology* (vol. 1), Chichester: Wiley Publishers.

Orbell, J., Dawes, R. and van de Kragt, A. (1990) "The limits of multilateral promising", *Ethics*, 100: 616–627.

Ortmann, A., Fitzgerald, J. and Boeing, C. (2000) "Trust, reciprocity and social history: a re-examination", *Experimental Economics*, 3: 81–100.

Ostrom, E., Gardner, R. and Walker, J. (1994) *Rules, Games, and Common-Pool Resources*, Ann Arbor, MI: University of Michigan Press.

Ostrom, E., Walker, J. and Gardner, R. (1992) "Covenants with and without a sword: self-governance is possible", *American Political Science Review*, 86: 404–417.

Page, T., Putterman, L. and Unel, B. (2005) "Voluntary association in public goods experiments: reciprocity, mimicry and efficiency", *Economic Journal*, 115: 1032–1053.

Penney, C. G. (1989) "Modality effects and the structure of short-term verbal memory", *Memory and Cognition*, 17: 398–422.

Plott, C. R. and Smith, V. L. (1978) "An experimental examination of two exchange institutions", *Review of Economic Studies*, 45: 133–153.

Putnam, R. (2000) *Bowling Alone: The Collapse and Revival of American Community*, New York: Simon & Schuster.

Rabin, M. (1993) "Incorporating fairness into game theory and economics", *American Economic Review*, 80: 1281–1302.

—— (1998) "Psychology and economics", *Journal of Economic Literature*, 36: 11–46.

Reiner, R. (director) (1987) *The Princess Bride*, A. Scheinman and R. Reiner (producers), USA: 20th Century Fox.

Roth, A. (1995) "Introduction to experimental economics", in J. Kagel and A. Roth (eds), 1995, *Handbook of Experimental Economics*, Princeton, NJ: Princeton University Press, pp. 3–109.

Roth, A. (1995) "Bargaining experiments", in J. Kagel and A. Roth (eds), *Handbook of Experimental Economics*, Princeton, NJ: Princeton University Press, pp. 253–348.

Roth, A. E. (1993) "On the early history of experimental economics", *Journal of the History of Economic Thought*, 15: 184–209.

—— (1994) "Let's keep the con out of experimental econ.: a methodological note", *Empirical Economics*, 19: 279–289.

—— (ed.) (1987) *Laboratory Experimentation in Economics: Six Points of View*, Cambridge: Cambridge University Press.

Roth, A. E., Prasnikar, V., Okuno-Fujiwara, M. and Zamir, S. (1991) "Bargaining and market behavior in Jerusalem, Ljubljana, Pittsburgh, and Tokyo: an experimental study", *American Economic Review*, 81: 1068–1095.

Rousseau, J. J. (1754) *Discourse on the Origin of Inequality*, trans. F. Philip, 1994 ed., Oxford: Oxford University Press.

Ruffle, B. J. (1998) "More is better, but fair is fair: tipping in dictator and ultimatum games", *Games and Economic Behavior*, 23, 247–265.

_____ (2000) "Some factors affecting demand withholding in posted-offer markets", *Economic Theory*, 16(3): 529–544.

Samuelson, P. and Nordhaus, W. (1985) *Economics*, New York: McGraw-Hill.

Schelling, T. C. (1957) "Bargaining, communication, and limited war", *Conflict Resolution*, 1: 19–36.

—— (1958) "The strategy of conflict: prospectus for a reorientation of game theory", *Journal of Conflict Resolution*, 2: 203–264.

—— (1960) *The Strategy of Conflict*, Cambridge, MA: Harvard University Press.

—— (1978) *Micromotives and Macrobehavior*, New York: W. W. Norton.

Schotter, A. (2003) "Decision making with naïve advice", *American Economic Review: Papers and Proceedings*, 93: 196–201.

Schotter, A. and Sopher, B. (2003) "Social learning and coordination conventions in intergenerational games: an experimental study", *Journal of Political Economy*, 111: 498–529.

—— (2006) "Advice, trust and trustworthiness in an experimental intergenerational game", *Experimental Economics*, 9: 123–145.

—— (2007) "Advice and behavior in intergenerational ultimatum games: an experimental approach", *Games and Economic Behavior*, 58: 365–393.

Seabright, P. (2004) *The Company of Strangers: A Natural History of Economic Life*, Princeton, NJ: Princeton University Press.

Siegel, S. and Fouraker, L. E. (1960) *Bargaining and Group Decision Making: Experiments in Bilateral Monopoly*, New York: McGraw-Hill.

Simon, H. A. (1955) "A behavioral model of rational choice", *Quarterly Journal of Economics*, 69: 99–118.

—— (1956) "A comparison of game theory and learning theory", *Psychometrika*, 21: 267–272.

Smith, A. (1776) *An Inquiry into the Nature and Causes of the Wealth of Nations*, London: Methuen and Co. Ltd.

Smith, V. L. (1962) "An experimental study of competitive market behavior", *Journal of Political Economy*, 70: 322–323.

—— (1964) "Effect of market organization on competitive equilibrium", *Quarterly Journal of Economics*, 78(2): 182–201.

—— (ed.). (1979) *Research in Experimental Economics*, (Vol. 1), Greenwich, CT: JAI Press.

Smith, V. L. and Williams, A. W. (1981) "On nonbinding price controls in a competitive market", *American Economic Review*, 71: 467–474.

Snijders, C. and Keren, G. (1998) "Determinants of trust", in D. V. Budescu, I. Erev and R. Zwick (eds), *Games and Human Behavior: Essays in Honor of Amnon Rapoport*, Mahwah, NJ: Lawrence Erlbaum.

Snijders, C. and Keren, G. (2001) "Do you trust? Whom do you trust? When do you trust?", *Advances in Group Processes*, 18: 129–160.

Stiglitz, J. (2002) *Globalization and its Discontents*, New York: W.W. Norton & Company.

Tindall-Ford, S., Chandler, P. and Sweller, J. (1997) "When two sensory modes are better than one", *Journal of Experimental Psychology: Applied*, 3: 257–287.

Titmuss, R. M. (1970) *The Gift Relationship*, London: Allen & Unwin.

Trivers, R. L. (1971) "The evolution of reciprocal altruism", *Quarterly Review of Biology*, 46: 35–57.

—— (1972) "Parental investment and sexual selection", in B. G. Campbell (ed.),

*Sexual Selection and the Descent of Man, 1871–1971*, London: Heinemann Educational.

—— (1974) "Parent-offspring conflict", *American Zoologist*, 14: 249–264.

Van Huyck, J. B., Battalio, R. C. and Beil, R. O. (1990) "Tacit coordination games, strategic uncertainty, and coordination failure", *American Economic Review*, 80: 234–248.

—— (1993) "Asset markets as an equilibrium selection mechanism: coordination failure, game form auctions and tacit communication", *Games and Economic Behavior*, 5: 485–504.

Van Huyck, J. B., Gillette, A. B. and Battalio, R. C. (1992) "Credible assignments in coordination games", *Games and Economic Behavior*, 4: 606–626.

von Neumann, J. and Morgenstern, O. (1944) *Theory of Games and Economic Behavior*, Princeton, NJ: Princeton University Press.

Weber, R. A. (2006) "Managing growth to achieve efficient coordination in large groups", *American Economic Review*, 96: 114–126.

Young, P. (1993) "The evolution of conventions", *Econometrica*, 61: 57–84.

Yunus, M. (1999) *Banker to the Poor: Micro-lending and the Battle against World Poverty*, New York: Public Affairs.

Zak, P. and Knack, S. (2001) "Trust and growth", *Economic Journal*, 111: 295–321.

# Index